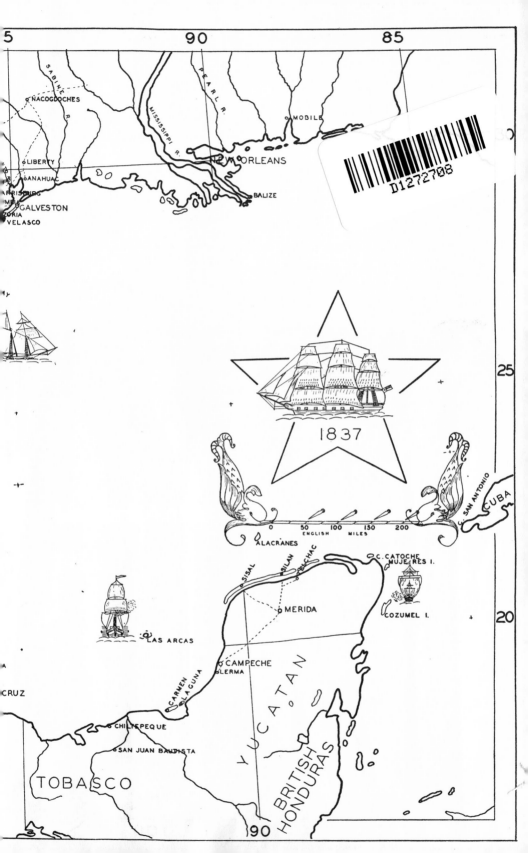

5   90   85

NACOGDOCHES

SABINE R

PEARL R

MISSISSIPPI R

MOBILE

LIBERTY

ANAHUAC

NEW ORLEANS

HARRISBURG

GALVESTON

BALIZE

VELASCO

1837

SAN ANTONIO

CUBA

25

ALACRANES

SISAL

DILAN

HECHAC

C. CATOCHE

MUJERES I.

MERIDA

COZUMEL I.

20

LAS ARCAS

CAMPECHE

LERMA

Y U C A T A N

CARMEN

LAGUNA

CRUZ

CHILTEPEQUE

SAN JUAN BAUTISTA

BRITISH HONDURAS

TOBASCO

90

THE TEXAS NAVY

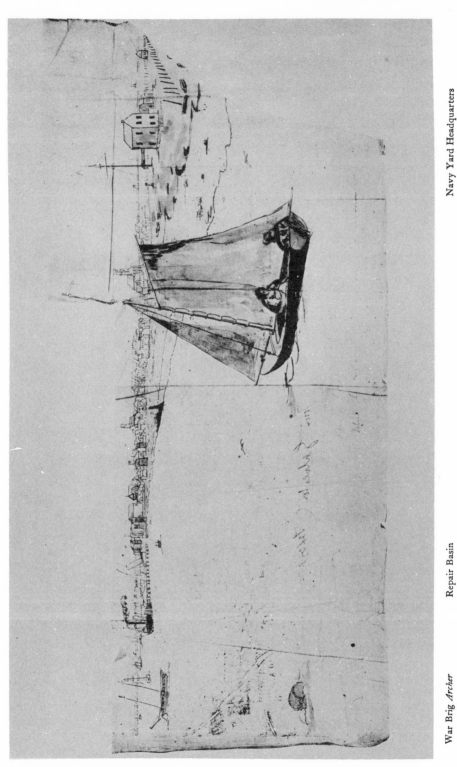

War Brig *Archer*   Repair Basin   Navy Yard Headquarters

GALVESTON ABOUT 1840, VIEWED FROM BELOW THE NAVY YARD

From a contemporary sketch by William Bollaert. (Courtesy of Newberry Library, Chicago)

THE TEXAS NAVY

IN FORGOTTEN BATTLES
AND SHIRTSLEEVE DIPLOMACY

By

JIM DAN HILL

1837

Facsimile Reproduction of the Original

STATE HOUSE PRESS
AUSTIN, TEXAS
1987

Library of Congress Cataloging-in-Publication Data

Hill, Jim Dan, b. 1897
  The Texas Navy.

    Reprint. Originally published: Chicago, Ill.:
University of Chicago Press, 1937.
    Bibliography: p. 206
    Includes index.
    1. Texas. Navy—History.   2. Texas—History, Naval.
3. Texas—History—Republic, 1836-1846.   I. Title.
F390.H57   1987   976.4'04   87-10017
ISBN 0-938349-17-1
ISBN 0-938349-18-X (pbk.)
ISBN 0-938349-19-8 (lim ed.)

State House Press
P.O. Box 15247
Austin, Texas 78761

To

ALMA HILL

*A Mother Who Has Done All in Her
Power to Transmit the Best of Her
Sturdy Texan Heritage to Four Daugh-
ters and Three Sons*

FOREWORD

In history there are happenings which have somehow "missed the accident of fame." Often these are among the most dramatic.

Not only that but some of history's greatest achievements are not given due credit for their influence on events because the spotlight was playing on some other actors at the moment. The half-back who tears down the field with the football tucked under his arm and makes the touchdown gets the headlines. The guard who opened up the hole which made the run possible gets never a sentence.

This has been the fate of the Texas Navy, the Navy of the Lone Star Republic. Books have been written on Sam Houston. The battles of the Alamo and San Jacinto have been celebrated in prose and verse. Hardly anyone, however, has heard of the contemporary Commodore Hawkins, the *Independence*, the *Invincible*, or the *Brutus*.

Doctor Hill in this book has rescued the Texas Navy from the shadowy obscurity in which it has lurked. He has given to it the importance it deserves, for it is no exaggeration to say that without it there would probably have been no Lone Star Republic and possibly the State of Texas would still be a part of Mexico.

The Navy was unquestionably largely responsible for the victory that Houston won at San Jacinto. It blocked reinforcements for Santa Anna. It forced him for lack of supplies to alter his plan of campaign at a crucial moment. While doing all this it was struggling under tremendous handicaps. It was makeshift. Its material was wretched. Its personnel was picked up haphazard. All this is pictured vividly by the author.

He has not merely given the bare bones of the naval narrative. He has also skillfully drawn the whole sequence of events in the fumbling but powerful movement of Anglo-Texans which led to Texan statehood.

He has shown the early attempts at compromise, the Constitution of 'Twenty-four and the inevitable treachery of Santa Anna. Even in those early days naval warfare played its part when the armed schooners the *Austin*, *Red Rover* and *Water Witch* aided in the attack on Fort Anáhuac.

True historian that he is, Jim Dan Hill has not attempted to paint those early characters as fabulous heroes. He has shown the good with the bad, the competent with the incompetent.

Indeed to me this book is far more than a history of the Texas Navy. It is a picture of the types and tribulations that were found everywhere on our frontier as the nation pushed westward. He has caught the genius of our people; the desire, often incompetent, always strong, to establish a parliamentary type of government, a democracy. He has shown the enormous vitality of these frontiersmen, who, in spite of blunders, venality and cowardice continuously pushed ahead towards a dimly-seen goal.

THEODORE ROOSEVELT

Oyster Bay, N. Y.
September 23, 1936

AUTHOR'S PREFACE

THAT TEXAS had a navy, along with her other trappings of sovereignty, is a fact mentioned in even the elementary state histories that the children of that commonwealth study in the grade schools. The extent, however, to which the neighboring Gulf of Mexico and its control were major factors in the economic, the military, and the diplomatic affairs of the Republic has escaped the attention of American historians. Only one or two writers seem to appreciate the importance of Texan control of the Gulf in the crucial Alamo-San Jacinto campaign of 1836, and the scope of their work did not permit them to go into the details of the naval operations.

Other students of southwestern history have unquestionably been aware of the naval actions and their importance, but they have not reduced their knowledge to a narrative. Certainly Dr. Alexander Dienst, a dentist in Temple, Texas, who for decades found pleasure and interest in collecting Texan historical materials, appreciated the importance of the navy, for much of his collecting had to do with it. He also wrote a monograph on the fleet that was published, twenty-seven years ago, in the quarterly of the Texas State Historical Association. His approach, however, was primarily that of the antiquarian, and he confined his research to Texan materials, which were of a fugitive character because of fires in the Texan capitol. Even so, his work from the sources available to him has long stood as the most scholarly effort to treat fully the Texan ships and their cruises. Since his interest was largely that of the antiquarian, he made no effort to integrate the maritime activities and naval operations with the complexities of the foreign and domestic affairs of the turbulent Mexican and Texan Republics —complexities that must be incorporated into the narrative if the operations of the Lone Star Navy are to be fully understood and appreciated. I feel deeply indebted to Dr. Dienst for his historical pioneering in the Texan sources.

To minimize interruptions for the general reader and at the same time keep faith with the scholar who is vitally interested in the sources, the notes and citations are relegated to an appendix. No attempt was made to validate every historical statement with pretentious documentation. Most of the more general facts mentioned are already established in such well known survey works as H. H. Bancroft's seven volumes devoted to a *History of Mexico* and *North Mexican States and Texas*, and G. L. Rives, *The United States and Mexico, 1821–1848*, not to mention the more recent historical contributions of such writers and scholars as Clarence R. Wharton and Dr. E. C. Barker. Because of the wide availability of these authentic general works, the sources specifically cited are for the most part confined to those that are directly quoted and to the more obscure materials that are highly pertinent to the naval narrative. Even so, not all the sources consulted and directly or indirectly drawn upon in writing this history are mentioned in the notes and citations. A supplementary bibliography is accordingly included.

Any historical work based upon far-flung sources leaves its author indebted to more people than he can adequately thank in a short preface. Dr. L. B. Shippee, of the University of Minnesota, was generous with aid and suggestions. Mr. J. S. Ibbotson, Librarian, The Rosenberg Library, Galveston, called my attention to available illustrations and sources. A like service was rendered by Mr. George B. Utley, Librarian, Newberry Library, Chicago. It is by virtue of his courtesy and the generosity of his institution that the William Bollaert drawings are reproduced in this volume. Mr. H. H. Fletcher, a most alert collector and rare book dealer, Houston, Texas, first told me of the Bollaert pictures. Incidentally, he was most generous in other helpful suggestions and this might well have been a better book had I followed his advice on more points. Professor Thorpe M. Langley, Geography Department, State Teachers College, Superior, relieved me of much tedious detail with reference to the final draft of the map and diagrams.

Mr. Allan Dawson, of the American Diplomatic Service, rendered valuable assistance in gaining my admission to the normally closed Foreign Office archives in Mexico City. Captains H. C. Cocke and Dudley W. Knox, U. S. N., were most generous in making available indispensable sources in the Navy Department Library, Washington, D. C.

To Mr. Clarence R. Wharton, Houston attorney, collector and historian, I am thankful not only for helpful suggestions and use of source materials in his private collection, but also for his hearty hospitality while I was using them. I am also quite grateful to Miss Winnie Allen and to her colleagues and associates on the staffs of the Texas State Library and the University of Texas archives. At no institution is a stranger received with a more generous welcome, encouraged with more enthusiasm, or aided with more patience.

Jim Dan Hill

State Teachers College
Superior, Wisconsin
August 12, 1936

CONTENTS

CONTENTS

ILLUSTRATIONS

THE TEXAS NAVY

CHAPTER ONE

TEXAN MARITIME TROUBLES
Trade Tariffs • Decrees • Bradburn at
Anáhuac • Resolutions • Velasco Fight

$\mathcal{A}$ SEA-FARING man, with enough salty characteristics to have rated him a forecastle berth alongside that of an Israel Hands or a Long John Silver, was one of the first individuals the bizarre Davy Crockett met as he, in 1835, cantered along the old San Antonio Trail.[1] Few have noted this as a significant episode because the annals of Texas are not among those to which one instinctively turns for swashbuckling sea tales or even plain, unadorned naval history.

Texas is so intimately associated with pony-riding plains Indians, French explorers, Spanish *padres*, fortress-like missions, boastful, buckskin-clad *Yanqui* intruders, Mexican counter-invaders, a romantic cattle frontier, cotton fields, and modern greasy derricks that no thought is given to ships and sailors.

The historians are at fault for the maritime omissions as well as for many other popularly held misconceptions. Until recent years they have clouded rather than clarified early Texan history. For three-quarters of a century nationally famous but provincial minded historians were so busy giving Texas an ignoble rôle in that great nineteenth century American drama, the Anti-Slavery crusade, that they could not be bothered with causes and activities that did not enlarge upon their thesis. For example: The Missouri Compromise and the Florida

3

Treaty in which the United States surrendered its claim to Texas "greatly reduced the area in which slave states might be formed, . . . and it became desirable to acquire the latter province for the benefit of the slave holding interest."[2]

In this summary fashion an able historian of the 'Eighties explained the colonization of Texas, her secession, independence, and the resulting Mexican War. Of course this war, in the minds of such prejudiced writers, was just a piece of gigantic, international highway robbery, for and by the slavocrats. Its one redeeming feature, they would have you believe, was that it helped to mobilize Northern opinion for the Great Abolition Crusade that achieved Negro freedom in the "Irrepressible Conflict" of 1861–65.

Following the lead of the smug and sedate historians, a myriad of hack writers on history textbook assignments and a host of perspiring platform patriots have perpetuated the Texan-Slavocracy-conspiracy myth down to our own day.

Dr. George P. Garrison's non-conformist opinions, the publication in 1919 of Justin H. Smith's erudite, scholarly and conclusive *War With Mexico*, the penetrating essays and studies of Dr. Eugene C. Barker supported by a small but growing group of lesser scholars have exposed the fallacy of the myth. Vestiges of it linger, however, in the minds of many well-informed, casual readers of history.

A new thesis is now well established, however, that the colonization of Texas was no conspiracy of the Slavocracy. It was rather the phenomenon of a rapidly increasing population expanding into a great geographical semi-vacuum—the West, of which Texas was merely a part. True, a mud fort at Nacogdoches, a cluster of missions near San Antonio, each surrounded by few settlers, gave Spain, and later Mexico, a nominal suzerainty over that vast but essentially vacant domain.

Had the incoming wave of Anglo-Texans at the very outset ruthlessly ignored the fiction of Mexican sovereignty in the same manner that earlier waves of frontiersmen had ignored the far more valid ownership of territories occupied for centuries by native, red skinned tribesmen, there probably would have been less trouble in the long run.

But the early Anglo-Texan colonists chose what appeared at first to be the easier path. They nominally accepted the Mexican suzerainty with its state religion, strange judicial concepts, stranger and often kaleidoscopic laws, and the mercurial instability of its officialdom. Thus, there soon developed a host of Anglo-Texan grievances, reciprocated by deserved Mexican suspicions, that led to secession and independence.

Although in actual practice the Anglo-Texan colonists enjoyed religious toleration, there was just enough reminder of a state religion to create a smouldering, mental unrest. Far more disconcerting was the failure of the Mexican legislature for the state of Coahuila-Texas, sitting in distant Monclova, to set up adequate courts for administering justice in the turbulent and rapidly growing Anglo-American communities. Compared to the inadequate courts and the desire for separation from Coahuila, the Mexican legal vagaries with reference to negro slaves, peonage and "contract labor" were of minor importance. But few Anglo-immigrants owned slaves, and that few were permitted to keep them. Disturbing to all and thereby a far greater irritant were the juristic uncertainties with reference to land titles. Every colonist was a landholder, and to such a degree a real estate speculator. Thus the Mexican Decree of April 6, 1830, which not only prohibited immigration from the United States but also gave the Anglo-Texans their first taste of Mexican military bureaucracy at its worst, is readily recognized as a major cause of conflict.

Though it is usually overlooked, the Anglo-Texans also had tariff, trade, and maritime grievances quite comparable to those of the Thirteen Colonies that paved the way, particularly in New England, for the American Declaration of Independence in 1776. In the American Revolution nothing drove the colonists to violence, i.e., the Boston Tea Party, burning of the King's cutter *Gaspee*, and the riots in commercial centers, as did the English tariff regulations and trade restrictions.

And so it was in the Texas of a century ago. The initial clashes of arms in Texas were consistently under the shadow of a storm cloud that formed and grew over a nearby customs house. Readers interested in other causes and factors leading to the Texan-Mexican clash are referred to Dr. Eugene C. Barker's excellent *Mexico and Texas, 1821–1835*. If the mental appetite demands more, the same author's *Life of Austin* provides additional diet. In this brief naval history it is not only necessary but is also fitting that the heretofore slighted maritime causes of the conflict be emphasized.

Contrary to the commonly held opinion, the majority of the first settlers came to Texas by way of the sea. Southwestern romance and historical travelogues have given an exaggerated importance to the old San Antonio Road, which constituted the one overland transportation link between American Louisiana and Spanish Texas. Individual adventurers often used that moss festooned trail, but the first Anglo-American colonists went to Texas by way of the Gulf of Mexico. The overwhelming majority of subsequent immigrants also embarked at New Orleans or Mobile, and coasted westward to Galveston Bay, the mouth of the Brazos or to Matagorda Bay. As the colonial population grew, surpluses of lumber, wool and cotton went from Texas to the factories of New Orleans over the same route. Later, west bound schooners brought not only additional colonists but primitive saw mill machinery, cotton gin equipment, rifles, ammunition, household utensils, fabrics and all the other manufactured needs of a rapidly growing West.

These early coasters were apparently unaware of the old Spanish custom of confining foreign commerce to limited channels. If any of them knew that Espiritu Santo Bay, a deserted lagoon, far to the southwest of where Texan colonists wanted to go, was the only official port of entry to the province of Texas, their actions showed no evidence of the knowledge. They continued to land passengers and cargoes where they willed. Thus, by 1825, Galveston, Brazoria and Matagorda were *de facto* ports of entry. Espiritu Santo Bay was still deserted.

Stephen F. Austin, the Moses of the Texas colonization movement and who, as an *empresario*, was personally responsible for the settlement of many families, saw impending trouble in this situation. In the above mentioned year, he requested that Galveston be made a legal port of entry. His good and powerful friend, General Manuel de Mier y Terán, departmental commander with headquarters at Matamoras, responded by making it a provisional port.[3] Later, Austin sought the official recognition of other shipping points, particularly Brazoria. In response to these later requests no action was taken. It left a situation made to order for some future, unscrupulous, Mexican official who might see fit to levy a tribute, private or public, upon Texan commerce using the non-recognized harbors or rivers.

On the other hand there was no reason why General Mier y Terán should have taken immediate action. Even after he had declared Galveston a provisional port, he did not deem it necessary to send a customs officer there. Since September, 1823, there had been in force a very generous decree from Mexico City to the effect that "all goods of every class, national or foreign that be introduced into the province of Texas for the consumption of its inhabitants be free of duty" for a period of seven years.[4] The purpose of the decree was obviously to stimulate colonization, and as long as it was in force there would be little occasion for the customs and port-of-entry question to cause difficulty.

Austin apparently came to this conclusion for he gave the matter no additional epistolary attention until 1828. His revival of interest in the question seems to have been initiated by a new Mexican tariff law passed in 1827. It contained no specific exemption in favor of the Texans. In addition to the *ad valorem* and specific levies there was a tonnage duty of 2.12\frac{1}{2}$ a ton on all foreign vessels entering a Mexican port. Though many of the vessels in the Gulf trade were owned by Anglo-Texans, their American registry had been retained. A rigid enforcement of this item alone was enough to give Texans great concern.

Austin's correspondence began to bristle in 1828 with reference to the tariff. Cautiously in his correspondence with Mier y Terán he showed that the tariff would set up an unsurmountable barrier to the New Orleans trade. This, he thought, would be all right when the Texan colonists had developed adequate commercial and credit relations with Tampico and Vera Cruz. Indeed, he saw great advantages to the Texans in prospective Vera Cruz connections, but until these were consummated the tariff of 1827 would be ruinous.[5]

In October 1828, General Mier y Terán decided that the free trade decree of 1823 still held. He accordingly sent no customs officer to the Texan coast, and Austin again lost interest in Mexican tariff schedules.

The famous decree against immigration, of April 6, 1830, was Mexico's first measure to counteract the Anglo-American influx, concerning which she had already shown much apprehension. This decree not only banned future Anglo-American emigrants but also called for a system of military posts throughout the settled portions of Texas, garrisoned by convict soldiers. The admitted duties of the garrisons were to enforce the non-immigration clauses of the decree and to enforce the collection of duties. The seven year free trade exemption period, as laid down in 1823, was to expire in October, 1830. It also seems that Mexican officialdom had decided that the Texans should have been paying the tonnage fees all along, even though Article 12 of the decree of April 6, 1830, opened Texan trade to foreign ships for a period of four years. In any case, May 18, 1830, before the soldiers had yet arrived, General Terán's subordinate, George Fisher, appeared at Brazoria, the busiest port on the coast, and began trying to collect tonnage fees.[6]

Fisher, a low adventurer of North American background but of Serbian extraction, turned out to be a self-important officious individual with a penchant for subjecting shippers to unreasonable demands and for openly denouncing his new neighbors to his Mexican superior officers. General Terán was, of course, the recipient of many protests against Fisher from his Texan friends. The sympathetic General at once disestablished the office on the apparent theory that the tonnage fee should not be paid.

Fisher was not ordered back to his duties as customs officer until 1831, but that does not indicate that all was quiet on the tariff front during the period of his suspension. Late in 1830, Mexican garrisons appeared at Velasco, between the mouth of the Brazos and Brazoria, and at Anáhuac, on Galveston Bay.

The latter garrison was commanded by another adventurer with an Anglo-American name, Colonel John D. Bradburn of the Mexican regular army. A native of western Virginia, this energetic ex-hillbilly had gone to New Spain as a filibuster in Mina's expedition. He had battled upward to preferment and rank in the turbulent armies of the Mexican patriots. With this record in mind we can readily understand the arrogance he displayed when he found himself lording it over several municipalities inhabited by his former compatriots of the old American frontier. They in turn considered him a renegade, overlooking with cavalier inconsistency their own Mexican citizenship that had been automatically acquired with their settlement upon an *empresario* grant.

Colonel Bradburn's offences against Anglo-Texans were numerous. In one way or another he aroused them against himself and against Mexican control by irritating anew practically every grievance the Texans had ever entertained against the Mexicans. First of all, however, he dusted off the legal port-of-entry question by entirely closing Brazoria, and opening a customs office under his own administration at Anáhuac. To his disappointment he discovered that although the Decree of Customs Exemption on consumption goods had expired, the Decree of April 6, 1830 had provided enough exemptions for two years to prevent his finding much traffic on which he could collect.

But the tonnage fee of $2.12½ on ships of a foreign registry that had been stipulated in the tariff of 1827 offered possibilities. With utter disregard for Article 12 of the Decree of 1830 which opened coastwise commerce to foreign ships for four years, he ruled, in January 1831, that a sixty-five-ton schooner owned and operated by S. Rhoads Fisher, soon to become Texan Secretary of Navy, had to pay that fee every time it entered Texan waters on a coastal voyage to Tampico. According to Mr. Fisher this would make his tonnage fees for a contemplated coasting voyage, not counting other port charges, come to $552.50. Fisher protested that "no vessel can stand this and unless a change is made the trade must be abandoned. I am not prepared to dispute the legality of Colonel Bradburn's demand, but Mr. Hiram and several other gentlemen here say they would not pay it, for Colonel Bradburn has nothing to do with this colony."[7]

In the meantime, the citizens of the closed port of Brazoria were pressing Colonel Bradburn to open that shipping point. This he reluctantly did when the Texan delegation would not listen to his plea that he had to consult Terán at Matamoras before he could act. The Texans, with justice, not only believed that Terán had never ordered the closing of Brazoria but also doubted strongly the legality of Bradburn's assumption of customs collecting duties.

This was the state of affairs when the pestiferous George Fisher arrived in Anáhuac, November 1831, to take over Colonel Bradburn's self delegated duties as customs collector. Bradburn remained as commander of the garrison.

Fisher brought little or no improvement. He permitted ships to continue entering and clearing Brazoria but ruled that before clearance could be legal the shipmaster would have to come to Anáhuac to get the papers signed. This meant an overland trip of about a hundred miles. The shipmasters in that region did not consider Fisher's signature worth that much trouble. In December 1831, the crews of two vessels overpowered the Mexican waterfront guards at Brazoria and put to sea without clearance documents. Most of the population of Brazoria participated in the rioting, and one Mexican soldier was wounded.[8]

All of this exasperated the fair-minded and just Mier y Terán. He cut the Gordian knot by holding the receivers of the ships' cargoes responsible for fees, ordering the detention of the ships should they return, and by rebuking Fisher for his unreasonable rules.

In February 1832, some two months after these disturbances, the government of Austin's colony forwarded a petition to the Mexican government which pretty well reflects the sentiment of the Anglo-Texan population at this time. The petition not only pleaded for relief from the immigration ban of April 6, 1830, but also for a renewal of the old tariff exemption for five years. It was also urged that George Fisher be relieved and a Mexican appointed in his place. Shortly thereafter, Fisher was relieved by Francisco Duclor. He chose to live in Brazoria to accommodate the bulk of Texan trade.

Bradburn continued at Anáhuac, however, and by June of that year had so antagonized the settlers over land titles, confiscation of supplies and peremptory and arbitrary imprisonment of prominent colonists that the populace decided that he could not be longer tolerated.

Many of the discerning frontier leaders thought they saw in Mexican national politics a chance to be rid of the odious Bradburn and all of his ilk. They and their garrisons had been sent into Texas by President Bustamante, who was a rabid Centralist. Indeed, the Decree of April 6, 1830, was characteristic of a number of measures whereby the Centralists, then controlling the government in Mexico City, had sought to ignore the states rights principles of the Mexican Constitution of 1824 and to exercise more and more direct governmental control over the masses of the Mexican people.

By the time Bradburn and Fisher were having their troubles with the Texans, discontent with Bustamante was cropping out all over Mexico. That political chameleon extraordinary and opportunist plenipotentiary, Antonio Lopez de Santa Anna, seized the leadership of the anti-Bustamante, states-rights faction with his Plan of Vera Cruz. The Texans saw in states rights under a Mexican federal constitution a solution to all their governmental troubles. Why not join Santa Anna's states-rights movement, kick out Bustamante's centralistic garrisons and as a reward receive from Santa Anna full statehood for the province of Texas? Thus argued Texan leaders at the village corners. More discerning and practical minded Texans foresaw that the immediate ousting of the garrisons at Anáhuac and Velasco would achieve immediate nullification of the odious ban against immigration and would return *de facto* free trade. What customs could Francisco Duclor collect without Lieutenant Colonel Ugartechea's garrison at Velasco? How potent would be his deputy in Galveston without Bradburn's garrison at Anáhuac?

Bradburn was aware of the rising tide of discontent in his area. Sensing the approach of a crisis, he made a military evaluation of the situation. He could hold his fort indefinitely against riflemen. The only two cannon not in the possession of Mexican garrisons were at Brazoria. The steamer *Ariel* had left them to lighten her cargo for getting over the Brazos bar. These guns could hardly be brought overland across the broad river mouths and marshes. They would come by sea and therefore necessarily pass Lieutenant Colonel Ugartechea's fort at Velasco.

Thus the first incipient clash of arms between the Texans and the Mexicans was of a distinctly maritime origin, involved ships and sailors, and brought up the age old military question of sea control.

Bradburn instructed his subordinate to get the cannon out of possession of the colonists at all costs, and continued with his arrogant policies toward the Texans in his immediate area. Bradburn should have been more cautious. He did not know that genial, good-natured and gentlemanly Ugartechea was already so thoroughly over-awed by rowdy Brazorians that ships came and went, such as the defiant schooner *Sabine*, with or without permission.

Apparently lulled by a sense of security, Colonel Bradburn

yielded nothing to the citizens of the Galveston Bay area. As a protective measure he arbitrarily imprisoned a Texan militia organizer. A frontier lawyer by the name of W. B. Travis, later hero of the Alamo, began talking an Anglo-legal jargon about a *habeas corpus*, and Bradburn incarcerated him for his trouble. Then a popular jokester played fast and loose with Bradburn's dignity. On vague charges the prankster was held in custody with the other two trouble-makers. When Mr. Jack, brother of the militia organizer, appeared before Bradburn in protest, he was given just fifteen minutes in which to leave Anáhuac. This he did and forthwith constituted himself a sort of pedestrian Paul Revere by touring the countryside and arousing the citizens to arms.

Soon bands from communities for miles around, under officers elected on the spot, were converging on Anáhuac. Colonel F. W. Johnson, a frontiersman who later succumbed to the urge of authorship and left an excellent compilation of his own and other narratives of his times, was selected as commander of the Texans. So rapidly did the Texans close in that on June 10, 1832, one of Bradburn's cavalry patrols was captured. Bradburn played for time by resorting to much vocal wrangling, promises, and efforts to shift responsibility; whereupon, the colonists withdrew a short distance and Bradburn strengthened his fort. This broke the truce. Blockade and preliminary siege operations began at once.[9]

The blockade was enforced by an improvised fleet consisting of the tiny schooners *Austin*, *Waterwitch*, and *Red Rover* which carried, all told, eighteen men. A small swivel aboard the *Waterwitch* seems to have been the only weapon in the "fleet" larger than a rifle. The operations of this squadron have been briefly summarized by one of the "captains":

We were ordered by the commander-in-chief Francis W. Johnson, to cruise up and down the bay of Galveston and the mouth of the Trinity River and make prizes of all vessels loaded with provisions for Fort Anáhuac.

About the 5th of June, 1832, Captain Kokernot discovered a vessel crossing the bay, in the direction of Anáhuac, and gave chase, overtook and captured her. She was loaded with butter, eggs, chickens and other provisions for the Mexican garrison at Anáhuac which was converted to the use of our little army.

Captain Scott (of the *Stephen F. Austin*) made prize of a boat near the mouth of the Double Bayou, loaded with beef and corn meal for the fort. About the same time Captain Spillman took two boats, off Cedar Point, loaded with corn and other provisions for Fort Anáhuac.[10]

While the "fleet" was capturing prizes, laden with butter, eggs, and chickens, some instinctive parliamentarian on June 13 transmuted Colonel Johnson's army into a civil body politic by improvising a gavel, pounding a stump with it and declaring that a deliberative body was now in session. Needless to say, the best American traditions were upheld by the passage of a cluster of resolutions, the Turtle Bayou Resolutions. These deliberations are important here largely because they, like other Texan documents that list or reflect grievances leading to revolt, show that the maritime trade situation was an outstanding source of complaint.

As would be expected, in view of the political situation in Mexico, allegiance to the Republic and her sacred states-rights Constitution of 1824 was pledged. Santa Anna and his decentralizing Plan of Vera Cruz were praised. Grievances were listed, among which those growing out of sea borne trade restrictions were not the least.

The most potent resolution, however, was the paragraph calling for a detachment to go to Brazoria for the two cannon. Captain John Austin and William Russell, two good, rabble-rousing frontier speakers, constituted the detachment. If their oratory prevailed, the sympathetic Brazorians would load the cannon on a ship and in personally delivering the artillery would also reinforce the Texans.

These two worthy captains lived up to their forensic reputations. The thoroughly aroused citizens of Brazoria asked Lieutenant Colonel Ugartechea if he would not be loyal to the

Constitution of 1824 (and disloyal to his *Presidente* Bustamante) to the extent of permitting them to carry the cannon
unmolested past his fort at Velasco.

Lieutenant Colonel Ugartechea's refusal increased the enthusiasm of the colonists for the Constitution of 1824. They
decided that the erstwhile affable Lieutenant Colonel must be an
enemy of that precious document. The Brazorians at once elected
Captain John Austin commander-in-chief on land and water.

No kin to the suave, pacific statesman-like Stephen F.
Austin, John was an ex-Connecticut Yankee sailor and an ex-
filibuster who knew the discomforts of a Mexican dungeon.
Willing to flirt with the dungeons again, he welcomed the command. His colleague, Captain Russell, was given command of
the fine large schooner *Brazoria* which had been seized, manned
by forty rifleman, and armed with the two cannon.

The morning of June 25, 1832, found this amphibious expedition, about 125 rifles afloat and ashore, making its way
down river to Fort Velasco. The fort consisted of a circular re-
doubt of sharpened uprights, backed by logs and sand. In the
center stood a high, keep-like bastion topped by a low parapet
which gave inadequate protection to the artillerymen that
served the long, lean 9-pounder swivel mounted thereon.
A smaller gun on the landward redoubts was better protected.

Under cover of darkness and aided by a diversion fire from
the *Brazoria*, an attacking party established itself within thirty
yards of the fort and set up a palisaded embankment. Dawn
came, and with it such a galling Mexican fire that Austin's men
could not show their heads to return it, let alone advance and
attack. Nevertheless, in good Latin-American revolutionary
style they kept up their spirits by shouting *"Viva* Santa Anna,"
to which the garrison of the small fort responded with equally
enthusiastic *"vivas"* for *"la Republica," "la Constitución y las
leyes"* and *"el Supremo Gobierno."*[11] The one-sided exchange of
leaden pellets and the reciprocal volleys of *"vivas"* ended at
eight o'clock when a torrential downpour wet the powder of the
Texan land forces. Austin withdrew.

Meanwhile Captain Russell had been relentlessly hammering the river side of the fort with the *Brazoria's* artillery. Of course, the Mexicans responded with their nine-pounder bastion swivel. About dawn the *Brazoria's* moorings were shot away. Left to the whims of the tide she drifted toward the fort, grounded and was left high within 170 yards of the hostile works. From this position the unerring aim of Russell's forty riflemen, shielded by bulwarks reinforced with cotton bales, drove the Mexican garrison from every vantage point. Successive Mexican gun crews, from the garrison of a hundred and twenty-five men, tried to serve the swivel and experienced such casualties that the artillerymen would not stand up to train the gun. They resorted to firing blindly by exposing only the wrist and the hand. So many Mexican forearms were shattered by the Texan riflemen that the garrison refused to fire the gun in even this haphazard manner.

In his disgust with his gun crews Ugartechea boldly exposed himself in pointing the piece. He was not killed, so claimed the American accounts, because of his popularity among the Texans and their admiration for his bravery. The Colonel's ability as a cannoneer, however, must have been as low as his courage was high, for the nine-pounder did not make a clean hit on the *Brazoria* after daybreak.

With the fort silenced by the *Brazoria's* riflemen and the Texan land detachment clearly beaten off, the situation was approaching a deadlock.[12] But conditions looked worse within the fort than the Texans suspected. At 10 A.M. Ugartechea hoisted the white flag. Texan bullets had induced the doughty Colonel to announce an endorsement of Santa Anna's Plan of Vera Cruz. With provisions and small arms he and his garrison were permitted to depart for Matamoras. The cannon and ammunition fell into the hands of the Texans.

Ugartechea reported to his superior that he had lost seven killed and nineteen wounded, ten of whom were shot in the hand or arm. The Texans had lost seven killed and fifteen wounded, but they had consummated a bold step toward nullifying tariff regulations, reopening the country to American immigrants and in ridding it of odious convict garrisons.

While Velasco was being captured, Bradburn's affairs at Anáhuac had taken a queer turn. Under orders from Terán that antedated the Texan mobilization, Colonel Piedras had arrived in the region with an appreciable force of Mexicans from the Nacogdoches garrison. His instructions were to relieve Bradburn and to pacify the colonists.

Bradburn forfeited his command in favor of Colonel Subaran and sought personal safety in a night flight to New Orleans. Piedras and Subaran released the prisoners, promised reforms, and announced themselves in favor of Santa Anna's Plan of Vera Cruz. Indeed, Subaran became so enthusiastic about the Plan that he and his garrison embarked for Mexico so that they might participate in the revolution against Bustamante. Piedras returned to Nacogdoches, encountered local hostility there, and he and his force shortly withdrew to Mexico. Meanwhile the Texan "fleet" off Fort Anáhuac had "sailed for Galveston Island, captured the deputy collector and his men, took possession of the customs house and other public property."[13]

Santa Anna's Colonel Mexía soon appeared off Brazoria with troop ships, 400 men, and the man-of-war *Santa Anna* from Matamoras. The Mexican revolutionists and supporters of the Plan of Vera Cruz were apparently suspicious of Anglo-Texan motives. But Mexía was quickly convinced that the Texans were simon pure devotees of a Federal union of Mexican states.[14] He furthermore got in touch with the remaining Centralist garrisons in the province, induced them to declare for Santa Anna and to withdraw to Mexico where their services were badly needed in the cause of Federalism. He and his forces soon followed suit.[15]

Thus by the end of the summer of 1832, the amiable customs collector Duclor, at Brazoria, was the only vestige that remained of the rigid, governmental regulations Bustamante had planned for Texas. During these months Duclor, without armed support, was unable to collect enough revenue to pay the expenses of his office. Within a few months he willed his official debts and the dubious assets of his office to the local anglicized *ayuntamiento* and departed for Tampico.

Thus ended the first open clash of arms between the Anglo-Texans and those who controlled the National Palace in Mexico City. Through the entire pattern of grievances and conflict there runs such a conspicuous thread of maritime grievances and struggle for sea control that one wonders why it has been so long slighted, if not completely ignored.

CHAPTER TWO

THE WAR BEGINS AT SEA • Politics and Customs Collectors • Cutters Clash • Austin • "Pirates" Incarcerated

FOR SEVERAL months after the clash of 1832, Santa Anna's states rights revolution in Mexico was achieving success and establishing its new train of politicians in the *Palacio Nacional.* The Texans naturally felt that they had contributed materially to the success of the movement and now was the time to reap their reward for having backed the right party in the recent gun-powder, national election. Statehood for an Anglicized Texas within a non-centralized, states rights, Mexican Union seemed to be their logical reward.

They resorted to the locally initiated convention, the usual political device of the American frontier for achieving statehood—but a device that in Mexico, with its heritage of bureaucratic New Spain, was sure to be viewed as a treasonable activity. In October 1832, a convention composed of delegates from the various municipalities met in San Felipe, the capital of Stephen A. Austin's colony, and drew up a list of grievances and adopted a petition for statehood. The usual plea for tariff exemption was included in the document.

A resolution of the convention also instructed the local councils, or *ayuntamientos,* in the absence of Mexican Federal officers, to bond officers of their choosing to collect tariffs at Matagorda, Galveston and Brazoria. These instructions from an extra-legal body were, of course, advisory and were probably put into the proceedings to create a good impression in Mexico City. In any case there is no evidence that such bonded officers of the *ayuntamientos* ever collected and sent to Mexico any funds derived from customs collections. Furthermore, the coastal merchants and ship owners were quiet for the next three years, a fact which is also good evidence that the Anglo-Texans enjoyed *de facto* free trade until 1835.

The convention of 1832 and its petitions yielded no results. In the meantime, the tariff laws, and the objectionable Decree of April 6, 1830, were still on the law books, and therefore were a constant menace to future tranquillity; a menace that increased as Santa Anna, after getting in office, was showing strong centralistic tendencies.

Accordingly in 1833 the Texans again resorted to a convention. Statehood was again petitioned, and resolutions against the decree of April 6, 1830, were adopted. The absolute necessity of legal free trade for an additional period of years was emphasized.

To lobby for these Texan desires, the highly influential and the cleverest diplomat of the American frontier, Stephen F. Austin, went to Mexico City. There he remained for the next two years, the latter part of which he spent in a Mexican dungeon for writing what an American would consider an innocent letter. He merely urged his friends in Texas to stage another locally initiated, statehood convention at which a tentative state constitution could be drafted for approval by the Mexican Congress.

Meanwhile in Texas the citizens were enjoying the State of Coahuila-Texas reform laws of 1833. And a cholera epidemic, in which turbulent John Austin died, was distracting local attention from affairs in Mexico City. At no time was the Texan horizon clearer of war clouds. The Anglo-Texans were willing to wait patiently for statehood unless the citizens were again aroused by the planting of "law despising garrisons, custom houses, etc., etc., amongst us."[1]

But it was the false calm that often comes before the storm.

The sending of Austin to a dungeon for proposing another Texan statehood convention was not the only evidence that Santa Anna was turning his back upon his Vera Cruz proclaimed states rights program. May 23, 1834, he openly discarded federal pretensions by announcing his highly centralistic Plan of Cuernavaca. At the time his trusted Colonel Almonte was making a tour of inspection through Texas and reporting unprecedented smuggling.

More significant for Texans were Minister of War and Navy José de Herrera's recommendations of April 11, 1834. He urged that the naval branch of his department should be expanded in order to patrol the coasts properly. He insisted that such expansion would make a rich return in customs collections and captures of illicit traders. Particularly did he regret conditions "on the Sea of the North" (the Gulf of Mexico adjoining Texas) where there were several examples of resistance to customs and Mexican officials. He considered it necessary to meet this condition "with ships of war ready to punish the transgressors."[2]

In harmony with the new centralistic trend and these recommendations, Santa Anna sought in 1835 to turn back the clock by re-establishing close control over Anglo-Texas. The Texans' old friend, Ugartechea, now promoted to Colonel, appeared in San Antonio with a large command which he, as province commander, quickly parceled out into smaller garrisons in the hinterland and along the coast. A rather genial Captain Tenorio appeared, with a garrison, at the ruins of Bradburn's old fort at Anáhuac. This was the supporting force for chief customs collector Gonzales, at Brazoria, and his two deputies, who re-established customs houses at Anáhuac and at Galveston. The Mexican Navy's schooner-of-war, *Moctezuma*, began prowling up and down the coast in the rôle of a revenue cutter.

For once history almost lived up to its alleged reputation for repeating itself. Gonzales at Brazoria interpreted his instructions as an order to collect tonnage and port fees only. The deputies on Galveston Bay insisted upon collecting according to the high rates of the Mexican Tariff in addition to the above-mentioned fees. This was rank discrimination against the people in the Galveston Bay area. As if regional discrimination were not enough, the Galveston Bay deputies indulged in individual discrimination by allowing "credit" to some merchants and demanding cash of others. The protests were loud and expressed in no uncertain language.

Nor did the Anglo-Texans stop with mere vocal protests. When a Texan ship captain found one of Tenorio's messengers among his passengers, he left the courier upon one of the deserted off-shore islands, where he remained for weeks. When the messenger finally got through to Tenorio's superiors, he attributed his treatment to the smuggling activities on that very voyage which the skipper did not want reported until his ship was clear of the coast.

Texans in the vicinity of Anáhuac tried to get rid of Tenorio's garrison by refusing to sell him supplies. Lumber collected for rebuilding the fort was deliberately burned. Tenorio repeated Bradburn's mistake of incarcerating a popular citizen. In retaliation a messenger from Colonel Ugartechea to Tenorio was seized and his dispatches read. The contents of the dispatches were not reassuring. Tenorio was urged to carry on, for reinforcements were en route so that "these revolutionists will be ground down."[3]

With these documents as a stimulus, the ubiquitous W. B. Travis aroused the militia to oust Tenorio even as Johnson had ousted Bradburn. But Tenorio was of softer metal than his predecessor. He vacated at once and did so with such courtesy that he at once became the social lion at a Fourth of July barbecue at Harrisburg. Instead of returning to San Antonio he lingered among the Texan settlements for some weeks. He was unquestionably expecting his Lieutenant Don Carlos Ocampo to arrive by water from Matamoras with money for paying local bills, and hoping to realize the possibility of the reinforcements that Ugartechea had promised. But more of these matters later. Meanwhile the withdrawal of Tenorio from Anáhuac once again left the customs collectors without support.

But what of the schooner-of-war *Moctezuma* that was to function as a revenue cutter? She, too, had been having turbulent moments. In line with her assignment early in June she had seized the Texan-owned but American registered *Martha* and had escorted her to Matamoras on charges of smuggling. She and her convoy were hardly clear of the coast when bumptious Captain Ezekiel Jones of the United States Revenue Cutter *Ingham* appeared at Matagorda—searching for slavers, the perennial American excuse in those days for cruising off a foreign coast.

The irate Texans regaled Captain Jones with a highly colored version of this latest outrage against the American flag. The testy American at once put to sea bent on punitive action against the *Moctezuma*. He found her at dawn June 14, 1835, well off the mouth of the Rio Grande. The Mexican captain apparently thought the American cutter was another smuggler, for the *Moctezuma* bore down upon the *Ingham* and fired. Captain Jones hoisted his American ensign, ran out his battery and gave the *Moctezuma* a broadside. At this show of teeth the *Moctezuma* fled toward the mouth of the Rio Grande. Twice the Mexican came about as though to give battle, but each time the *Ingham* presented her broadside, and the *Moctezuma* had a change of heart.

The chase continued for six hours and a half, and ended off the forts at the mouth of the Rio Grande. The Captain of the port sent thirty men in small boats to reinforce the crew of the *Moctezuma*, but her commander still deemed an engagement so inadvisable that he put his ship aground at the harbor entrance to avoid an action. He managed to get her across the bar, however, by throwing some of the cargo overboard. But his vessel was so damaged in the operations that she was not seen again on the Texas coast for months.

Not satisfied merely with putting the *Moctezuma* out of commission, doughty Captain Jones proceeded into port and pressed the "rights" of the so-called American citizens aboard the *Martha* so effectively that the captain of the port not only reprimanded the *Moctezuma's* skipper, but apologized to the Americans and delivered up the prisoners.[4]

While the foregoing events were in progress, the Permanent Morelos Batallion of the Mexican Army was being sent into Texas by the conventional sea route, Matamoras to Copano, Matagorda or points still farther east.

And here it is well to remark and to urge the reader to keep in mind that most troop movements of any size into Texas were over this route, because of the twelve days march over dry, barren lands, between Monclova and San Antonio. It was already an accepted principle with the Mexican War Department that to maintain an army in Texas, supplies (and preferably the troops as well) should be transported by ships to a point on the Texan coast nearest the ultimate destination.

Admittedly a raiding column of troops could be marched successfully across the barren wastes but even so, additional supplies for a sustained campaign would have to be transported by water. These hot, dry and flat barrens, then void of bivouac facilities and often subject to Indian raids, particularly if slow moving burrow trains were in transit, gave a basic military importance to the control of the Gulf that is not apparent from a casual glance at a map. Nor would a motor trip through the region today lead one to think it was once a forbidding, desert-like barrier to military movements. Unlimited supplies of subterranean water and irrigation projects have transformed some of the barrens into highly productive gardens, orchards and farms.

But let us return to the Permanent Morelos Batallion. It was being moved into Texas to constitute the reinforcements Colonel Ugartechea had in mind when he advised Tenorio to carry on. The small flotilla carrying this battalion consisted of the *Josefa*, *Ana Maria*, and the war schooner *Correo de Mejico*.

The latter was commanded by Lieutenant Thomas M. Thompson, of the Mexican Navy. Born an Englishman, he had become an American citizen while sailing out of New Orleans as a mate on the J. W. Zacharie ships. Came days of adversity during which he sank to a levee tavern proprietor.[5] Then fortune smiled again and Mr. Thompson achieved the gold braid of a duly commissioned *Teniente Segundo de Marina, Republica de Mejico*. In short, he was a sort of a seagoing Bradburn.

After convoying the flotilla to Copano, Lieutenant Thompson was to continue to Galveston where he would support Tenorio and the customs officers in the enforcement of the revenue law, and spend his spare time making an accurate chart of the coast. Indeed, Lieutenant Thompson had aboard his ship Tenorio's Lieutenant Ocampo who had one thousand dollars in his custody for retiring some of Tenorio's bills[6] and perhaps partially paying the garrison.

Upon their arrival in Galveston Bay, Thompson and Ocampo were astounded to find that Tenorio had departed and that the customs houses were not functioning. They were told that Tenorio and the remnants of his detachment (desertions had been heavy) were at Austin's capital, San Felipe, as they really were. A special courier was sent to Tenorio with letters reporting the arrival of Ocampo and Thompson and urging his return. But Tenorio either did not stomach the idea of again occupying his unhappy former position or the Texans were still addicts to their recently formed habit of intercepting Mexican dispatches, for Thompson waited through much of July and all of August without word from Tenorio.

During this time Thompson tried to restore Mexican authority on the troubled coast. In a proclamation dated July 26, 1835, he warned the citizens of Anáhuac against maintaining a militia company.[7] When they ignored his warning, Thompson threatened to burn the town. In a deposition A. C. Allen of Brazoria swore that his tiny sloop had been confiscated at Galveston by Thompson and illegally converted into a tender of the *Correo*. Mr. Allen furthermore testified that Thompson had boasted that he was "commander of the coast from Tampico to the Sabine."[8] As far north and inland as Nacogdoches, in mass meetings of discontent, resolutions were passed against Lieutenant Thompson and his schooner-of-war.[9]

While Thompson was thus harassing the rugged citizenry, Stephen F. Austin, whose pacific technique in leading turbulent frontiersmen is still one of the most amazing phenomena of the frontier, had been released from the Mexican dungeon and was returning to Texas by way of Vera Cruz and New Orleans.

From what he had seen of the Mexican government in general and of Santa Anna's operations in particular, he had become a changed man. For the first time in his career he had decided that the unnatural bonds between Mexico and Anglicized Texas had to be severed. Though prepared to follow a strict "observance of appearances" toward Mexico until the time to throw off the mask, he saw no hope for Texas without complete Americanization. "The fact is," he wrote, "we must and ought to become a part of the United States."[10]

Austin, with his powerful influence over the Texans, had chosen the path to secession. To what extent he was responsible for the cargo of munitions and for the armed character of the *San Felipe*, upon which he returned to Texas from New Orleans, cannot be learned from sources now available. His sojourn in a Mexican dungeon for writing an ill advised letter gave him a literary restraint not revealed in his letters prior to that experience. In any case, it is significant that shortly after he wrote the above-quoted cautious confidences to a trusted relative, we find him late in August, 1835, bound for Brazoria aboard the munitions laden, armed *San Felipe*, commanded by swashbuckling, arrogant Captain W. A. Hurd.

For the moment let us leave the *San Felipe* as she plows through the gentle Gulf swells toward the mouth of the Brazos river and return to Thompson, his revenue cutter, and the fractious citizens of Brazoria.

On the morning of September 1, the brig *Tremont* was outward bound, loaded with lumber, for Pensacola. She was hardly over the Velasco bar when Thompson brought her to. The *Tremont's* commander was unable to present a manifest of his cargo. For this reason Thompson declared the ship seized, put a prize crew of eight men aboard, and ordered them to carry the brig to Vera Cruz. The Texans were apparently expecting something like this. Perhaps they had been the beneficiaries of another one of Thompson's premature boasts, for a group of them had assembled at the mouth of the river to see what would happen when the *Tremont* cleared.

In any case, a large number of Texans witnessed the proceedings from the shore and were filled with such indignation that shortly the small steamer *Laura* was standing to sea manned by a party of volunteers, armed for boarding, and bent upon recapturing the *Tremont*. She, like the *Correo*, was becalmed close inshore.

So lively was the fire from small arms aboard the *Laura*, augmented by a cannon from the shore, that Thompson recalled the prize crew and thereby abandoned the *Tremont* to strengthen his own ship.[11] Under the stimulus of a counter fire from the *Correo*, the *Laura* took the *Tremont* in tow and withdrew to shallow water beyond the *Correo's* range.

At this stage of the game a sail was noted on the eastern horizon. Thé *Laura* at once laid a course for it and in about an hour returned with a schooner in tow. It was the armed *San Felipe* with her distinguished passenger, Stephen F. Austin, and a cargo of munitions.

The *San Felipe* was towed to the bar and there lightened for the crossing by the usual transfer of cargo and passengers to the *Laura*. During these activities the almost becalmed *Correo* had been patiently working her way close enough in shore to use her cannon. By 8 P.M. she had gained the desired position. But even earlier, the *Laura* had taken such passengers, Austin among them, and freight as were desired, and had steamed up the river. But she had left on board the *San Felipe* the volunteers who had originally come out to retrieve the *Tremont*.[12]

By the time the *Correo* had got within half a cannon shot, a gentle but fitful off-shore breeze enabled the *San Felipe* to bear down upon her in an effort to board. This Thompson avoided by veering his ship and presenting a broadside. There followed a heavy exchange of cannon and rifle fire that lasted more than an hour in which the lighter armed *Correo* was completely worsted. Her two guns were dismounted, most of the crew wounded. Thompson himself was struck twice in the legs by Texan rifle balls.

In this plight Thompson shook out his sails to catch the night breeze and stood seaward in hopes of getting to Matamoras. The *San Felipe* gave hot pursuit. The *Correo* lost her pursuer during the night, but dawn, September 2, revealed both ships becalmed within sight of land. The ever obliging *Laura* at once steamed out and towed the *San Felipe* into a raking position within half a cannon shot of the *Correo's* stern. "In this state, with a flat calm, . . . cannon dismounted without munitions, the boatswain and the larger part of the crew wounded," explained Thompson to the Mexican War and Navy Department, he and Ocampo decided to parley.

Ocampo shoved off in a small boat for a conference but the arrogant Hurd would have no conversation with anyone other than Thompson. When he proved reluctant to leave the *Correo*, the Texan fired a cannon into the air, and Thompson struck his colors—unconditional surrender.

In taking possession of the prize, the Texans joyously discovered that Thompson did not have on board a copy of his commission in the Mexican navy. Notwithstanding an ample packet of official orders that were in his possession, Hurd insisted that Thompson must be a pirate. Following this rather strained line of logic, he put the entire Mexican complement beneath hatches, transported them to New Orleans and, by virtue of the *San Felipe's* American registry, pressed charges of piracy against them in the American federal court.

Thus while Austin toured the Texan settlements urging them to form a government for concerted action, be it compromise or resistance, and while Colonel Ugartechea in San Antonio published proscribed lists of Texans who were to be seized for resisting customs officers and tampering with official messages, Thompson and his crew languished in a New Orleans jail.

Of course Mexican Consul Martinez at New Orleans quickly claimed Thompson and his men as Mexico's own.[13] That should have been enough to effect their release, but Prosecutor Carleton did not think so, and they were held for trial. When the court finally got to the matter in January, 1836, the proceedings degenerated into a case of Texas vs. Mexico, upon which the jury disagreed, with blissful indifference to application of justice to the imprisoned men.

The chances for an impartial trial were thrust still further into the background by the character and antics of the attorneys. Felix Huston was associated with the United States attorney. In this suit he was apparently grooming his fractious disposition for the time when he was to make real duelling history by almost killing Albert Sydney Johnston in a field-of-honor decision as to which of them was to be commander-in-chief of the Texan army. Across the table, and for the Mexicans, sat P. Soulé, none other than the inimitable Pierre Soulé, who later, as President Pierce's fiery Minister to Spain, challenged, duelled and insulted his way through Europe to the bombastic Ostend Manifesto.

Any trial with these two embryo duelling reputations opposed to one another could not be without color. Hence, books and inkstands were used as missiles, with dark hints of pistols at dawn, every time a rule of evidence was discussed. The judge became disgusted and gave both of them a jail sentence. After the furor of the trial died down, the court released the men and the officers of the *Correo*. Thus the New Orleans *Courier* lamented that the "pirates" were "set at liberty and the attorneys were put in jail."[14]

Though the American federal court phase of the *San Felipe-Correo* affair ended with a touch of the comic opera, the clash between the ships off Velasco was a very significant and important event in Texan history when it is viewed in its proper setting. It was far more than a southwestern edition of the *Gaspee* affair off Rhode Island that heralded the American Revolution and with which the *San Felipe-Correo* affair is usu-

ally compared, if it is mentioned at all. It is not too much
to say that the clash between the *San Felipe* and the *Correo*
was a naval engagement in significance—in fact, the opening
shot of the Texan struggle for independence.

The complete change in attitude on the part of the Texan
leader, Stephen F. Austin, has already been mentioned. The
significance of the war-like character in armament as well as
the cargo of the *San Felipe* has been described. To that degree
the *San Felipe* was just another gun-runner. She departed from
the rôle of a mere gun-runner after she disposed of her cargo.
Then it was that she, under the direction of the Texan leaders,
took the offensive against the Mexicans, and in what was essentially the naval engagement that followed, proceeded to
clear the coast of Mexican naval hindrances to the importation
of additional munitions from friendly New Orleans. In short,
the Texans appreciated the necessity of keeping that maritime
highway open and therefore disposed of the *Correo*, the only
representative of Mexican sea power present, in the summary
manner described.

The Mexican Minister of Foreign Affairs, de Costilia y
Lanzos, appreciated this fact from Mexico City when he protested the detention of Thompson and his crew in New Orleans.
The coming court decision "will, in the meantime, have served
to divert from service on that coast a vessel destined to protect
it as far as its weak powers would allow."[15] That the Texans
were thus able to jockey the United States into the embarrassing position of holding the *Correo's* men, thereby relieving
themselves of the burden, was merely a stroke of good fortune;
but of which they made the most. Had not the peculiar circumstances enabled them to pass their embarrassing prize
Correo and the prisoners to the custody of the United States,
some other procedure of perhaps a cruder sort would have been
used to keep this little man-of-war out of service. The sea lane
between Texas and New Orleans had to be kept open to the
traffic of warfare at all costs.

Furthermore, the attack on the *Correo* by the Texans aroused

Mexican officialdom as did no other episode prior to that date. One whole issue of the *Diario del Gobierno*,[16] the official daily, was devoted to the "outrage." There were many editorial comments in successive issues. Hundreds of comments flowed into the Foreign Office alone. They took the form of translations of clippings from Texas and New Orleans newspapers, reports of consuls, and depositions from sundry individuals—all offered as evidence of the "*sublevación de los colonos en Tejas.*"[17] Had the Texans tried to stop with the *San Felipe-Correo* affair without adding the battles of Gonzales, Concepción, and the capture of San Antonio, they would not have escaped the campaign of subjugation Santa Anna launched the following year. Whether the mass of Texans realized it or not, the die was cast with this overt attack upon the petty man-of-war *Correo*. Unquestionably the outstanding Texan leaders fully realized it.

In our enthusiasm for the maritime aspects of the Texan revolt, we must not lose sight of the other fundamental causes: lack of autonomous government, land frauds in the Coahuila state government, growing centralism of Santa Anna's party, clash of legal concepts and justice, and the ban against American immigration. But even so, none of these had the unhappy faculty for precipitating the immediate letting of blood as did the maritime situation, interlocked though it often was with one or more of the other factors mentioned. And certainly the first fight in the successful Texan campaign of 1835 had all of the essentials and results of a naval engagement for sea control, or naval supremacy, in which the Texans were victorious.

CHAPTER THREE

LEGISLATION AND LETTERS OF MARQUE • State Politics • Bid for Private Capital • Privateer • Failure

THE MEXICANS had come to a realization of their impotence on the Gulf even before September 1, 1835, the date of the clash between the *Correo* and the *San Felipe*. In March of that same year Minister of War and Navy Herrera's vigorous successor, Tornel, not only endorsed his predecessor's recommendations of 1834,[1] which we have already noted, but also submitted proposals for an even bigger fleet. He insisted that it was imperative that Mexico extend a maritime domination from Vera Cruz to the mouth of the Sabine. He thought the augmentation of the Mexican naval service by two 12-gun brigs, six 6-gun schooners and eighteen 2-gun pilot boats (small schooners) would be about right.[2] Though this ambitious program was but partially consummated at the close of 1836, the Mexican Navy became much more active immediately after the *Correo-San Felipe* affair. Within six weeks two Mexican men-of-war, the *Moctezuma*, soon renamed the *Bravo*, and the *Veracruzana* were operating on the Texan coast.

These two ships did not take the offensive, however, by blockading Brazoria and Galveston against the constant flow of volunteers and military supplies from New Orleans to these Texan ports. Instead, their operations were of a defensive character! They were protecting water communications and convoying supplies and troops with which General Cos was reinforcing Colonel Ugartechea at San Antonio through September and October of 1835. During this period an appreciable Mexican supply base was established at Goliad, the strategic importance of which will be readily perceived by a glance at the map.

But against what were the Mexican men-of-war protecting these coastal lines of communications? Had the Texans already created a Navy?

To answer these perfectly logical questions it is necessary to take a brief glance at the military and political events in the hinterland which, by the way, were happening with spontaneous and chaotic rapidity. Kaleidoscopic and often confused though they may seem, all had a basic motive—termination of Mexican military occupation and political domination in Texas. They mark the path of revolt and secession.

On October 1 and 2, 1835, one hundred sixty Texans drove off a party of eighty Mexicans that Colonel Ugartechea sent to Gonzales to retrieve a small brass cannon. This party of resisting Texans became the nucleus for volunteer bands from all over Texas. By October 12, Stephen F. Austin found himself elected to the command of an appreciable and growing rustic, undisciplined army.

He accepted, though his talents were better suited to statesmanship. Moreover such powers as he may have had for quick military decisions were being hampered by one of the most serious illnesses of his life. Instinctively and in response to a sort of mass psychology he led the men toward San Antonio. By October 19, all Mexican outposts had been driven in and the city put under seige.

Although General Cos had arrived in person two days earlier with considerable reinforcements and had superseded Colonel Ugartechea at San Antonio, the Mexicans still did not take the offensive. Any chances he might have had to win by a brisk offensive, Cos lost in the battle of Concepción, October 27, and the Texans settled down to the collection of cannon for seige operations.

By November 21, General Austin was ready to attack. He sent out an order to that effect only to be told by his two popularly elected division commanders and their subordinates that the troops were against it. The temper of the Texan soldiery throughout the revolution is perhaps well reflected by a sort of an enlisted man's Magna Charta adopted by the Goliad volunteers on this very day: "We claim, and can never surrender but with life, the right to elect, and elect freely, our immediate commander." Shortly, thereafter the Texan Consultation asked Austin to lead a three-man diplomatic mission to the United States. On November 24, the broken-in-health Austin gladly witnessed the election of Edward Burleson to succeed him. That the same civilian Consultation had named, October 16, one Sam Houston, a Major-General and commander-in-chief of the Texan forces was ignored by the undisciplined troops before San Antonio.

While the army debated, under the chairmanship of General Burleson, whether to press the seige or to move into winter quarters at Goliad or Gonzales, a Mexican deserter arrived in camp with lurid stories of Mexican dissension, weak fortifications, and diminishing supplies. With a burst of enthusiasm a rugged Kentuckian with a long background as a filibuster in Mexico and as a member of the Coahuila legislature, wanted to know with a shout who would "go with old Ben Milam into San Antonio." Colonel Francis W. Johnson, Bradburn's old Nemesis, and several hundred soldiers thought that they would enjoy Milam's company on such a jaunt. It was decided that Milam command one attack division and Johnson the other.

Five days of fighting and infiltration by breaking through the walls of adjacent Mexican residences enabled them to sweep the barricaded plaza with their rifles. General Cos sought refuge in the fortress-like mission Alamo, but found his position so uncomfortable that December 10 he surrendered. Old Ben Milam's suggestion of a trip "into San Antonio" had been a good one, but the joke was on him. He was the only Texan killed in the five days fighting.

Four days later Cos's column with only sufficient arms to beat off Indians and to guard a column of six hundred convict soldiers, began a terrible return march across the dry barrens to the Rio Grande. In the meantime, October 9, a small party of volunteers from the Matagorda area, acting on their own initiative, captured the Mexican garrison and supply base at Goliad. Another small Mexican detachment at Lipantitlan had been disposed of similarly November 13. Thus Cos's withdrawal, shortly before Christmas 1835, left Texas without a Mexican garrison.

While the Texans were fighting Mexicans with one hand they were organizing a government with the other. The spontaneous desire for a sovereign body to direct their concerted efforts against Mexico resulted in the selection of delegates from each settlement to meet in "Consultation." This group has been mentioned above as the one which assigned to Austin his diplomatic mission to the States.

The Consultation should have met in October, 1835, but due to the chaos of the times, with one set of delegates going to Washington, Texas, as the central point, and others to San Felipe, and still others to make speeches to the army that was forming before San Antonio, there was but a nucleus of the delegate-consultants at San Felipe prior to November 1. This small group assumed sovereignty and transacted business under the very inappropriate title of "The Permanent Council."[3] Its permanency ceased November 1 when a quorum of fifty-five delegates arrived in San Felipe.

But before the Permanent Council relinquished its nebulous sovereignty, it took under advisement the pressing coastal situation. The solution chosen was the issuance of letters of marque to privateers. To what persons and to what ships the several letters were issued is not clear—probably to coastal ship operators who sought legality to resist any Mexican war ships that might attempt to interfere with their passages to and from New Orleans.

The Consultation in its turn had hardly assumed the mantle

of the defunct Permanent Council when A. C. Allen, mentioned in connection with the *Correo-San Felipe* affair, petitioned the Consultation for a letter of marque for a ship sufficiently manned and equipped for an aggressive cruise. The petition was approved and the executive instructed to issue it.[4]

The executive referred to was the governor created by the Texan Plan of Provisional Government that the Consultation delegates were then preparing. By November 14, they had finished the task and adjourned.

Upon their departure all governmental activities under the constitution-like plan fell upon the shoulders of the General Council, composed of "one member from each municipality." This General Council in turn chose a governor and a lieutenant governor. The latter was to be the presiding officer of the Council. The former was vested with the usual executive functions including "commander in chief of the army, the navy and all military forces of Texas by sea and by land."

Notwithstanding these implied functions of sovereignty, the Plan did not declare Texas an independent republic. Indeed, undying allegiance to that palladium of Texan liberties, the Mexican Constitution of 1824, was declared.[5] The fact that the precious document denied a Mexican state the right to organize a regular army, a navy and to issue letters of marque was overlooked by the Texans. The continued allegiance to the decentralizing Constitution of 1824 was a bid for aid from the many Mexican Federalists below the Rio Grande. And that bid might have been effective had not the increasingly powerful Santa Anna recently stamped out the last vestige of Federalism by sending a conquering and devastating army into the revolting state of Zacatecas.

The office of governor went to Henry Smith, a contentious, militant individual with a rugged and often vituperative vocabulary. He was hardly elected before he felt called upon to make a speech.

The General Council listened sympathetically to this initial executive message. Among sundry other recommendations,

Governor Smith advised the "granting of letters of marque and reprisal: by doing which we can not only prevent invasion by sea, but we can blockade all the ports of Mexico, and destroy her commerce, and annoy and harass the enemy more in a few months, than by many years of war, carried on within our own limits. My own mind is satisfied that the whole of our maritime operations can be carried out by foreign capital and foreign enterprise. Already applications for commissions have been made. . . ."[6] Upon receipt of these admonitions the General Council at once created standing committees, including one on "Affairs of the Navy."

The General Councilmen were fast workers, for by November 18, only four days after the Consultation had adjourned, the Naval Affairs Committee reported an outline of a maritime policy. That they were stimulated by the operations of the *Veracruzana* and the *Bravo* in the vicinity of Matagorda there can be little doubt.[7] A definite and detailed policy on issuance of letters of marque, disposition of prizes and the division of prize money accruing therefrom was recommended. The committee closed with a proposal for the establishment of a publicly owned and operated navy consisting of four schooners, two of 12 guns each and two of 6 guns each, "for the security of our extended coast and the protection of our commerce."[8] By November 24 an ordinance based upon this report was in the hands of the Governor for his signature. Already at odds with the Council, he vetoed it because of its liberality to privateersmen, but expressed himself as favorable to the creation of a regular Navy.

As a result of the veto, two new bills were quickly passed and received the executive approval. One was for the creation of a navy of the size designated above, and one regulated privateering affairs. The latter represented a compromise with the views of the Governor. Later the privateering bill was liberalized by an amendment so that blank letters of marque could be issued, the same to be filled in by the favored party, when, where and if the armed ship was fitted out.

Major Samuel Whitney, preparatory to a trip to New Orleans, was issued six such blank letters and Messrs. McKinney and Densmore were issued three.[9] Two other letters of marque were issued after December 1, 1835, one to the owner of the schooner *William Robbins*, December 5, and another to a certain B. F. Smith on the day following. Though a duplicate or two were issued thereafter, this seems to have ended the issuance of original privateering commissions. On the strength of this sheaf of issued letters only a few privateersmen actually made predatory cruises.

Protective cruises by privately armed craft were in progress, however, while the legislators were still bickering about the details of a policy. This was natural, for in a crisis of a people, naval activity, as demonstrated by the action of the *San Felipe* against the *Correo*, cannot be delayed by lack of duly enacted legislation any more than armies were kept from forming before Boston, 1775, and before San Antonio, 1835, by the absence of laws calling for such armies. In revolutions men act and clothe their deeds with legality by subsequent legislation. Thus the citizens of Brazoria and Matagorda were engaged in a limited amount of privateering even before the opinions of the politicians were crystallized into a naval policy in the form of laws creating a navy and regulating privateering.

Early in November, 1835, when the Brazorians suspected a strange ship of being a successor to the *Correo*, a heavy gun belonging to the city was placed aboard Captain Hurd's *San Felipe*. She at once stood to sea to come to grips with the stranger.[10] Details of what followed are lost to history, but apparently the sequence of events were not so happy as they had been with the *Correo*. The next we know of the vessel she was aground in Matagorda Bay and being hotly cannonaded by a Mexican man-of-war, which finally withdrew.[11] Could the doughty Hurd have been chased there by the attacker? It is enough to say that the *San Felipe* must have suffered from the experience, for the borrowed heavy gun was returned to the Brazorians by the schooner *William Robbins*.

This episode and the repeated appearance of the *Bravo* and *Veracruzana* in those waters filled the Matagordans with alarm. To protect shipping the local Committee of Safety bought and armed the *William Robbins* and retained Captain Hurd as her skipper. They hoped eventually to sell her to the Texan Navy Department, if and when one was created. Until then a letter of marque would do. Not until December 5, was such a commission granted. Incidentally it was one of the last letters issued by the General Council, or by the yet unborn Republic of Texas, for that matter.

Shortly thereafter the *William Robbins* made her first and last prize as a privateer. The inward bound American schooner *Hannah Elizabeth*, laden with two cannon and munitions for the Texan army at San Antonio, was chased ashore at Paso Caballo by the *Bravo*. Lieutenant Mateo with a prize crew was put aboard. Before the prize could be floated, a stiff "norther" came up and the *Bravo* stood off shore for safety. On December 19, 1835, her plight became known to Captain Hurd. He augmented his crew with volunteers, proceeded to the Paso, and received Mateo's surrender.

There was no admiralty court in which to condemn the questionable prize that flew a neutral flag and was loaded with cargo consigned to their own troops. But S. Rhoads Fisher, commanding the volunteers, and Captain Hurd were not men to quibble over legal details. To settle their claims they sold a part of the cargo on the spot to one of the *Hanna Elizabeth's* passengers and advertised an auction of the remainder.

All was well until the Texan military commander in that area, Colonel J. W. Fannin, the illegitimate son of a Georgia planter and who had been known in 1819–21 to the cadets at West Point as J. F. Walker, decided to deal himself a hand in the game. One would like to believe that he resented the profiteering upon munitions for his troops, but his prior record at Velasco (dealer in slaves with Congo accents) suggests that he wanted a different division of the spoils. He credited the recovery of the cargo to soldiers—one Somers and two com-

panions, who had, he claimed, virtually recaptured the prize
before the *Robbins* appeared.[12]

A denunciatory letter from Governor Smith, accusations and
personal recriminations between Fannin and S. Rhoads Fisher
followed. Investigations by a committee of the General Council
filled the air.

The malodorous features of this episode probably had much
to do with the General Council's coolness toward privateering
the following January. Probably of more importance was the
failure of American privateering capital to come out of New
Orleans to fight Texan naval battles for private gain. And, of
course, little, if any, American capital went into privateering
because there was no rich Mexican trade in the Gulf to prey
upon. Mexican port records during this period show that practically all the foreign trade was in American and English
bottoms. This meant that any privateersman that touched one
of their flags was courting seizure by the American or British
Gulf and West India squadrons. There was a lively Mexican
coastal trade carried mostly by ships owned in Yucatan, the
New England of Mexico, but these cargoes were of cheap raw
materials or crude handicraft products turned out by the natives. The Spanish Main had sadly degenerated since the gold
laden galleon prizes of Hawkins and Drake.

Whatever the motives of the General Councilmen were on
the subject, Mr. Barrett, one of the *Robbins* investigators,
secured the passage of a motion, January 7, 1836, asking the
Naval Affairs Committee to consider calling in all outstanding
letters of marque. Nothing came of the motion, for on January 11, the Provisional Government was wrecked by a terrific
row over military policy. One faction, composed of hot heads
and people with axes to grind south of the Rio Grande, wanted
Texas to invade Mexico. There the invading army supposedly
would be a rallying point for thousands of Mexican Federalists,
still loyal to the Constitution of 1824, and who were waiting
to ally themselves with any movement strong enough to break
the centralistic tyranny of Santa Anna.

Smith and his adherents wanted to have nothing to do with mercurial Mexican alliances. Had not Texans allied themselves with Santa Anna and his federalistic Plan of Vera Cruz only to find that his centralism was harsher than that of Bustamante? For his sound but injudiciously presented logic, Governor Smith was deposed. But he clung to his seal and records and ably defended himself in an imbroglio of insults and abusive words. So many disgusted Councilmen withdrew that but a shadow of a government, composed of the Lieutenant Governor and a rump of the General Council (not a quorum) remained. Thus, from January 18 to March 1, 1836, when a newly chosen convention met to declare independence and adopt the constitution of a republic, Texas had no potent body exercising a sovereign leadership.

The immensity of this ghastly governmental mistake was soon brought home to the Texans. During those very months Santa Anna was concentrating at Monclova his victorious columns from the Zacatecas spoliations for a similar and personally conducted subjugation of Texas—the Alamo-San Jacinto campaign, in which the Texan regular navy and armed merchantmen (with and without letters of marque) played an important but often overlooked rôle.

In the meantime, to answer a question raised at the beginning of this chapter, the aggressive show of impromptu naval force demonstrated by the capture of the *Correo de Mejico* by the *San Felipe* followed by other abortive coastal privateering activities and a threatening bale of public legislation designed to create a navy and draw a swarm of privateers out of New Orleans all apparently contributed to make the Mexican ships *Bravo* and *Veracruzana* over-solicitous of Cos's water lines of communication at a time when they should have been intercepting volunteers and supplies from New Orleans. Indeed, they might have intercepted one or more of the war schooners with which the Texans were soon to seize naval supremacy in the most vital campaign of the Texan-Mexican War.

CHAPTER FOUR

THE NAVY AND SAN JACINTO
Four Schooners • Invasion • Sea Power and Mexican Retreat • Its Importance

I T WILL BE recalled that Governor Smith and the General Council had agreed upon and consummated the enactment of an ordinance sending agents to the United States to procure, fit out, and commission into the Texas navy four vessels: "two schooners of twelve guns each and two schooners of six guns each."[1]

Acting under this authority, the designated naval agents hastened to New Orleans and were delighted to find the former United States revenue cutter *Ingham* on the open market.[2] They had hardly bought her when there appeared in New Orleans a certain "Major" Charles E. Hawkins, recently from Texas and the bearer of a letter of introduction to them from Governor Smith. He had apparently applied to Smith for a naval command and so impressed the Governor with his qualifications and record that the Governor sent him to the commissioners in hopes that they had not filled all the captaincies of the ships authorized.

They had not, and they were equally impressed by the "Major's" maritime credentials. In the American navy, Hawkins had waited years for the coveted promotion from the stagnant list of midshipmen to the still more stagnant list of lieutenants. Then of a sudden in 1826, his hero, Commodore D. D. Porter, U. S. N., of the *Essex* cruise fame, resigned in a huff and accepted supreme command of the Mexican Atlantic fleet, which, still fighting to sustain Mexican independence, was operating against a Spanish squadron based at Havana. With a few other young blades Hawkins had resigned, followed Porter south, and soon he became commander of the *Hermon*. In this capacity he had distinguished himself in a severe naval engagement off the Cuban coast.[3] With Porter he had resigned from the Mexican service, 1828, and for a time was a river captain on the Chattahoochee. He left this prosaic and no doubt muddy environment for service as a filibuster under the Mexican liberal, Colonel Mexía, an association which seems to explain the title of "Major." He was fortunate enough to survive Mexía's abortive and distastrous Tampico expedition,[4] and now sought a commission in the Texan navy. He was given command of the *Ingham*, rechristened *Independence*, and by January 10, 1836, was off the Texan coast.

While the *Independence* was being sent to sea, the commissioners had bought the *Brutus*. Captain W. A. Hurd, of *San Felipe* and *William Robbins* fame was made her commander. Much overhauling was essential before she could accommodate a battery and sufficient crew to work it. The finances of the commissioners were exhausted before the work was completed. Indeed, the private purse of Commissioner Green was opened to finish the job. In the meantime merchants and insurance companies with a big Mexican patronage sought to prevent her from sailing. She finally got clear of legal difficulties and appeared in Texas waters early in February, 1836.[5]

It will be recalled that the Matagorda Committee of Safety had made a privateer of the *William Robbins* with the hopes of selling her to the government as a man-of-war. An active lobby not only for her purchase but also for buying McKinney and William's *Invincible* continued right up to the break between Governor Smith and the Council.[6] In truth, these two ships were a minor element in the disagreement. The Council was strongly in favor of their purchase but Smith, on legal and fiscal grounds, resisted. With impeachment near at hand, he, in his last message to that body, acquiesced January 9, to their purchase. In doing so, however, he garnished his remarks concerning the ships with dark hints of "corruption" and the "shrine of plunder"[7]—very mild language for the Governor. "Judas," "parricides," "scoundrels" and "wolves" were more typical of his epithetical style. In his peroration he was sure that some of his Councilmen were bothered with "a tickling and contraction of the muscles of the neck, anticipating the rope."

The *William Robbins* was renamed the *Liberty* and Captain W. S. Brown, who had succeeded Hurd on her quarterdeck, carried on after her admission to the Navy. His older brother, Captain Jeremiah Brown, an ex-coaster with a good record for badgering and defying Mexican officials, was assigned to the *Invincible*.

Thus was created the first Texan fleet that could claim an official naval status. And here we might pause to examine the units as to size, complements, and armaments. Because of two destructive fires in the Texas Adjutant General's office, one must, for even those basic details, depend primarily upon reports of Mexican prisoners taken from their prizes.

Captain W. S. Brown's 70- or 80-ton *Liberty* was the smallest of the fleet. Even so she carried "six small guns and twenty to fifty men," according to Captain Chandler of the American schooner *Harriett*, which in March, 1836, was stopped on the high seas by the *Liberty*.[8] Captain Hawkins's *Independence* had twice the tonnage of the *Liberty* and mounted nine or eleven guns all told. To Captain Hurd's *Brutus*, also of about a hundred and sixty tons, was attributed, in 1837, a long 18-pounder swivel and "nine short guns." Captain J. B. Brown's *Invincible*, in 1837, carried a 9-pounder swivel and six carronades.[9] Each of the three last mentioned ships were manned by about forty men.

The *Invincible*, of deep draught and fine lines, was considered the fastest sailer and the crack ship of the fleet. But Commodore H. L. Thompson, ranking officer in 1837, complained dolefully of the poor sailing qualities of the *Brutus*. And the speed of even the smart *Invincible* he insisted, "with an open heart . . . is not nor never was what they have been cracked up to be."[10]

While the Texan fleet was being acquired and chaos reigning supreme in the Texan army and government, Santa Anna, now self-styled "the Napoleon of the West," had not been inactive. That the distrusted *Yanquis* in Texas were now revolting in the name of Federalism had made his régime of Centralism all the more popular.

Even so Santa Anna did not want to launch his Texan campaign of subjugation until the spring of 1836. The Mexican treasury was in a bad condition. Though Minister of War and Navy Tornel was working upon his naval expansion program, which in time would be fully adequate to control the strategically important sea route, little had as yet been accomplished.

But news of the Texan forces besieging Cos in San Antonio stirred Santa Anna to action. October 31, 1835, orders to General Ramírez y Sesma started that officer's forces in Zacatecas on a march to reinforce Cos. Ramírez covered the four hundred and fifty miles to the Rio Grande at Laredo by December 26. There he met the ousted and retreating Cos. These two columns retreated still further into Mexico and were soon merged with the forces Santa Anna was personally organizing at San Luis Potosí, Saltillo and Monclova.

News of Cos's evacuation had further stimulated "the Napoleon of the West." He would wait for neither spring nor Tornel's ships-of-war. Santa Anna brushed aside the critical forebodings of second-in-command Filisola, an able Italian soldier-of-fortune, who viewed with reluctance sending six thousand men across one hundred and ninety leagues of dry, Indian infested barrens without first establishing a well protected and navy supported supply base on the Texan coast and as near to San Antonio as possible.

It was February 16 before Santa Anna's main army, already short of supplies and badly jaded by the barren wastes of

Northern Mexico, reached the Rio Grande at the impoverished mud village of San Juan Bautista. An additional eight days of tedious marching across the rough, dry Texan barrens, subject to the violent winter changes in temperature so characteristic of that region, lay between them and San Antonio. The Mexican accounts of the campaign portray this march as being one of the worst hardships to which the army was subjected. The troops were forced to subsist on half rations. Hunger, sickness, thirst and sheer exhaustion caused the gun carriages and combat wagons to become loaded with helpless stragglers. Some undernourished soldiers died in the painful eight-day march from the Rio Grande to San Antonio. The latter place was reached by the advance detachments February 23, 1836.

Simultaneously a column of about a thousand men under General Urrea was advancing along the coastal plain from Matamoras toward San Patricio, where Colonels Johnson and Grant commanded a small Texan force. Further along Urrea's route, at Goliad, Colonel Fannin commanded four hundred men—the largest single Texan force in the field. Supply ships were to parallel Urrea's column so that a base of operations could be re-established at Goliad or Victoria.

Notwithstanding their hardships, the advance of the land forces of the Mexicans was rapid and well coördinated. San Antonio was surprised with a garrison of less than one hundred and fifty men under Colonel W. B. Travis, who in desperation vacated the city and withdrew to the Alamo. At the same time he sent out pleas for help, which brought only enough aid to raise Alamo's garrison to one hundred and eighty-four men. Urrea caught Johnson unawares, February 27, and wiped out his entire command. Only Johnson and four companions escaped. Grant and his fifty men fared no better March 2.

Now that San Patricio was in his hands, Urrea rested on his arms and awaited word from Santa Anna at San Antonio. Not until March 12 did he resume the advance toward Fannin at Goliad. Fannin wavered between first one decision and then the other. As a result Urrea, March 20, reinforced by six hundred men from San Antonio, captured Fannin and his entire force on the nearby Coleta river. In accordance with a special dispatch from Santa Anna, almost all of the prisoners were shot.

Meanwhile, and herein explains Urrea's long delay at San Patricio during which Fannin should have escaped, Travis, Crockett and Bowie, with their 181 companions in the Alamo, had fought the most desperate, spectacular and, though every man was killed, the most successful delaying action in American military history. From February 23 to March 6 they held at bay, and in doing so greatly crippled and further delayed, Santa Anna's entire army.[11]

Though the Alamo's garrison was not perhaps aware of the full significance of their stand, theirs was far more than the conventional delaying action behind which a friendly main force escapes, advances, makes a flank movement, or digs in at a strong point. Theirs was a holding action behind which a republic was created, a government established, and the nucleus of an army recruited.

At Washington, Texas, on March 1, a convention of delegates with plenary powers was being called to order. It had been authorized by one of the ordinances passed by the now defunct General Council. The convention had full, sovereign power and proceeded to exercise it. Independence was declared. While one committee prepared a constitution other executive committees on war, naval and fiscal affairs proceeded to organize the country for resistance. Sam Houston was again named commander-in-chief of the Texan army which was to be called into existence by liberal land grants to volunteers. The Naval Affairs Committee confirmed practically all that had been done by Governor Smith and his Council.

By March 16 the Committee on the Constitution had finished its labors and the Convention as a whole declared the document submitted to be the Constitution of the Republic of Texas. It of course followed the American pattern. A frontier lawyer by the name of David G. Burnet was named President, *ad interim*.

A Yucatecan liberal, Lorenzo de Zavala, became Vice-President. A cabinet of State, War, Navy, Treasury and Justice departments came into existence. Robert Potter of the Naval Affairs committee became the first Secretary of Navy.[12] Shortly the new President and his Navy Department was addressing Captain Chas. E. Hawkins of the *Independence* as "Commodore."

While these stirring events were in progress, Commodore Hawkins, from January 10 to March 1, was cruising up and down the coast between Galveston and Tampico. On this cruise he destroyed "a considerable number of small craft, with all material on board that could be used to the injury of Texas."[13] By March 12 he had completed the cruise and was refitting in New Orleans.

Meanwhile the *Liberty* had taken the offensive. On the night of March 3, Captain Brown found the fine Mexican schooner *Pelicano* anchored in the roadstead at Sisal. Boarding parties in two boats were sent in (probably under cover of darkness) to cut her out. The Mexican garrison commander countered by reinforcing the *Pelicano* with twenty soldiers. The result was a severe boarding action in which seven of the defenders were killed. Many of the remaining Mexicans capitulated by way of the ship's rail and a brisk swim for the shore. Others preferred a Texan prison to the shark infested waters. They sought safety beneath the hatches.

Had we no other evidence available, the character of the *Pelicano's* cargo indicates that the Mexicans were already feeling the Texan naval policy with its threat of privateers and state owned warships. This cargo was composed largely of munitions packed in the hearts of barrels of flour, apples, and potatoes. To add to the confusion of any Texan warship or privateer that might intercept her, this false cargo was covered by manifests showing it to be the property of J. W. Zachari of New Orleans. Incidentally, the correspondence of New Orleans Consul Martinez to the Mexican State Department shows that this firm sometimes coöperated with Lizardi and Company, also of New Orleans. The latter company was openly the agent for Santa Anna's commissariat.

The cruise of the *Liberty* made Consul Martinez particularly irate. He provided the Mexican Minister in Washington with all kinds of grounds for a protest to the American government. A rebel ship of an unrecognized people making such seizures, he insisted, was nothing short of piracy. If His Excellency, the Minister, could not induce the American State Department to accept this principle, he might present further evidence that the *Liberty* was in reality the erstwhile *Rambler*, of Pensacola, which he felt indicated a breach of America's treaty of amity. In any case, he thought that this was "no trivial incident" to be passed over lightly. The good consul then prepared duplicate copies of his dispatches to be forwarded to his own foreign office in Mexico City. It is significant that he decided not to mail them on the regular packet, but preferred to hold them until they could be carried by the *Moctezuma*, which he thought would be in New Orleans soon.[14]

General Sam Houston also considered the *Liberty's* prize no trivial incident. "Captain Brown with one of our vessels," the retreating General declared in Proclamation dated March 31, 1836, "has taken a Mexican vessel with four hundred and twenty barrels of flour, three hundred kegs of powder and other supplies for the army."[15]

Immediately after this successful cruise, the *Liberty*, with her prize, joined Commodore Hawkins. He was now back from New Orleans, and his ship was, with the remainder of the Texan fleet, then based at Matagorda. Incidentally, the prize *Pelicano* was wrecked crossing the Matagorda bar, but the cargo was saved.

In order to keep in constant contact with the military advance of the enemy, which by this time was known to be as far east as San Antonio and Goliad, and at the same time protect the flank of a rapidly growing but retreating army of aroused Texans who were mobilizing under Sam Houston, Hawkins held most of his fleet at Matagorda. To check any hostile movement by water, he sent Captain Jeremiah Brown's fast *Invincible* on a patrol to Matamoras. It was a fortunate assignment because at this very time two thousand additional troops were being mobilized at Matamoras for reinforcing Santa Anna in a troop movement by sea. Furthermore, supplies, some by water from New Orleans, for the entire force were being concentrated at the same port. So important did the Mexicans consider this potential movement that the city was put under an embargo lest information thereof fall into the hands of the Texans. The only ships that were permitted to leave were those with supplies for the army already in Texas, and each of these was being escorted by a Mexican man-of-war.

Thus, when the *Invincible* arrived off the mouth of the Rio Grande April 3, Captain José Maria Espino of the *Bravo* was standing out of the river mouth with the *Correo Segundo* in convoy. In crossing the bar, Espino lost his rudder and was thus caught outside and almost helpless by the *Invincible*. Instead of closing and engaging at once, Captain Brown, probably with an inkling of mysterious movements at Matamoras, sought to gain some information about the enemy.

He hoisted the stars and stripes to his main gaff, boldly stood closer in, lowered away a boat and sent Lieutenant William H. Leving aboard the *Bravo*. This gentleman, clad as an American naval officer, pretended that the *Invincible* was an American revenue cutter from Pensacola. In testy tones Lieutenant Leving wanted to know why the American consul at Matamoras had been subjected to undue vexations and why American shipping there had been victimized by capricious changes in port regulations.

But it so happened that aboard the *Bravo*, supervising the shipping of a new rudder, was none other than *2° Teniento de Marina* Don Thomas M. Thompson, late of the *Correo de Mejico* and still later from the New Orleans jail on piracy charges. Captain Espino sent him aboard the *Invincible* to make arrangements for sending ashore the alleged American officer with communications to the proper port authorities.

The Texans on the *Invincible* must have recognized their old acquaintance and decided that the jig was up. They let Thompson come aboard, clapped him beneath hatches and then gave the *Bravo* a broadside. Captain Espino very naturally put Mr. Leving in the brig (to hold for a firing squad) and returned the cannonade.[16]

The engagement lasted for about an hour, in the course of which neither ship appears to have suffered severely. Certainly the *Invincible* was not seriously injured; and Captain Espino reported no injuries to his *Bravo* beyond a round shot in the poop and two minor injuries to the rigging. The battle was cut short by the appearance, well off shore, of the square fore royal of a sizeable brig. Both contestants viewed it with suspicion. Captain Brown pulled out of the engagement and approached the stranger for a showdown.

She turned out to be the fine American owned brig *Pocket* with a false manifest in favor of Lizardi and Company and carrying a contraband cargo.[17] She was also under contract to transport a large number of troops in the anticipated movement from Matamoras to Copano.

Of particular interest was her passenger list. On board was Lieutenant Don Carlos Ocampo, Tenorio's former junior officer and Thompson's associate aboard the ill-fated *Correo de Mejico*. After his release from the piracy charges he had lingered in New Orleans longer than had Thompson. It will also be recalled that during this same period Minister of War and Navy Tornel was rapidly expanding the Mexican Navy. Indeed, he was procuring ships faster than he could find trained officers to man them. We are therefore not surprised to find that the same passenger list included certain Lieutenants Somers, Hogan, and Taylor, recipients of recent commissions in the Mexican navy.

Now that they had fallen into the hands of the Texans they suddenly remembered that they were American citizens.[18] In addition to many incriminating letters that Captain Jeremiah Brown found in possession of Lieutenants Ocampo, Hogan, *et al.*, he found an excellent and recent map of the Texas coast. It was the result of the recaptured Thompson's survey work while he was patrolling with the *Correo de Mejico*. Truly the engagement off Matamoras and the taking of the *Pocket* constituted a veteran's reunion for those who had participated in the *Correo-San Felipe* affair.

In company with her valuable prize, the *Invincible* hastened back to Matagorda, found none of the Texan fleet there and continued along the coast to Galveston. At this port Captain Brown found the fleet and a number of commandeered merchantmen, laden with inhabitants of the coastal settlements and all their strictly personal effects. One commandeered ship, the *Flash*, had aboard Acting President Burnet, his cabinet, and a few records—in short, the government of the Republic. All had narrowly escaped capture at Harrisburg a few days before. Everyone was wildly excited.

The President and the Cabinet had not heard of the dramatic fall of the Alamo, March 6, until a few hours before Acting President Burnet's inauguration, at 2 A.M., March 17. Immediately thereafter the Convention was adjourned and the alarmed delegates returned to their homes, thereby spreading a mounting contagion of alarm throughout the Anglicized settlements in Texas. Sam Houston had hastened to Gonzales, March 7, to take command of a small army that had come into a more or less spontaneous existence at that point. But this did not allay the alarm among the civilians, because Houston at once began an aimless retreat to Burnham's Crossing on the Colorado, thence along the east bank of that stream to a point opposite Columbus. The appearance of hostile forces across the river from him had caused a further retreat to San Felipe on the Brazos. For reasons known to no one, he continued his aimless and pointless retreat by marching out of the smouldering ruins of Austin's colonial capital northward to Groce's Ferry. The latter was certainly a pointless maneuver. Gauging its pace more or less to keep itself in step with the east bound progress of the army, the Texan government had remained on wheels and horse back long enough to reach Harrisburg, whence it could easily seek safety and the protection of the Navy by transferring to Galveston.

With the army in aimless retreat, with the government concerned for its own safety and the advancing Mexican columns marching without opposition from San Antonio into the heart of the Anglicized area, it was natural that the population, stimulated by the constantly arising contagion of fear engendered by news of the Alamo and the Goliad atrocity, took to horses, wagons, river boats, and commandeered coastal vessels to proceed eastward toward the safety of United States soil just beyond the Sabine. To the Texans at the time it was the retreat of a people before a devastating, hideous horde of Mexican vandals. Often they destroyed their own homes, barns and food supplies to keep them from falling into the hands of the enemy. To the frightened civilians it was the uprooting of a civilization. Later they looked back upon it with jocular reminiscences and called it the "Runaway Scrape."

These events explained why Captain Brown and his prize *Pocket* found Galveston Harbor so crowded, the government aboard the *Flash*, and excitement in the air. As a part of this military, governmental, and civilian retreat, Hawkins had shifted his base from Matagorda to Galveston. Before doing so, however, the tiny *Liberty*, on an off shore patrol, had made a prize of another fine American brig, the *Durango*. Like the *Pocket* she was laden with a contraband cargo, whitewashed by a false manifest. Also like the *Pocket*, she was chartered to aid in the general Mexican troop movement in which the *Pocket* was to have participated.

On a similar patrol, immediately prior to the naval retreat from Matagorda, the *Independence* had encountered and had a brush with two Mexican men-of-war, the *Urrea* and the *Bravo*, which were convoying a supply ship along the coast in hopes of contacting one of Santa Anna's columns. The appearance of Mexican ships in force no doubt hastened the withdrawal from Matagorda.

When Houston so pointlessly marched north from San Felipe to Groce's Ferry, Santa Anna, with one of his advancing columns, reached the former settlement hot upon the heels of the retreating Texans. Instead of following them, however, he turned southward and again stood upon the banks of the swollen Brazos at Thompson's Ferry, several leagues north of Brazoria. This put Santa Anna in the heart of the Texan region of discontent and near the sea whence badly needed supplies could be received. Without waiting for a junction with a column under General Gaona that was marching from Bastrop to Richmond by way of Columbus, or for General Urrea's reinforced column that was advancing to Brazoria by way of Victoria, and Matagorda, Santa Anna dashed forward with seven hundred and fifty men of his personal command to Harrisburg in an effort to capture Burnet and his Cabinet. Needless to say, by this time they were safe aboard the *Flash*. Bitterly disappointed Santa Anna burned Harrisburg.

From the smoking ruins of Harrisburg, Santa Anna and his column marched to New Washington, on an arm of Galveston Bay. There is no military explanation for this disastrous maneuver other than the Mexican Army's need for provisions. A foraging cavalry detachment under Colonel Almonte had reported some Texan supplies in a New Washington warehouse. Thus the Mexican failure to keep a naval supported service of supply abreast of the Mexican advance was responsible for Santa Anna's subsequent misfortunes.

The most recent biography of this self styled "Napoleon of the West" insists that *El Presidente's* real motive in going to New Washington was that he might board a coasting vessel and return to Mexico City and the plaudits of his followers while his Alamo and Goliad laurels were still fresh. Santa Anna, unaware of the Texan fleet's presence in the lower stretches of the vast bay, went so far as to negotiate with the German owner of a small schooner anchored at New Washington. But one of the Texan war schooners appeared that very day at New Washington and captured the schooner before Santa Anna and his staff embarked upon her.[19] If this analysis of the Dictator's motives be fully accepted, the Texan navy may claim further credit for forcing Santa Anna to remain in Texas to the bitter end of his impetuous advance.

With the New Washington supplies in his possession and the Texan fleet dominating Galveston Bay, Santa Anna continued northward along the shores of the Bay toward Lynch's Ferry, just above the mouth of San Jacinto River. Without any apparent knowledge as to the whereabouts of the Texan army, with which he had been out of contact since leaving San Felipe, he intended to continue his advance along the coast to the Sabine or until he was able to establish connections with a Mexican man-of-war, or some other craft suitable for returning him to Vera Cruz.

In the meantime Houston's motley army of seven or eight hundred had vacated its bivouac on the west bank of the Brazos at Groce's Ferry. Once across the river, Houston continued his retreat along the old San Antonio Road toward Nacogdoches. Mass eagerness for a battle with Santa Anna's column rather than orders from Houston caused the army to take the fork of the road leading toward Harrisburg. The Texan force reached the ruins of Harrisburg April 18 and found itself between Santa Anna's personal command and the supporting columns of Gaona near Richmond and Urrea at Brazoria. Fortuitously the Texans had become the pursuers rather than the pursued. They pressed onward toward Lynch's Ferry across the San Jacinto near which, it was hoped, Santa Anna would be found.

By April 20 there was spirited skirmishing between minor parties of the two hostile columns converging on Lynch's Ferry. Santa Anna fell back into a defensive position and, because of Houston's reluctance to attack, was reinforced by General Cos and four hundred men. Houston hoped the Mexicans would attack him. But Houston's captains urged an offensive, to which the General reluctantly agreed. When the motley Texan troops were paraded, shortly after noon of the 21st, a number of rabble rousing speeches were made, at the end of which the

Texans stealthily advanced through the woods and noisily hurled themselves upon the Mexican encampment.

Fortunately for the attackers the Mexican officers were taking their afternoon *siesta*. Enlisted men were working about routine camp duties. Though a bayou cut off a Mexican retreat, no sentries were posted. The rout was complete. Less than twenty surviving Mexicans reached the Brazos and Gaona's main column, now commanded by General Filisola. All other Mexican survivors, including Santa Anna, were captured. The Texans lost but two killed and a number severely wounded. Sam Houston was among the latter.

The recently returned Captain Brown of the *Invincible* was the first naval officer in Galveston Bay to get the glad tidings. So happy was Brown when Houston's messengers paused at his ship to tell the news that he rent the air with three salutes from the long, midship's gun before he paused to reflect: "Hold on boys or old Hawkins will put me in irons again." It seems that immediately after taking command of the fleet at Matagorda the thirty-six year old Commodore Hawkins had disciplined his exuberant subordinate with just such treatment.

After suspending the gunpowder phase of the celebration, Brown fortified the two famished bearers of the tidings, an army captain and one Hon. Ben C. Franklin, soon to sit as the first admiralty judge in Texas, with drinks of the "best liquor on the ship." Captain Brown then called away his gig and sent the messengers to the flagship. They partook of Hawkins's hospitality to the extent of a sumptuous meal, and perhaps more choice liquor. Not until Commodore Hawkins "hinted" that they had better proceed to Galveston Island and tell President Burnet did they move on. Afterward they thought His Excellency was a little "miffed" because everybody on the Island knew all about the glorious victory before he did.[20]

Smashing though the victory was, the Texans followed it up with neither a military nor a naval advance. Dame Fortune had given them Santa Anna in person. They satisfied themselves by negotiating a "treaty" with him. Because of the

Alamo and the Goliad massacre the rabble was crying for his execution. Thus the Texan leaders found the Mexican President in quite a receptive mood for such negotiations—as if a captured executive could make a treaty alienating over a quarter of a million square miles of territory. There was then, as well as now, an accepted rule of warfare that a captured commander or executive lost all authority the moment he fell in the hands of an enemy.

Nevertheless the Texans, with Santa Anna's hearty and fervent coöperation, ignored this principle. Santa Anna sent messengers to Filisola and Urrea ordering them to retreat, and then sat down to negotiate.

The orders to Generals Filisola and Urrea were wholly unnecessary because they had already started the retreat. General Filisola was a much better general than he has received credit for being. In evaluating the tactical situation the moment he heard of Santa Anna's complete defeat, he found himself confronted by the following factors.

He had every reason to believe that Santa Anna's overwhelming defeat indicated a counter attacking Texan army of far greater strength than it really was. His immediate command, no bigger than that Santa Anna had lost, was on half rations consisting largely of hardtack and corn crackers. He was in a devastated country upon which no army could live. His officers, who bought their food from their own foraging cavalry were paying what were then famine prices. "A load of *maize* came to sell for ninety pesos; a cake of bread, three reales . . . a little sugar loaf, twenty reales and a pint of liquor, eight pesos."[21] Moreover there was much sickness and a shortage of medical supplies.

As if these were not enough troubles for an army in a strange land, cutting across his and Urrea's line of retreat were two deep, and at that season, frequently swollen rivers. Much of the intervening land was low and swampy. These factors combined with the Texan control of the sea made his position perilous. The enemy, to quote Filisola's own estimate of the situation, "possessed, furthermore, three steamboats and several schooners, with which, situated at Galveston or the Island of Culebra (near Matagorda) he should have been able with impunity to make up-river incursions upon the right flank and rear guard of our troops, and also to place in jeopardy the detachments at Copano, Goliad and Matagorda . . . cutting all communications whereby provisions could be received."[22]

General Filisola, in the above quoted remarks, was not far wrong in evaluating the Texan maritime strength. True there were no steamboats in the Texas Navy but at least three had been commandeered during the flight of the coastal settlers to Galveston. They would have proved valuable in transporting troops, or towing the small war ships into strategic positions in the rear of the Mexican columns. The Texans truly missed a golden opportunity. Their foolish negotiations with Santa Anna saved Mexico two armies, each of which, when outlying detachments were called in, was larger than the one lost at San Jacinto. Santa Anna's "treaty negotiations," reached fruition in the so-called Treaty of Velasco, May 14, in which Mexican withdrawal and Texan independence was promised.

Meanwhile smart Filisola coöperated with Santa Anna's blandishments by assuring Texans that his retreat was in response to orders from his chief. At the same time he was correctly instructing his subordinates that Santa Anna had lost all authority and that they should at once look to him for orders.[23] The only Texan force to keep in contact with the retreating Filisola was a detachment of twenty Texan rangers. This well mounted band does not appear to have followed the retreating Mexicans immediately.

Filisola and Urrea took from April 23 to May 9 to gain a position west of the Colorado. The swampy muddy roads and swollen streams had taken their toll of animals, provisions and cannon. The Mexicans had to pass one entire night standing in water. After crossing the Colorado May 9, conditions were not so bad. Thus by May 14, Filisola was able to establish his headquarters at Goliad where he found provisions for ten days.

These supplies that brought such badly needed relief to the now completely famished soldiers had been brought to Copano but a few days before by two vessels from Matamoras. One was the *Correo Segundo* the sailing of which had been so seriously delayed by the already discussed action between the *Bravo* and *Invincible*. The other supply ship was the *Bravo Segundo*,[24] probably the one being escorted by the *Urrea* and *Bravo* at the time of Commodore Hawkins's little brush with those vessels and before his withdrawal from Matagorda.

From Goliad, Filisola's aids scurried off to San Antonio to supervise the evacuation of that place and to procure what provisions they might from the Mexican population there. Still fearing that a Texan force of size might be pursuing, Filisola threw up temporary fortifications at Goliad to protect his forces then preparing for the long march across the desolate unoccupied area between him and the Rio Grande.

Meanwhile the Mexican government had heard of San Jacinto. Vigorous War and Navy Minister Tornel at once wrote to Filisola instructing him to hold San Antonio and to concentrate at a suitable point near the coast for receiving supplies and reinforcements of four thousand men. The messenger traveled over the slow overland route and did not reach Filisola until May 28. By that time he had evacuated San Antonio, Victoria, and Goliad, and with a rapidly dwindling commissary had retreated as far south as the Nueces River.

Urrea, in a subsequent wordy row with Filisola, claimed that he alone of Filisola's generals proposed that they march back into Texas when these orders were received. General Urrea forgot to say that Filisola offered to surrender the command to him if he really wanted to make such a countermarch and thereby throw the already famished army upon the known to be devastated region around San Antonio, Goliad and Victoria. Urrea was unwilling to accept the command, according to Filisola. In any case the army continued to retreat.

Had they about faced and returned to Copano, Goliad and San Antonio they might not have fared so badly as most of the

Mexican generals thought. That is, they would have found supplies, granted that they had beaten Major Burton and his detachment of twenty mounted rangers to them.

The Major and his detachment were on a reconnaissance to ascertain whether Filisola had really retreated south and west of the line of San Antonio and Goliad. Near Copano about June 1, they received news of a suspicious appearing craft in the offing. Before dawn of June 3, Burton concealed his detachment in the brush and signaled the merchantman to send a boat. It was seized the moment it touched the sand. The concealed detachment used the boat to board and take possession of the ship. She was the *Watchman*, laden with provisions for Filisola.

In the face of contrary winds it seemed that the rangers didn't know what to do with their suddenly acquired white elephant. While they pondered the question and waited for the winds to change, the *Comanche* and *Fannie Butler*, likewise laden with supplies for Filisola, dropped their anchors in the harbor.[25] Their skippers were decoyed aboard the *Watchman*, imprisoned and their commands seized by the small boat parties of rangers. In due time the flotilla of prizes made its way to Velasco and were legally condemned in Judge Franklin's admiralty court.[26] Of course, Major Burton and his twenty rangers were at once dubbed the "Horse Marines."

For such a detachment to invade its maritime field so successfully should have brought shame to the proud officers and tars that constitute the traditional navy. But the Texan fleet had not been in existence long enough to acquire traditions. Furthermore, the navy had been as active during the post San Jacinto weeks as was the sister service, the army, of which the rangers were not a part. In fact, the Texan army lay in camp near modern Harrisburg eating up the cargoes of the *Pocket* and *Durango* and from sheer boredom generating quarrels within its own ranks as to who should be commander-in-chief now that the wounded Houston was in New Orleans and seemed to be slated to succeed Acting President Burnet.

The Navy was kept busy, though put to but little better use than was the Army. The *Liberty*, commanded by Captain Wheelwright, was sent to New Orleans as a convoy to the merchant vessel *Flora* on which arrived, May 22, the wounded and now popular idol, General Houston. While at the Crescent City, the schooner was refitted but the Republic of Texas could not raise enough hard cash to pay the bill. The ship, months later, was sold to satisfy the claims against her. With this ignoble ending her name disappears from the Texan Navy list,[27] and Captain Wheelwright, who had succeeded W. S. Brown, became available for another assignment.

Captain Brown's *Invincible* and Captain Hurd's *Brutus* also went to New Orleans, presumably for supplies, immediately after the Battle of San Jacinto. Spurred on by the underwriters and owners of the brig *Pocket*, Commodore Dallas, commanding the American Gulf Squadron, ordered the sloop-of-war *Warren* to seize the *Invincible* for her depredations against "American commerce." Because of this, May 1, Brown, his officers and crew were incarcerated on charges of piracy that were filed by the Louisiana and Marine Fire Insurance Company. The Texan agent in New Orleans, William Bryant, quickly employed an able attorney and by May 7 the crew and ship were again at liberty. This did not, however, keep Captain Brown from becoming enmeshed in a private suit instigated by the same company.

Contemporaneous with this seizure, the Texans, apparently trying to dodge legal difficulties, bought the *Pocket* from her owner so that by the time Judge Franklin's prize court adjudicated her case in June or July, the court was in reality rendering a decision upon a cargo that was first consumed and afterward bought by the capturing republic.

But the United States cared little for a purchase with such coercive characteristics. The adjudication of the prize in Judge Franklin's admiralty court was held in still higher disdain than was the purchase. Hence the American Department of State continued to press vigorously the claims of not only the owners of the *Pocket* but also of those who had owned the *Durango*. The United States government also picked up its diplomatic cudgels in behalf of Messrs. Taylor, Hogan and Somers, the Mexican "naval officers" that had been captured with the *Pocket*.

By 1838 the Republic of Texas was so assiduously courting favor from the United States that on April 11 of that year a treaty between the two republics was signed in which Texas agreed to pay in full, with accrued interest, for the losses suffered by the owners of the *Pocket* and of the *Durango*.[28] Thus was closed that minor episode.

While the *Liberty*, *Invincible* and *Brutus* were being overhauled in New Orleans, Commodore Hawkins's *Independence* was transporting President Burnet, his Cabinet and the still negotiating Santa Anna to Velasco. Upon the return of the *Brutus* and *Invincible*, the former to Matagorda and the latter to Velasco, the *Independence* sailed for New Orleans early in June with diplomatic commissioners Grayson and Collinsworth aboard. They were en route to Washington to negotiate for American recognition of Texas, hence they should travel aboard a warship.

The *Independence* had hardly cleared for New Orleans when the *Invincible* was ordered to take Santa Anna aboard, now that he had signed the "Treaty" of Velasco, and return him to Vera Cruz. Turbulent soldiers at Velasco would not have it so, and to avoid a threatened dissolution of the government, President Burnet had to acquiesce to the forceful removal of Santa Anna from that vessel.[29] *El Presidente's* person continued to be the center of plots for assassination or execution by radical Texans; and of efforts for deliverance by patriotic Mexicans.[30] Finally Houston returned from New Orleans and persuaded the people to permit Santa Anna to return to Mexico by way of Washington, D. C. He spent the following winter and spring on this circuitous and leisurely return trip.

Meanwhile one of Tornel's newly acquired and heavy gun brigs, the *Vencedor del Alamo* was cruising off Copano looking for the three ships that had been captured by Major Burton's Horse Marines. Finding herself too late she ran up the coast to Matagorda where she found the *Brutus* at anchor. The latter feared the result of an engagement and sent out a cry for help that was quickly heard as far east as Galveston. The privately owned steamer *Ocean*, manned by volunteers and barricaded with cotton bales, took the *Invincible* and the privately owned *Union* in tow and hastened to the aid of the *Brutus*.[31]

Apparently alarmed by the approach of this hybrid flotilla, the commander of the *Vencedor del Alamo* cracked on all sail for Vera Cruz. The *Invincible* promptly pursued her. By July 25 she was cruising off Vera Cruz and inviting an engagement. The Mexicans could not believe that the *Corsario America-Tejano* would have so promptly followed the *Alamo* were she alone, and for that reason the *Invincible* was permitted to blockade the port for several days without a battle being offered.[32]

Without considering the appearance of the *Vencedor del Alamo* on the coast, sufficient reports of preparations for a super-vindictive vengeance upon *los colonos Tejanos* were emanating from Mexico City to warn President Burnet's government that Santa Anna's "Treaty" of Velasco was not worth the paper required to bring it into existence.

When the temper of Mexico became apparent in the late summer and fall of 1836, many Texans thought that their new Republic should take the offensive. In man power she was affluent beyond her previous happiest dreams. Adventurers and potential settlers were arriving on every boat and joining the army individually, by companies, and even by batallions. There were more men than the infant Republic could pay, or even feed, but for the fortuitous captures made by Major Burton's Horse Marines. With nothing else to do they fell into quarreling and duelling over relative ranks, powers, and prerogatives and debating whether or not the army should invade Mexico or anticipate Wilson's subsequent policy of watchful waiting.

They did the latter. In well informed Texan circles it was recognized that Texas could not keep an army beyond the Rio Grande in the face of increased Mexican sea power, as typified by the new heavy brig *Vencedor del Alamo*. Thus when the Naval Affairs committee of the Texan Congress, October 26, 1836, recommended expansion of the fleet to include, among several other ships, one steamer of ten guns, Congress passed a bill, November 18, based on the report but which called for *two* such steamers. Both were to be of ample capacity for transporting large bodies of troops. The solons of the Republic were obviously impressed by the impotency of their greatest army in the face of a rising Mexican naval force and with it the passing of sea control to the enemy. These founding fathers did not have to wait for the publication of A. T. Mahan's writings on the influence of sea power to appreciate its potency.

But as early as July 21, 1836, the *Vencedor del Alamo* was the only cruising unit Minister Tornel's new *esquadrilla para el mar del Norte*, which was to "blockade the ports of the rebellious Texans, to facilitate the movement of supplies for the army, and also of troops in case it should be convenient to transfer them quickly to some point on the coast."[33] Hence President Burnet felt safe in ordering his available three-schooner fleet to blockade Matamoras. On the above date, the world was duly informed that enough warships for the strict maintenance of a blockade were being ordered to the mouth of the Rio Grande.[34]

This assignment kept Hawkins and his flotilla busy for the next six weeks. Early in September Burnet's government ordered the *Invincible* to New York for a refitting. While Hawkins and his *Independence* were in New Orleans a week or so later, the Commodore was surprised to learn that Hurd and his *Brutus* were en route to New York in hopes of a refitting at the metropolis. With only the *Independence* remaining in the Gulf, it is obvious that the Matamoras blockade became a farce.

Notwithstanding the short duration of the "effective blockade," it produced an immediate diplomatic reaction. Mexico read Burnet's blockade manifesto and at once begged the principal maritime powers not only to ignore it but to capture and treat as pirates the rebels who were placing in jeopardy the commerce of the friends of Mexico. The plea was received with marked sympathy at the British Legation but by the time Mr. Pakenham had transmitted it to his government, October 3, 1836,[35] the blockade had reached its farcical stage. The canny British Foreign Office seems to have taken advantage of this development to avoid committing itself one way or the other. Certainly a definite reply cannot be found today in the Mexican Foreign Office Archives.

The Hanseatic cities immediately assured Mexico that the blockade would be ignored; but Venezuela gave the most immediate and soul stirring reply. She waxed eloquent in her sympathies for Mexico and ended with a few salty, diplomatic tears over the possibility of a part of the once gloriously free (since the ousting of Spain, it is assumed) territory of Mexico slipping back into the abyss of slavery should Texas make good her independence.[36]

In Washington, Minister Gorostizo pointed to this blockade and its brief maintenance by ships armed and fitted out in United States as a major Mexican grievance. He considered it on a parity with General Gaines's recent, unexplained movement of troops across the Sabine. Getting no satisfaction on either point he soon called for his passports.[37]

Except for the petty cruises in 1836 of the privateers *Terrible* and *Thomas Toby*, it is believed that the foregoing pages record, notwithstanding the shortage of official Texan naval documents caused by early fires in the Texan capitol, with a fair degree of accuracy and emphasis the maritime factors and naval activities that contributed to the failure of Santa Anna's Alamo and San Jacinto campaign. Whether or not the reader concedes the significance of, and the overwhelming importance of, Texan maritime supremacy in this campaign is beside the point. The important fact is that the fathers of the Texan Republic did.

The following extract from the Naval Affairs Committee's evaluation of the situation, October 26, 1836, is conclusive:

"The *Brutus* and *Invincible* are both in New York, in a situation which prevents their services from being immediately available; and the *Liberty* is detained in New Orleans. Thus while momentarily in expectation of a blockade from the enemy, our whole line of seacoast is defended by but one national vessel, the *Independence*, mounting seven guns. . . . While our navy remains in this condition, it is in the power of the enemy, at his pleasure, to cut off our supplies, and seize upon our seaports. . . . So far in our struggle with Mexico, our navy has proved adequate to the protection of our seacoasts, and to the annoyance of the enemy. But the navy of the enemy has lately been increased by the addition of several vessels of the most splendid description; it therefore becomes imperiously necessary that our navy should be increased by the same ratio.

Your committee, therefore, suggests that the immediate building or purchase of the following description of vessels:—

One sloop-of-war, 600 tons, mounting 24 guns; probable cost.............................	$ 60,000
One steam vessel, mounting 10 guns...........	45,000
Two schooners, 200 tons, mounting 11 guns.....	30,000
	$135,000[38]

That the Texan Congress and President Houston more than concurred in this opinion is evidenced by the immediate passage, November 18, of a bill to increase the navy. As mentioned above, the congressional bill went the committee one better and called for two steamers (capable of transporting troops) instead of the one. Otherwise it followed the proposals of the Naval Affairs Committee.

Naval supremacy really did pass to Mexico in the winter of 1836–37, but why Mexico failed to coördinate her supremacy with a second invasion of Texas is another story.

CHAPTER FIVE

THE MEXICAN BLOCKADE • Mervine of the U.S.S. Natchez • Battle off Velasco • Defeat • The Wharton Saga

T HE TEXAN congress which in November, 1836, passed the naval bill calling for a 24-gun sloop-of-war, two steamers capable of transporting troops and two heavy schooners mounting 11 guns each, is known in the history of the buckskin Republic as the First Congress. The same election that called it into existence under the recently adopted Texas Constitution had also elected Sam Houston President. His was the first constitutional term, which was to run for two years, after which the regular term was to be for three years. It might also be added that a President was not permitted to succeed himself. Sam Houston was inaugurated upon the resignation of President *ad interim* Burnet, October 22, 1836.

While the Texans were thus getting their government on a more permanent basis and authorizing the purchase of ships (without raising sufficient money to buy them) Mexico was not wholly inactive. Powhatan Ellis, the American *Chargé* in Mexico City, reported that some 4,000 raw levies set forth from Mexico City under General Nicolas Bravo, who boasted that he would have 12,800 men before he reached the border.[1] Bravo probably never achieved the latter figure, but for the next several months he was in command of a large force that was concentrating at Matamoras with the reconquest of Texas its definite objective.

But the capture of Santa Anna had left Mexico leaderless. Whatever else may be said against that mercurial, chameleon-like individual, he had what so many Mexican (and American) politicians lack—the power of decisive and aggressive action. His Texan failure and "Treaty" of Velasco had left him a broken idol at the base of a very high pedestal. There is little wonder that he lingered in the United States before returning to Mexico. His absence and disrepute created a field day for lesser Mexican leaders who sought the laurels he had lost at San Jacinto. Political unrest became rife throughout the Mexican republic. The proponents of states rights and Federalism used the failure of the Centralists to swell the ranks of their followers. A revolution seemed imminent and Minister of War and Navy Tornel became so alarmed about the domestic situation that he refused to give the orders that would have launched Bravo and his army into a Texan subjugation campaign during the winter of 1836–37.[2]

By the spring of 1837 Tornel had built up an appreciable naval force and Bravo's command was ready to be on its way as soon as Mexican affairs became a little more stabilized. In the meantime, Tornel knew that Texan powers of resistance were being greatly increased by the rapid influx of soldiers-of-fortune and war munitions. Why not use the naval strength for a Texan blockade? A decree proclaiming such a blockade had been drawn as early as January, 1836, but had been permitted to lie unpublished in the dusty archives until the day came when more than a "paper blockade" could be maintained. That day was at hand. Thus in March and April, 1837, the world was informed that the shipping of sinews of war to *Los Colonos de Tejas* was at an end.

And so it was for the time being. By April 15, Houston's Secretary of Navy, S. Rhoads Fisher was writing Col. A. H. Thurston of the Texan army that since the 5th of that month Galveston had been blockaded by three brigs-of-war and two schooners. The garrison had supplies for only three more weeks and was in danger of being starved out. He ended with the alarming statement that should Mexico get footholds at Galveston and Matagorda Bay, Texas was lost.[3] The blockading Mexican squadron, in addition to filling the Texan coastal settlements with alarm, was being rewarded by a number of good prizes. Of course, many of these prizes from New Orleans were flying the American flag.

Immediately Commander Mervine, of the United States patrolling sloop-of-war *Natchez*, decided to put in his oar. That he did so was a distinct advantage to the Texans for at this time their three-ship navy was conspicuously absent from the Gulf. The *Invincible* and *Brutus*, though en route, had not yet returned from refitting at New York. Commodore Hawkins's *Independence* was still in New Orleans where she had lain since January, 1837, without a captain. The Texan Commodore had died of smallpox in the home of a Mrs. Hale.

Among the first Mexican prizes to be sent to Matamoras for adjudication was the United States merchantman *Champion*.[4] A few days later, April 9, there appeared almost simultaneously off the mouth of the Rio Grande three vessels. One was the Mexican brig-of-war, *General Urrea*, which had captured and was escorting into Matamoras the American merchantman *Louisiana* for adjudication.[5] The third was the U.S.S. *Natchez*, a 22-gun sloop-of-war of Commodore Dallas's West India and Gulf squadron, which was arriving at the port in response to a message from the industrious and quarrel-loving D. W. Smith, American Consul in Matamoras who was greatly concerned over the seizure of the *Champion*. As the courses of the three ships converged at the mouth of the Rio Grande, Commander Mervine became interested in the *Louisiana*.

Accordingly he sent Lieutenant Peck alongside the *Louisiana* with a boarding party. Mr. Peck learned that she was a Mexican prize, but decided to do some investigating himself. He rowed to the *General Urrea* and asked if the *Louisiana* had been warned off the coast, as stipulated in the American-Mexican Treaty of Amity and Commerce, prior to her capture. Captain Machin of the *Urrea* answered in the negative. Lieutenant

Peck then desired to see the papers of the prize but was told that they had already been sent ashore to the port captain of Santiago de Brazos.

Upon receiving Peck's report, Commander Mervine became dissatisfied and returned Peck to the *Urrea* with a request that Captain Machin remove the prize crew. Otherwise he intended to recapture the *Louisiana*. At the same time Lieutenant Moor was sent with an armed party to the *Louisiana* to carry out the threat. Captain Machin refused, whereupon the *Louisiana* was seized by Mr. Moor's detail; her skipper was restored to command, and the vessel convoyed by the *Natchez* to a point well off shore for a safe start on her return voyage back up the Texan coast.[6]

Having seen the *Louisiana* well on her way, Commander Mervine returned to the mouth of the Rio Grande to see what he could do about the recently captured *Champion*. Since the *General Urrea* was still outside the bar, Mervine anchored the *Natchez* so that the Mexican man-of-war would be under his guns and therefore a hostage to the success of further negotiations. Commander Mervine then sent a letter to the captain of the port warning him that the *General Urrea* could not be moved until satisfaction concerning the *Champion* was received. Efforts were made to communicate with the crew and passengers of the *Champion*, but to no avail. The port captain in the temporary absence of General Nicolas Bravo, did not feel at liberty to act in the matter and continued to hold the Americans *incommunicado*.[7]

While matters were thus in a deadlock the Mexican gun brig, *General Terán*, appeared, with two additional American prizes —the *Julius Caesar* and the *Climax*, both captured by the Galveston blockaders. The highly incensed Mervine wished to intercept them but to do so would permit the *Urrea*, still under his guns, to escape. He met the situation by capturing the *Urrea* before going in pursuit of the brig-of-war *General Terán*. A boarding party was lowered away under Passed Midshipman D. McDougal, who demanded the surrender of the Mexican man-of-war. Mr. McDougal returned with the report that Captain Machin, of the *Urrea*, would strike his colors if the *Natchez* would fire a shot in his direction. The obliging Lieutenant Peck sent a round shot about fifty feet athwart the Mexican's bow, and down fluttered the Mexican ensign.

Thus left free to give pursuit, Commander Mervine chased the *General Terán* aground "on the worst part of the bar, where she remained during twenty-four hours." Meanwhile, the *Natchez* was under artillery fire from the land forts, from the *General Terán* and from the *General Bravo*, which happened to be in port. Commander Mervine returned the fire and a spirited artillery engagement resulted. The Mexican gunnery did not keep the *Natchez* from retrieving the *Climax* but the Mexican prize crew of the *Julius Caesar* put her beyond reach of the Americans.[8]

The *Climax* was set free, as the *Louisiana* had been; and the *Urrea* was sent to Pensacola under a prize master. In a day or two, Commander Mervine lost hopes of getting another Mexican ship under his guns, and cruised northeasterly along the Texan coast looking for blockaders. He reported seeing none, hence claimed that the Mexican blockade was of the "paper" variety which, had it been true, would have tended to justify his actions at Matamoras. His best justification lies in the above mentioned terms of the American-Mexican trade treaty and in the apparent practice (partially admitted by Captain Machin, of the *Urrea*, and unanimously asserted by the Americans) the Mexican naval officers had of appropriating property from the prizes before they were condemned.

That the activities of Mervine and his *Natchez* made an indelible impression upon the Mexicans and adversely affected the efficiency of their blockade there can be no doubt. In the first place one of their men-of-war, the *Terán*, had been chased aground; the *General Bravo* had practically been blockaded from April 9 to the 18th. Two prizes had been retrieved and set free; and the *Urrea* had actually been carried away as a prize to Pensacola. These were tangible losses that the Mexicans could not offset in any way, vent their spleen though they did by embargoing the regular American coasters that happened to be in port.[9]

The aggressiveness of the *Natchez* made the Mexican commanders far more cautious in making prizes than otherwise would have been the case, and did more than anything else toward reducing the blockade to a farce. For example, the *Libertador* and *Vencedor del Alamo* arrived at Matamoras with a bona fide Texan prize captured after an engagement off Velasco only a few days after the departure of the *Natchez*. Instead of at once returning to their blockading stations, as one should expect, they sailed *at night* for Vera Cruz with both of the men-of-war acting as a convoy for the captured Texan. The Mexican naval officers frankly considered Matamoras an unsafe base henceforth. The very day that these ships stole away under cover of darkness, a great protest was signed by "all the Mexican residents of Matamoras,"[10] in which the episode and general situation was reviewed without loss of flavor. The protest expressed the fear that the *Natchez* was not gone for good. She was merely lying well offshore to ensnare other inward bound units and prizes of the Mexican squadron.

Though other American men-of-war frequently hove to off the port and disconcerted the population to such a degree that Mexican merchantmen were often afraid to sail, the *Natchez* did not return. Indeed, a naval court of inquiry had not only shaken Commander Mervine's confidence in himself, but the Department of State had decided to return the *Urrea* with apologies.

Thus it was that on the morning of June 7, 1837, General Vicente Filisola, who had succeeded General Bravo at Matamoras, got the fright of his life. Off the bar the preceding evening there had appeared a "ship of the line and four corvettes" one of which was recognized as the odious *Natchez*. Filisola at once rushed 1600 men to the defenses at the river mouth along with all the artillery he could muster. At 1:00 A.M. he was still rushing dispatches hither and thither and making final troop dispositions. The Yankees had come! They were after the *Champion* and *Julius Caesar*, in the recapture of which Mervine had been thwarted.

It was, of course, Commodore Dallas, with a part of his Gulf Squadron, who had run down on a diplomatic mission to smooth over the whole affair and to tell the local officials that the U.S.S. *Vandalia* was following with the *Urrea*. The genial Commodore was not making a show of force for he knew General Filisola was a man who would do the right thing. Therefore he would leave only the usual corvette (not the *Natchez*) off that port and would depart with the assurance that Filisola would release the *Champion* and *Julius Caesar* with their crews.

The equally pleasant and suave Filisola was delighted to inform the Commodore that the crews and passengers had been released and permitted to sail for New Orleans, but that the prizes must continue in Mexican possession. And that was how the situation stood when the 21-gun salutes were fired,[11] and Dallas continued down the coast to Vera Cruz for another stop on this "courtesy cruise."

He dropped anchor in Vera Cruz June 24, 1837, and reopened the matter with General Antonio de Castro and the naval authorities there. But Dallas did not get past the fundamentals of his conference with Filisola. Though de Castro expressed something savoring of gratitude that America should send ships into those waters to maintain order, the editorials in the official daily during the following month were not so polite. "We have seen Commodore Dallas come to Matamoras and negotiate with our Filisola with the most indecent deceit, and a few days later to Vera Cruz to quarrel with General Castro and insult the entire Mexican Nation. We have seen returned to us the brig *Urrea*, and that far from disapproving the conduct of him that captured her with such notorious injustice, it seems that they only try to fill to the brim the measure of our grievances."[12]

It took Minister of War and Navy Tornel, however, to sum up adequately the full results of these American naval activities:

"Later the United States was notified that, having the necessary maritime force to enforce the blockade (of Texas) Mexico would take the necessary steps to make it effective. All nations have respected this inherent right of sovereignty of our country except the United States, who escort all ships going to the Texan coast with their Florida fleet. This enables such vessels to carry contraband of war such as arms, munitions, and volunteers for our enemies."[13]

But the operations of the American "Florida fleet" were not wholly to blame for the failure of the Mexican blockade of 1837. The Texan navy was by no means inactive, though its first efforts against the Mexican blockade did result in the loss of the flagship, *Independence*.

It will be recalled that following the battle of San Jacinto the tiny war schooner *Liberty*, Captain Wheelwright, convoyed the *Flora* with Sam Houston aboard, to New Orleans. After a refitting, there was such a heavy bill against her that the Texan treasury could not retire it, and months later she was sold and disappeared from the Texan naval lists. Upon the death of Commodore Hawkins, Captain Wheelwright was transferred to the *Independence*. Simultaneously the Texans were making strenuous efforts to pay the bills of the *Brutus* and *Invincible*, refitted in New York, so that they might return to the Gulf and counteract the Mexican blockade.

These two ships safely avoided the blockaders and had reached Galveston early in April. Captain Hurd of the *Brutus* and Captain Brown of the *Invincible* had been forthwith and immediately relieved from duty. Sam Houston's Commodore, H. L. Thompson, succeeded Brown and one Captain J. D. Boylan was assigned by Secretary of Navy Fisher to the *Brutus*. Should the *Independence* reach the Texan coast safely, Commodore Thompson would have his entire fleet, newly refitted, under his immediate command.

She sailed from New Orleans April 10, with W. H. Wharton, Minister to the United States, aboard. The preceding March 3, he had secured American recognition and was returning to receive the thanks of the Republic.

At 5:30 A.M., April 17, the *Independence* encountered the Mexican blockaders off the mouth of the Brazos River. They were the *Vencedor del Alamo*, Captain D. Blas Godines and the *Libertador*, Captain D. F. R. Davis. The latter flew the pennant of Commodore Lopez, who was on board. When sighted, both the Mexican brigs-of-war were six miles to windward, which gave them a distinct advantage for closing in action. Furthermore, the wind was brisk and the sea running so lively that the lee guns of the low free boarded Texan schooner were continually under water, and those to windward occasionally "dipped their muzzles quite under."[14]

It was a running cannonade, with the *Vencedor del Alamo*, taking station astern so that projectiles from her chase guns would rake the *Independence* from the stern forward. The *Libertador* took station more or less on the port bow of the *Vencedor del Alamo* and on the weather quarter of the *Independence*.

By 9:30 A.M. the ranges had been reduced to a mile and the fireworks began in earnest. Marksmanship must have been poor on both sides, and the sea decidedly choppy for no harm seems to have been done to either antagonist until Commodore Lopez closed the *Libertador* to within two cables length (400 yards) of the slow sailing Texan's weather quarter. Lopez then luffed, or threw his ship's head toward the wind, and thereby presented his broadside. In the comparatively close action that followed, the Texans replied warmly with the three sixes and the long nine-pounder pivot—the only guns that would bear. Since the *Libertador* bore to windward in order to present all her teeth, the distance between the vessels was materially increased within fifteen minutes of sailing on such diverging courses, and the Texans took unearned credit for having beaten off a superior craft while at the same time under a raking fire, ineffective though it was, from the *Vencedor del Alamo* astern. In fact nothing but the rigging of either ship suffered.

As the distance increased between the *Libertador* and the

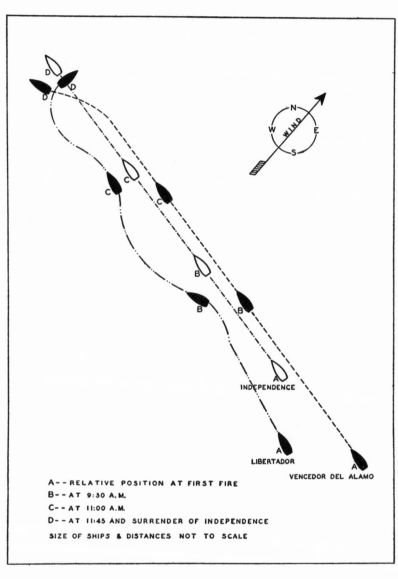

A -- RELATIVE POSITION AT FIRST FIRE
B -- AT 9:30 A.M.
C -- AT 11:00 A.M.
D -- AT 11:45 AND SURRENDER OF INDEPENDENCE
SIZE OF SHIPS & DISTANCES NOT TO SCALE

Capture of the *Independence*

Independence, Lopez put his flagship on her original course at the same time drawing slightly more abeam of the Texan. In the meantime, the *Vencedor del Alamo* was creeping up astern. Thus by 11 A.M. Lopez was again in position to luff the *Libertador* and present her full broadside. Both ships sustained some deck and hull injuries; and Captain Wheelwright was wounded during the cannonade as the paths of the ships diverged once again. He was the only Texan injured and was at once carried below for medical attention. Lieutenant Taylor continued to fight the ship.

But the minutes of the *Independence* under the Texan flag were already numbered. Commodore Lopez had drawn in his two ships so close that by about 11:45 he was able to signal Captain Godines for the execution of the final maneuver that was to bring the Texan colors fluttering down without serious additional loss in life to either side. On execution of the signal, the *Vencedor del Alamo* luffed to a position on the weather quarter of the *Independence* while the *Libertador*, well up abeam of her victim when the evolution started, bore down before the wind into a perfect raking position within a pistol shot of the Texan's stern.[15] The Texans very judiciously struck their colors, and Commodore Lopez came aboard to receive their surrender with courtesy and pleasant reassurances.

With Commodore Lopez it was not an empty formula. So long as they were in his charge, Captain Wheelwright, his officers and crew and their distinguished passenger, William H. Wharton, were treated with extreme courtesy and consideration, each in proportion to his rank.

Nevertheless, it was the beginning of a series of interesting adventures for all of them. The *Independence* had struck her colors almost within sight of Eagle Island, whose fields and broad, well wooded acres constituted the plantation of the captured Texan minister. His devoted brother, John A. Wharton, began putting every possible political pressure upon President Sam Houston to do something in his brother's behalf. At the same time he was planning a personally conducted expedition, the objective of which would be the immediate release of his brother from the *adobe*, Mexican prison in Matamoras.

Meanwhile the wife of the diplomat had mounted her favorite horse and, accompanied by Dr. Branch T. Archer, had started a slow overland trip to Washington, D. C., where it was hoped the United States Government might be urged into bringing pressure to bear upon Mexico to extend the usual diplomatic immunity to William H. Wharton. It was only a short year since the massacre of the Alamo and Goliad forces, hence the friends and families of the prisoners were very apprehensive, particularly since no word was at once received through either Mexican or Texan channels as to the disposition of the prisoners.

In the "piney woods" just before reaching the Louisiana line Mrs. Wharton's horse fell. Mrs. Wharton's leg was broken in the accident and she returned to Eagle Island on a litter.

A week later and still incapacitated, she boarded an oyster boat at Velasco. Before it sailed for New Orleans she heard from her captured husband.

He reported that he was being treated with kindness and suggested that if it were compatible with Texan interests, some of the Mexican prisoners captured in the battle of San Jacinto might be exchanged not only for himself and the crew of the *Independence* but also for a number of other Texans who had fallen into Mexico's hands one way or another and were then incarcerated at Matamoras. In a postscript he remarked that the Mexicans may "require Gen'l Cos in exchange for me."[16]

This stopped all of Mrs. Wharton's further plans but gave John H. Wharton his cue. By May 8, 1837, he had wangled from President Sam Houston authority to charter a vessel at a cost not to exceed five thousand dollars in which he might proceed to Matamoras under a flag of truce and effect an exchange of thirty prisoners.

July was well advanced before he had chartered the schooner *Orleans*, from the firm of McKinney and Williams, for four thousand dollars. Aboard her he and Captain Clendenin, Field Artillery, Texan Army, had in their custody thirty Mexican soldiers, who, since they had been bagged in the battle of San Jacinto, had been kept in the "bull pen" at Liberty.

They arrived at the mouth of the Rio Grande, October 2, and hoisted a white flag of truce on the foremast and the Texan ensign to the main. The *Orleans* was boarded by a Mexican port officer who would not permit the Texans to enter the port, or leave, until permission was received from the Port Commandant.

Before this permission was received, a gale blew up and all through the night Mexican prisoners as well as the Texan crew battled to save the *Orleans*. They were unsuccessful and had to abandon her, fast ashore south of the river mouth. In the struggle for life against the hammering surf, all personal effects were lost and two men were drowned.

Ashore at last, John A. Wharton quickly learned that weeks before his brother had escaped. He had donned a priestly garb, smuggled into the jail by Father Muldoon, and walked out into the desert. The friendly padre had served in Texas and had many acquaintances there.

From the remaining Texan prisoners the younger Wharton further learned that Captain Wheelwright and most of his officers had also escaped. Strangely enough these men had been aided in their flight and were accompanied by none other than Lieutenant Thomas M. Thompson, Mexican Navy, and erstwhile commander of the Mexican war schooner *Correo de Mejico*. Apparently this English adventurer had forgiven the Texans for throwing him into the New Orleans jail on piracy charges after his defeat by Captain Hurd's *San Felipe*. Perhaps his change of heart was because Captain Wheelwright had promised him a commission in the Texan Navy. At least that is what Thompson wanted. Nevertheless, he was not rewarded upon the successful arrival of his party in the Texan settlements.

Meanwhile John A. Wharton, his ship wrecked and his former Mexican prisoners at large in Matamoras, had nothing to trade on. A Catholic padre, probably Muldoon, who was no doubt weary of the constant stream of Wharton troubles, urged and aided the second Wharton, Captain Clendenin and some of their seamen, in an unannounced flight from Matamoras. It was late in October before the younger Wharton and his party ended their Odyssey at Velasco, to be greeted by William H. Wharton, who had completed his return almost two months earlier.

In reviewing the whole affair connected with the capture of the *Independence* by the *Libertador* and the *Vencedor del Alamo* it seems that the Whartons got a lot of hardship, and the Texan naval officers got some satisfaction from pointing out that they had been defeated only by overwhelming odds. Lieutenant Taylor attributed sixteen 18-pounders and a hundred and forty men to the *Libertador*. According to him the *Vencedor del Alamo* had one hundred men, six 12-pounders and a long 18.

Of course the Mexicans got another warship out of the engagement. But their pride over this achievement was far exceeded by their elation over recapturing a certain gun they found aboard the *Independence*. It was the Mexican cannon captured by the Texans at San Jacinto almost exactly a year previously.

It had engraved upon it the "initials of the leading ladies of Texas; where the cannon is esteemed as one of the best trophies capricious fortune conceded to them."[17]

A small part of San Jacinto had been avenged. So proud were the Mexicans of their victory that they were intensely eager that their prize reach Vera Cruz without mishap. Matamoras, with the *Natchez* suspected of being in the offing, was considered unsafe. Both victor ships were used to convoy the prize from Matamoras. The *Independence* was incorporated into the Mexican Navy, as a member of which she escaped falling into the hands of the French in the Pastry War, only to figure prominently in a revolutionary outbreak at Tampico a few years later.[18]

CHAPTER SIX

THE TEXAS NAVY COUNTER
ATTACKS • Lone Star Imperialism
Battle off Galveston • Saucy Privateer

T HE THUNDER of the cannonades between the *Independence* and the Mexican blockaders attracted the entire population of Velasco to the seashore. The spectators assembled just in time to see the Texan flag flutter downward from the main gaff. The populace considered it an ignominious affair. The most embarrassed man present was Houston's Secretary of Navy, S. Rhoads Fisher. Intent upon doing something about this awful stigma upon his own arm of the service, he proceeded to Galveston and conferred with his immediate subordinate, Commodore H. L. Thompson of the *Invincible.*

These two worthies decided that the two remaining effective Texan warships should make a cruise. Strong argument could have been presented for such a use of the tiny, two-ship fleet. A weak naval detachment at large on the high seas has more than once drawn many times its equivalent in strength from strategically chosen blockading stations.

By rushing to sea before the orders of a timid government could keep his small squadron on the American coast, Commodore John Rodgers, in 1812, drew after his tiny command so many British blockaders that practically all the American merchant fleet that was on the high seas when hostilities started entered their home ports in safety before the English cruisers returned to form a cordon along the coast. Otherwise

Rodgers's squadron might well have been blockaded and the inward bound shipping snared as well. The great strategist, Mahan, considers the voyage of Rodgers the only really sensible use of the American high seas men-of-war during that conflict.

Of course Fisher and his Commodore could not cite Mahan as an argument for a cruise, but they were endowed with common sense, which is the basic qualification of every good strategist. With the Mexican Gulf Squadron, now augmented to eight men-of-war by the capture of the *Independence*, the two Texan ships were as much in danger of being rendered useless by blockaders as were those of Commodore Rodgers in 1812. In fact, the situations were analogous. A cruise to the Mexican coast could be expected to draw the Mexican fleet in pursuit and leave Texan commerce and supplies from New Orleans free to go and come.

But the vital question that confronted Secretary Fisher and Commodore Thompson was whether or not Constitutional commander-in-chief of the Army and Navy, President Sam Houston would approve such a cruise. Whatever Houston's homespun virtues as a frontier leader and statesman may have been, there is no conclusive evidence that he knew the meaning of the word strategy. As an infantry lieutenant under Jackson he perhaps learned a little about military tactics though he never gave evidence of such knowledge. Let the hero worshipping writers who spread the delusion that he was a military man explain his vagaries in the San Jacinto campaign—particularly his refusal to attack while his forces equalled those of Santa Anna; his permitting Cos to march past him with reinforcements, and then his attack upon the combined hostile columns in a presumably barricaded or entrenched position. Houston did not win the San Jacinto victory; the Latin *siesta* habit lost it. Thus in an even more abstruse problem of naval strategy one would expect Houston to be wrong. And so he was. He insisted that the only way ships could defend a coast was for them to remain on that coast.

Fisher and his Commodore were reluctant about further

urging a cruise upon the President because of his known touchiness concerning matters having to do with the army and navy. Even then he was in a quarrel with Congress over the proper use of the fleet.

Right after the capture of the *Independence* the ever aggressive Texan solons had taken under advisement a resolution to send the two remaining ships to the mouth of the Rio Grande to see what could be done about getting Wharton and the other prisoners exchanged. Houston nipped the idea in the bud by telling them ahead of time that he would ignore the resolution. Sending the ships to Matamoras would leave the coast unprotected; the approach of Texan squadron might lead to harsh treatment of prisoners, and furthermore, trying to direct ship movements by resolution was a gross encroachment upon the Constitutional powers of the Executive.[1] If he, as President, was commander-in-chief of the Army and Navy he would function as such; Congress would not. And that was that!

By June 10, 1837, Mr. Fisher and Commodore Thompson had apparently evaluated all the pros and cons of the situation and decided to make a cruise anyway. Moreover, the Secretary of Navy decided to go along as "a volunteer." He explained such strange action for a Secretary of the Navy by saying it was to "inspire great confidence in the men and stimulate our Congress to do something for us."[2] Nevertheless, one suspects that it was partially from a desire for a little adventure and a natural reluctance to return and face the certain ire of his President after the ships were gone.

Before formally beginning the cruise, the *Invincible*, Commodore H. L. Thompson, and the *Brutus*, Captain J. D. Boylan, convoyed the *Texas*, laden with army supplies, to Matagorda. They were back in Galveston by midnight of June 10. A boat was sent ashore with dispatches from Secretary Fisher, and both vessels stood to sea at 1 A.M., June 11.

Sailing in company, the two little cruisers ran eastward to the mouth of the Mississippi where they lingered for two days in apparent hopes of intercepting some Mexican vessels homeward bound. When this yielded nothing, they stood southward toward the Yucatecan coast. On July 1, they parted company with the understanding that the island of Mujeres, on the northeast corner of the Yucatan peninsula, should be the rendezvous.

Captain Boylan, of the *Brutus*, chose a more easterly course; and when off Cape San Antonio (the western end of Cuba), he hove to for a few days; but no potential prize came in sight. Accordingly he laid a course for the rendezvous. Mujeres was reached July 8. The *Invincible* had steered a more direct course, hence had been waiting for several days.

From Mujeres boat expeditions made short excursions to nearby islands, on which were found an abundance of turtles that the natives had collected in pens for food. With larders restocked (without payment being made) from this convenient source, the little fleet continued southward to the much larger island of Cozumel.

So infatuated were the Texans by this tropical gem that they went imperialistic with a vengeance. They liked its "delightful situation and the salubrious trade wind which blows without cessation . . . the richest of soils which produces the finest kind of timber." All of which convinced Thompson that it would "be one of the greatest acquisitions to our beloved country that the Admiral aloft could have bestowed upon us."

In accordance with this spirit, Thompson hoisted the Texan flag (which, by a slip of the pen, he called the "Star Spangled Banner") to a "height of forty-five feet with acclamations both from the inhabitants and our little patriotic band."[3] With the jungle quivering from the echoes of a twenty-three gun salute, he took possession of the island for the Republic of Texas.

From Cozumel, July 16, with full water casks, the fleet doubled back northward, and passed once again the island of Mujeres. Off Cape Catoche, a number of sails were sighted from time to time, but because of the sailing qualities—"which I can with an open heart assure you is not nor never was what they have been cracked up to be"[4]—of the two schooners, none of them were overhauled. Beginning at Cape Catoche, boat parties were sent ashore at sundry points such as at Silan and Telchac; but no resistance was met. Off the latter port the first prize, the schooner *Union*, of Sisal, was captured. Other ships were boarded but all were neutrals.

By the 24th they were off the town of Chilbona near which the usual boat party, this time with Captain Boylan and the Secretary of Navy among its members, went ashore for a reconnaissance. A hundred yards from the beach they were charged upon by a detachment of cavalry. Armed only with pistols, they fled to their boat, which was gotten afloat just in time. Secretary of Navy Fisher seems to have offered the most effective resistance to this charge. He whipped out one of his pistols while the boat was being shoved off and unhorsed one of the riders.[5] For this "rascally reception" the Commodore got indignant and burned two small towns in the vicinity.

While these operations were in progress the gig of the *Brutus* made a two-day trip to the nearby city of Sisal. Favorable reports were made as to conditions there. At once the two war schooners stood for that port and were rewarded with the prizes *Telegrafo* and *Adventure*, both of Campeche.[6]

The next day, July 26, the Commodore sent a canoe ashore with a letter to the Mexican commandant of the castle at the harbor entrance. The message was "that I had sufficient force to take the town, and requesting him to remove to some place of safety the women and children and the old and the decrepit persons; as I intended bombarding the town, unless they paid the government of Texas the small sum of twenty-five thousand dollars, in consideration of which I would guarantee immunity from molestation for six months."

The commandant's "first reply" to this mild demand "was a twenty-four pound shot close under our main chains, our white flag still flying at the fore; this want of respect to our flag of truce induced me to open our broadside on the town and castle, and the action became general, lasting three hours and thirty minutes, we receiving no damage."[7] Captain Boylan, however, admitted that the fire from the castle and a "large gun near the mole" finally began to get the range with such precision that it was deemed advisable to withdraw.

Some forty prisoners, taken from the prizes, were sent ashore, however; and the schooner *Adventure* was burned because she was a dull sailer. The Commodore also salved the wounded feelings of his officers and crews by passing out $527.37 as "prize money."

And injured feelings there were aplenty, for during the engagements with the Sisal batteries, the Commodore had climaxed his already established custom of ranting about the decks by clapping his boatswain in irons and "God damning" all hands (with occasional provocative references to the ancestry of some of his crew) until the pious Purser of the *Invincible*, filled with thoughts of the troubles Jonah brought upon his shipmates, "feared the Almighty would inflict some punishment on us for his wickedness."[8]

The distribution of the "prize money" must have had some assuaging effect. At least that was about his only major act upon which no accusation was based by his subordinates after the return of the vessel to Galveston. But the Navy Department called him to account for that, for five hundred dollars of the distributed funds were acquired by "ransoming" the prize *Union* shortly after the burning of the *Adventure*. The Department considered this very irregular. The prize should have been sent to Matagorda or Galveston, with cargo unbroken, for adjudication.[9]

With the *Adventure* and *Union* off his hands after bombarding Sisal, the Commodore laid a course northward for nearly a hundred miles to the Alacranes, which were reached July 21. The same evening the Texans captured the Mexican schooner *Abispo* which was sent, in company with the *Telegrafo*, to Matagorda, for adjudication.[10] A few other sails were chased, but no additional capture was made until August 8, when the English schooner *Eliza Russell* hove in sight. Though the well defined Texan policy was against the molestation of English

merchantmen, when Thompson found that her cargo was consigned to a Mexican and the risk borne by him, the Commodore
could not resist taking her and she was sent to Galveston under
a prize crew for adjudication.

Before leaving the Alacranes, Captain Boylan was sent
ashore to search the main island. He "found many articles of
various description buried in the sand which we took on
board." He then hoisted the Texan flag on the barren beach
and modestly took "possession in the name of the government."[11]

From the Alacranes, the small fleet doubled back to the
Yucatecan coast, passed again in sight of Sisal, rounded the
northwest corner of the peninsula to Campeche (where were
sent ashore the prisoners); cruised by Laguna and inter-
mediate points, without taking more than an occasional open
fishing boat until near Tobasco. Off that port, August 12, the
mail schooner, *Correo de Tobasco*, laden with a light cargo and
four passengers was captured. Moreover, she was but a day
out of Vera Cruz. Efforts were made by the Mexican skipper
to destroy his dispatches,[12] but the Texans captured enough
to learn therefrom full details as to the location of the Mexican
fleet. All of it by this time had been concentrated in Vera Cruz
harbor, whence it might launch a counter attack when news
of the position of the Texan fleet was received. The *General
Terán*, *General Bravo* and *Independence* were to sail eastward,
as a result of reported Texan depredations off Yucatan.

Captain Boylan claimed, in his official report of the cruise,
that the two Texan men-of-war spent the next three days in
cruising in the path of that squadron in hopes of meeting it.
Thompson makes no such claim; and depositions of Mexican
prisoners show that in reality the Texans immediately ran inshore to a position off the bar of Chiltepeque. The prisoners
were landed, under a flag of truce; and the port commander
considered it expedient to order his meager garrison to aid in
the watering and provisioning of the small hostile squadron.

Had the Texan fleet actually laid itself athwart the conventional route from Vera Cruz to Yucatan, it would have very likely found all the Mexican men-of-war it would have cared to meet. At the very time the Texan Commodore was lingering near Chiltepeque, Commodore Aldana, in command at Vera Cruz, was clearing from that port with the brigs-of-war *Iturbide* and *Libertador* and the ex-Texan schooner *Independence*. He arrived in Campeche and made inquiries as to the whereabouts of the Texans August 17.[13] By that time Thompson had beaten his way along the Mexican coast to the vicinity of Vera Cruz where the *Brutus* captured a little schooner named the *Rafaelita* which on investigation, turned out to be none other than the renamed *Correo de Mejico*, which had been released in New Orleans after her capture by the *San Felipe*.

Vera Cruz, where still remained a strong naval detachment, was given a wide berth. Between Vera Cruz and Tampico, a number of sails were chased, but none proved to be good prizes. An American craft was boarded by an officer from the *Brutus* at the very bar of the latter port, but there is no evidence that the *General Terán*, which had been sent to Tampico,[14] made an overt gesture toward the audacious Texan.

Thence the Texans ran up the coast to blockade Matamoras. But with the weather getting rougher and the supply of water low, they continued up the coast, passing Brazoria at 5 P.M., August 26, and at 9 o'clock anchored, with the prizes, outside the Galveston bar. Nightfall and the stiff offshore wind that had made such a fast passage possible must have made the treacherous bar too dangerous for an immediate crossing.

Early in the forenoon of the day following, August 27, the little fleet was still outside the bar. By 10 o'clock the *Brutus*, with the Honorable Secretary of Navy Fisher, and in company with the *Correo de Tobasco* (the *Rafaelita* had been lost at sea), crossed the bar and furled their sails off the Navy Yard. The Commodore and his deep drafted *Invincible* would wait awhile.

But the waiting was not to be inactive. About noon there appeared on the horizon three sails. They were the merchant-man, *Sam Houston*, with two Mexican brigs-of-war in hot pursuit.

They were the Commodore Aldana's command that the Texans had missed while watering and provisioning at Chiltepeque. After his arrival at Campeche, August 17, Aldana had scouted along the Yucatecan coast in search of news and had at last decided that his quarry would soon be running for the home port. Accordingly, he had augmented the crews of his two fine brigs from the personnel of the slow, ill-conditioned *Independence*, which had already detained him more than he thought she was worth. He had reached this decision August 21. By daybreak of the 27th he was approaching Galveston Island, but with land not yet in sight. It was at this time that he sighted the brigantine, *Sam Houston*, and cracked on sail in pursuit. So great was the start of the merchantman that she reached the bar still some five miles ahead of her two pursuers.

Upon approaching the bar, Commodore Aldana reduced his canvas to the mainsail, boomsail and the jib, when he found the *Invincible*, and the merchantman, still outside the bar. He desired to approach the situation slowly and make a reconnaissance with an eye to cutting out the two ships in a night, boat attack. To the great surprise of the Mexican Commodore, the Texan war schooner set her sails, exchanged signals with the distant *Brutus*, off the Navy yard, hoisted her colors and the broad pennant of a Texan commodore and stood out toward him.

The first phase of the ensuing engagement was featured by an effort on the part of Commodore Aldana to put his *Iturbide* between the *Invincible* and the shore, at the same time leaving the *Libertador* far enough in the offing to keep the Texan from running to sea. The direction of the wind and shoaling water, (very disconcerting because of inaccurate maps) defeated this movement. Thompson claimed that it was two of his lusty broadsides that defeated the move, but since the Mexican commander reported no casualties and no damages during the entire engagement, this statement may well be discounted.

In the second phase the Mexicans stood well off shore, after a sharp exchange of gun fire, in hopes of luring the *Invincible*

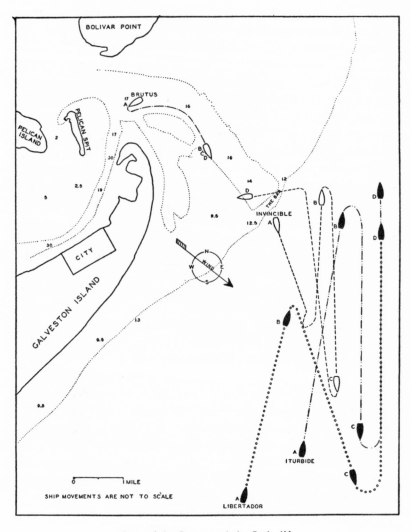

Loss of the *Brutus* and the *Invincible*

after them. At about the same moment, Commodore Thompson decided to try luring the *Libertador* and *Iturbide* inshore where uncharted sand bars might work to his advantage. He furthermore had a right to expect the *Brutus* to come out in accordance with his signals.

But his consort, while leaving her anchorage, had run aground. The steamer, *Branch T. Archer* hastened to her aid, only to get a hawser afoul of the stern post of the *Brutus* so that the rudder was completely unshipped. Mexican gun fire could not have more effectively put her out of action.

Since the *Invincible* would not follow him, nothing remained for Commodore Aldana but to try closing with the now withdrawing *Invincible*. This he did until shoaling water brought his rudder in contact with the bottom. In dismay he hauled off. At the same time, Thompson was trying to follow the escaped merchantman across the bar. A sharp bump against the sandy bottom unshipped his rudder and the helpless *Invincible* piled herself upon a shoal just within the bar.

Within the next forty-eight hours, heavy seas swept over her from stem to stern and pounded her to pieces. Though all hands were saved, Commodore Thompson was much distressed over the loss of his ship, but he could not resist stating again that "she never was the vessel she was cracked up to be."[15]

Though the little Texan fleet at the outset of its cruise had freed the coast of Mexican blockaders, thanks to the rare hunch that carried Commodore Aldana straight to Galveston, the cruise had ended in the essentials of a Mexican victory. The *Invincible* had been caught outside of the bar, and though she escaped destruction by enemy gun fire, she found it expedient to attempt the treacherous harbor entrance under circumstances that led to her destruction. In hastening to her aid, the *Brutus*, sole remaining effective Texan cruiser, was rendered helpless by loss of the rudder, until, a few weeks later, a second terrific storm pounded her to pieces. The only satisfaction that the Texans could derive from the situation was that the same boisterous weather that had finished Commodore Aldana's work, also drove the *Iturbide* and *Libertador* to shelter at Matamoras, but not until they had witnessed the wrecking of the *Invincible.*

Without a single national ship that could be sent out to patrol the coast, the Texans became frantic.

But as usual with republics, the immediate attention was given to the serious business of showing disapproval of those who had participated in the unfortunate closing phases of the cruise. Hence, while the President tackled the problem of putting Secretary Fisher in his place, Captain Boylan was given the task of collecting depositions for court martialing the Commodore.

But Fisher found champions in the Senate who admitted the right of the President to suspend a cabinet officer (as Houston had already done) but doubted whether the circumstances warranted such strong action. Efforts were made at Fisher's impeachment by friends of the President but with no success, until finally the Senate expressed the wish that he would resign because "the breach between him and His Excellency is such that it could not be for the interest of our common country that he should retain the station."[16] The Senate further resolved that the President did not have a valid case against the erstwhile seagoing Secretary. A Mr. William M. Shepherd accepted the portfolio of the Navy Department which now, instead of containing a list of ships, held nothing but unpaid bills and court martial proceedings against Thompson.

Meanwhile Commodore Thompson had rendered the proceedings useless by dying and thereby cheated his many enemies of the pleasure of seeing him tried on charges ranging from excessive profanity to embezzlement. The latter charge was largely based upon his unauthorized distribution of the "prize money" from the ransomed schooner *Union* and his alleged habit of annexing liquors from the prizes, not to mention personal effects, such as a pair of pantaloons belonging to the Mexican mate of the *Correo de Tobasco.*

But all of this did nothing toward solving the problem of

naval defense, to which the new Secretary Shepherd was turning. An effort to solve the problem by purchase of the American owned steamer *Pulaski*, was frustrated by the refusal of the owner to make delivery in Galveston. He feared that a renewed Mexican blockade might close the port.

Thus for the time being, if a fleet was to be created quickly it was necessary that it be done from resources at hand. These consisted largely of the recently captured prizes and the privateer *Thomas Toby*, which also offered a prize in the form of the brig *Fenix*, or *Phoenix*, as the Texans called her. And in connection with this mention of the *Thomas Toby* and her prize, we might well pause to review briefly the history of this one outstanding Texan privateer.

Originally she was the *De Kalb* but some time after the acquisition of a letter of marque, issued by the Consultation, she appeared on the Gulf early in 1836 as the *Thomas Toby*, Hoyt commanding. In the fall of 1836 she was cruising off the ports of Vera Cruz, Sisal, Campeche, Matamoras, and Tampico. According to a journal entry of November 10, 1836, Lieutenant Tennison, then a midshipman in the Texan Navy, credited her with having been so bold as to play "her long Tom upon" a fort at Tampico. He also credited her with a prize or two on this cruise, but they could not have been very important.

She got to sea again in the spring of 1837 just before the commencement of the effective Mexican blockade. On May 24, she was off the port of Sisal where she captured the fine Mexican brig *Fenix*. Boat parties from the *Toby* were pulling into Sisal harbor to cut out the *Correo de Campeche* when the Texans sighted "the sail of the Spanish brig *Emilio*. Expecting that this might be some ship-of-war that came in pursuit, the force was made to return"[17] declared the Mexican accounts of the *Toby's* operations off Sisal. The Texans probably thought the *Emilio* was one of the new Mexican gun brigs, for the *Toby* and her prize *Fenix* soon vanished from the Yucatecan coast. Not only the privateer, but the *Fenix* as well, were anchored in Galveston Bay when the *Invincible* was lost.

With the erstwhile navy in the hands of creditors, captured, or defeated by the enemy; and the coast so endangered that the owners of the steamer *Pulaski* refused to consummate a sale, it was natural that the Houston administration should authorize Lieutenant Wright to make a survey of the situation and see what could be done toward utilizing the *Toby* and the prizes on hand.

Lieutenant Wright considered the brig *Phoenix*, recently built at Campeche of cedar and ironwood, 274 tons and capable of a battery of twelve 12-pounders, an excellent potential addition to the fleet. He also thought the *Thomas Toby*, considering the situation, to be a bargain at the demanded price, though at the moment he felt she was too heavily armed. Even the little *Correo de Tobasco*, 65 tons and Baltimore built, could do yeoman service if armed with the "Widow Porter," a long 18-pounder then at Victoria, and the two small brass sixes from the over-gunned *Thomas Toby*. "As it is absolutely essential and requisite that an addition be made to our navy without delay I would earnestly and respectfully recommend the immediate purchase of these vessels. At any other time I should be loath to advocate the purchasing and equipping vessels for service which are not built expressly as vessels of war."[18]

Though Secretary of Navy Shepherd heartily endorsed the recommendation of Lieutenant Wright, and wrote at length upon the absolute necessity of maintaining control of the Gulf, these ships were not bought. Early in 1838 the merchant brig *Potomac* was purchased from L. M. Hitchcock. She was never fully converted into a man-of-war, although Captain Wheelwright did bankrupt a prosperous Galveston ship chandler, Mr. H. Sanderson, by procuring for her, on governmental credit, over ten thousand dollars worth of equipment and naval stores. The *Potomac* never made a cruise. To the end of the Republic she was the receiving ship for the Galveston Naval Station.

When Congress met in regular session, it responded to the general naval scare by re-enacting the essential features of the unexecuted naval bill of the previous year. This new bill, autumn of 1837, called for a ship of 500 tons, eighteen guns; two brigs, 300 tons, 12 guns each; and three schooners, 130 tons and five to seven guns each. Payment therefore was "solemnly pledged" by the "public faith" and new agents were to be sent to the Atlantic seaboard to let the contracts, for such warships were not to be found on the open market.

Thus in summarizing the Texan-Mexican naval activities for the year 1837, we may safely conclude that the year opened with a distinct naval advantage in favor of the Mexicans. They were unable to make the most of their opportunities by blockading the Texan coast because of the meddling of the United States fleet which was unwilling to see American ships captured by such a blockade and adjudicated in Mexican courts. After the repudiation of the United States naval officers in the Gulf by the American State Department and the return of the gunbrig *Urrea*, the Texans frustrated a future blockade with a cruise of the *Brutus* and *Invincible*, which with the operations of the privateer *Thomas Toby*, gave the Mexican fleet something to do besides hovering on the Texas coast.

The effect of the cruises of these two Texan warships and the *Thomas Toby* cannot be over-emphasized. The editor of the *Diario del Gobierno*, official daily for the Centralists in Mexico City, lamented that the Texan privateer and cruiser custom of hoisting American colors prevented proper policing of the Mexican coasts by Tornel's new navy. But in Yucatan, the New England of Mexico where most Mexican ships were owned and where merchants were dependent upon the carrying trade and where the philosophy of states rights was deep rooted, there was no disposition to explain away Centralist failures with weak excuses. One Yucatecan newspaper boldly editorialized as follows:

The crew of the *Toby*, so we are informed, is only thirty men, and her armament only one pivot gun, eight-pounder, two brass guns, rifles and small arms. . . . The evils that a pirate so insignificant as the *Thomas Toby* causes daily to our extended commerce are very grave, and most painful in that it has not been many months since

Yucatan, in spite of her poverty, contributed EIGHTY THOUSAND PESOS, MUNITIONS, SAILORS, etc. etc. for the repair and equipment of the squadron of the Republic.[19]

What the same editor thought after the far greater depredations of Commodore Thompson's a few weeks later could not be ascertained from sources now in Mexico City. Perhaps, by that time the Centralists had suppressed his sheet and wrested his irritatingly squeaky quill from his indignant hand. It was just such editorials that were rapidly building up Yucatecan sentiment for the subsequent revolt and secession of the maritime provinces—events that were to play such a prominent part in later chapters of Texas naval history.

Notwithstanding the successful Texan cruise of 1837, the successes of Commodores Aldana and Lopez and the autumnal storms, left the Texans without a serviceable ship with which to protect the long coast line. From a military and naval standpoint there was nothing to keep Tornel from sending troop laden ships to strategic points on the Texan coast.

But the Gods of fortune again favored the Texans. The same international depression, or panic, that was paralyzing the United States (and Texas) was playing havoc with Mexican revenues. Moreover, the interior of the Mexican Republic was visited by a series of long remembered earthquakes; a fish shortage skyrocketed Mexican food prices on both coasts; and an abortive revolt in North Central Mexico was just serious enough to draw Filisola's Matamoras command into the hinterland.

As if these were not troubles enough for Mexico, the French Minister was beginning a sword rattling program in an effort to collect $600,000 on some old claims and to get justice for some imprisoned Frenchmen. Hence the restored Centralist President Bustamante and Minister of War and Navy Tornel were in no position to launch a navy supported military offensive against Texas in the months that followed the Mexican supremacy at sea.

CHAPTER SEVEN

THE FRENCH IN THE GULF
Claims Ignored • Vera Cruz • Santa
Anna • Revolution • Texas Fortunate

THE ACTIVITIES of the French in the Gulf of Mexico during 1838–39 are so intimately entwined with the naval history of the powder burnt Republic of Texas that they cannot be ignored. During the period in question the French fleet combined with the Mexican incompetence to constitute the first line of Texan defense.

Trouble between Mexico and France had been long abrewing. Within the sixteen years of intermittent civil strife within Mexico, it was inevitable that some resident foreigners should suffer. Two Frenchmen had been shot in "the butchery of Tampico in 1835." At Atenzingo in 1833, five Frenchmen, "who enjoyed the general esteem, and who followed an industry useful to the country . . . were beheaded, made in fragments and dragged at the tail of the horses (including a woman that was found among them) by known Mexicans, that did the deed publicly in the middle of the day and crying: 'Mueran los Estrangeros.' "[1]

Of course French Minister Baron Deffaudis was making the most of one version of a gruesome episode when he typified French grievances in the above quoted lurid rhetoric. By the same token the Mexicans did not select a representative case when they derisively singled out the petty claim of a French baker in Parian, who sought an indemnity for a few dozen confiscated chocolate eclairs, as typical of all French claims and

97

therefore wrote the resulting trouble with France into Mexican history as the "Pastry War."

Irrespective of the merits of the claims, by 1837 France was speaking in earnest. Unable to get any satisfaction, Baron Deffaudis once again submitted an itemized bill for damages totaling six hundred thousand dollars. Unless Mexico made immediate arrangements for a settlement, his government would have to resort to maritime reprisals.

That proud old Centralist, President Bustamante, who had regained the leadership of his party and nation after the fall of Santa Anna, was indignant; and well he might be. Since all the lesser *politicos* were prattling wildly about national honor and the strength of the fortress at Vera Cruz that had defied the mightiest efforts of Spain, it would have been political suicide to bow to France. Consequently Baron Deffaudis received his passports January 16, 1838.

By March of the same year, a French squadron under Admiral Bazoche was off Vera Cruz. Mexican custom receipts dropped to practically nothing and the foreign trade was paralyzed.[2] Abiding faith in the strength of San Juan de Ulúa, the protecting castle at Vera Cruz and "the Gibraltar of America," combined with the news that the French Fleet was being wracked by scurvy and storms during the hot, yellow fever season, was all that kept the Mexican cup of bitterness from over-flowing.

But in October Admiral Baudin brought strong reinforcements and assumed supreme control of the French diplomatic and naval operations. Before making the Mexican port feel the vengeance of his fleet, the dapper, one armed French Admiral reopened negotiations with Bustamante's Minister of Foreign Affairs, Cuevas. Through November 17–21, 1838, Admiral Baudin conferred with Cuevas at Jalapa. His demands were simple. He merely wanted the six hundred thousand dollars Deffaudis had demanded plus an additional two hundred thousand for the cost of collection. A French fleet could not operate so far from the Bay of Biscay without additional expense. Unless his terms were met, November 27 would find him thundering at the walls of San Juan de Ulúa.[3]

The Mexican answer was reinforcements for Vera Cruz under General Arista, war hymns in the streets of Mexico City, and a flat refusal of both chambers of the Mexican Congress to make any concessions.[4] Meanwhile, the crafty and disgraced Santa Anna, ever the opportunist, hastened to the troubled beach at Vera Cruz. Hopefully he looked for a high crested wave upon which he could ride, surf-board fashion, back into the good graces of his people.

Through the forenoon of November 27 Baudin's steam tenders towed the heavy sailing ships-of-the-line into a perfect position for bombarding San Juan de Ulúa. For diplomatic reasons, and a continued confidence in the strength of the fortress, the garrison commander, General Gaona, held his fire until 2:00 P.M. when the first blasts of the initial French broadsides shook the ancient castle.

The shells from Baudin's one hundred and four modern guns went deep into the old musty walls where their detonation sent heavy débris tumbling down about the ears of General Gaona's gunners. By nightfall great breaches in the walls were everywhere. All the Mexican guns were silenced and the morale of the garrison was broken as much by the obvious inferiority of their own guns and ammunition as by the punishment they had taken.

General Gaona asked his chief, General Rincón, in Vera Cruz, if he should vacate the highly prized castle. Rincón dodged the responsibility by referring the matter to a commission headed by the ubiquitous Santa Anna. With responsibility apparently well enough divided to protect all reputations, the Mexicans withdrew, agreed to reduce the Vera Cruz command to one thousand men, and pay damages to French nationalists recently expelled from the city. In return the French Admiral was to relinquish San Juan de Ulúa and to discontinue the blockade for eight months.[5]

The Mexicans had driven a good bargain, but not good

enough for the astounded jingoes in Mexico City. Notwithstanding his carefully designed machinery for making Santa Anna and the other prominent Mexicans share his responsibility, Rincón was disgraced, to be succeeded by the. selfsame Santa Anna. Even so, the Cabinet was forced to resign, and Bustamante saved his régime only by giving two portfolios to hated leaders of the Federalist, states rights opposition. The chagrined Baudin refusal to take vengeance by shelling the city.

Instead, in the early foggy hours of December 5, 1838, he landed a raiding expedition of fifteen hundred troops and marines. In three columns it quickly penetrated to the barracks near the southwest corner of the city. In this advance General Arista was captured. Santa Anna escaped a like fate by fleeing down a fog shrouded back alley clad only in his underwear.

As Mexican resistance formed, Baudin's raiding columns fell back in good order to their boats with a loss of but eight killed and sixty wounded. As the French retreated Santa Anna quickly acquired a pair of trousers and a sword. He then placed himself at the head of a Mexican column that was marching through the now vacated city toward the waterfront. His forces arrived just in time to receive the last whiff of grape shot fired from the covering boat howitzers as the main landing party shoved off for the return to the ships.

Santa Anna took credit for driving the French into the sea. Even luckier for his political future, this last volley so severely wounded him that his leg had to be amputated. The political surf bather had found his crested comber. Within three weeks it was a frothy tidal wave that so completely engulfed Mexico that the masses forgot the humiliating presence of the French fleet. They thought only of Santa Anna's heroism. His return to Mexico City was accompanied by ovations, ceremonies, and adulation, that were not exceeded until the subsequent arrival of his revered, exalted, and hallowed, amputated leg. To the echoes of florid, effervescent forensic eulogies it was buried, under a noble monument, in the National Capital.[6]

But what of Baudin? Though he had twenty-six ships, not counting prizes, and four thousand men he did not feel able to invade Mexico. He contented himself with tightening the profitable blockade and incorporating the Mexican Navy, captured with San Juan de Ulúa, into his own squadron.

The acquisition of the Mexican fleet was the biggest prize the French thus far had to show for their efforts. Recently brought into a state of efficiency by Tornel, the French found it in exceptionally fine condition. An officer on Baudin's staff described these ships as consisting of "the beautiful corvette *Iguala,* of twenty-four guns, three beautiful brigs and two schooners." He beamed over their *charmante* construction and modern equipment so new from the ship chandlers of Baltimore.[7] Their seizure by the French was a great victory for the Texans.

As if this were not enough good fortune for the Lone Star Republic, Admiral Baudin decided to bring the stiff-necked Centralists to heel by fomenting a revolution in the predominantly states-rights, or Federalist, regions north and northwest from Tampico. He accordingly raised the blockade from Tampico northward as soon as the revolting Federalists were in control of the custom houses. In this way the enemies of Santa Anna and Bustamante were being subsidized for the powerful armed revolt against Centralism that came in 1839. As a by-product of these efforts Admiral Baudin was setting up a temporary buffer state between Texas and her bitterest enemies in Mexico City.

That the Texans were thoroughly and happily aware of this turn in their fortunes there is ample evidence. In August of 1838, even before Baudin was setting up the revolutionary "buffer state," President Sam Houston's Secretary of State was writing to his diplomatic agent to France:

The blockade of the Mexican ports by France is reducing Mexico to a deplorable state. She cannot live without commerce, which is now cut off. . . . This emergency has induced them to attempt smuggling goods into their own country through the ports of Texas. . . . You may say in truth to all, that Texas is prospering to an extent that no one could have reasonably anticipated when you left us.[8]

But all good things must come to an end, even the Texan luck that characterized the first presidential administration of General Sam Houston. Eventually, an enormous English squadron, outweighing that of Baudin, hove up on the horizon to investigate this French barrier to good British trade. When the fleet of Commodore Douglas R. N. arrived, English Minister Pakenham offered "mediatory" services between Baudin and the Mexicans.

The French Admiral was quite willing for he had no hankering for another stormy season on that pest ridden coast. Hence after a bit of quibbling with the English, the size of whose fleet Baudin felt was a discourtesy to France, several British ships were detached (but not sent too far away) and negotiations went forward at a rapid rate.

Thus by March 9, 1839, Baudin, aided by the English, had come to an agreement with two Mexican representatives— Señor Gorostiza and ex-President Victoria. Under the agreement France got the six hundred thousand dollars. Whether or not France should retain the fruits of the blockade, including the handsome Vera Cruz fleet she had annexed, was to be determined by a mixed commission.[9] Pending the action of this commission, in the dim distant future, France kept the Mexican Navy.[10] Again Texas was the beneficiary of the vagaries of Mexican-French-British diplomacy.

CHAPTER EIGHT

*A NEW PRESIDENT AND A NEW
NAVY • Commodore Moore • Mexican
Chaos • "Great Ex" • Fleet Retained*

WHILE FRANCE was fortuitously guaranteeing Texas against
a Mexican invasion, Sam Houston was maintaining a régime
of strict economy within the Lone Star Republic. This meant
that he had to avoid armed conflict with both Indians and
Mexicans.

Prior to his Texan career he had lived several years as a
Cherokee tribesman and as such had served on diplomatic
missions to Washington. Naturally he experienced little trouble
in keeping his old friends to northward puffing at the peace
pipes. But toward the end of his régime, agents of General
Filisola at Matamoras were active among the hard riding plains
Indians to westward, and frontier settlements felt their forays.
Western citizens rightfully complained about the lack of military protection.

The Mexican naval blockade and invasion scare that followed Commodore Aldana's victory off Galveston, August 27,
1837, and caused the prospective arming of the prize brig
Phoenix and the proposed purchase of the privateer *Thomas
Toby* has been noted. The saber rattling of the French soon
allayed those alarms so that the *Thomas Toby* was never bought.
The brig *Potomac*, previously mentioned, was bought, but she
was never completely converted into a seaworthy warship. She
soon declined to the status of a "receiving ship." Through her

naval career she remained tied up at the Galveston navy yard.

Before the hostile naval and military scare was allayed by the arrival of the French, however, the Texan Congress passed and President Houston reluctantly signed, November 4, 1837, a naval bill appropriating $280,000 for the acquisition of a fleet. The bill also stipulated that the Secretary of Treasury should make those funds available to whomsoever the President might name as naval agent. There is an insistent tone in the measure as passed. Indeed, the earlier drafts of the bill had vested the designation of the agent in the hands of Congress, which, combined with the specific instructions the final draft of the measure carried to the executive branch of the government, indicates that the representatives of the people were getting tired of passing naval bills that listed ships to be bought and getting no navy merely because of executive ideas on economy.

The insistent tone of the naval bill was also engendered by Houston's known antipathy for those who go down to the sea. His row with seagoing Secretary of Navy Fisher was largely responsible for that attitude. Furthermore the solons felt that he was often parsimonious to the point of false economy. The truth is that Houston wished to solve all Texan troubles, frontier, fiscal, maritime and diplomatic, by the very economical device of becoming annexed to the United States.

But the domestic situation in the States during the latter half of Andrew Jackson's second administration, made annexation of Texas by that sturdy old expansionist inadvisable. Such a policy might wreck the presidential chances of the President's favorite apostle and heir apparent—unctuous, cautious little Martin Van Buren. With his favorite duly elected and inauguration day at hand, Jackson, as the last act of his second administration in March, 1837, formally recognized Texas as a republic. Because of party strife and rising sectionalism, Van Buren was decidedly cool toward Texas and the annexation courtship became strictly a one sided affair.

Chagrined by this turn of affairs and perhaps a bit disturbed by the congressional insistence for a navy to the point of almost taking from his hands the selection of a naval agent, Houston finally appointed Peter Grayson to the mission. Grayson did little or nothing and eventually resigned to announce for the Presidency of Texas in the Election of 1838. Constitutional provisions had set the first President's term at two years. Thereafter terms of three years were stipulated. No President could succeed himself. This situation invited a good field of candidates.

Thus the Houston administration had luckily muddled through to a close with little to show for two formative years in office. The army had been permitted to decline until Mexican incited Indians raided the frontier at will. Mexico had repudiated the Houston sponsored "Treaty" of Velasco. Mexican invasion had been prevented by factors strictly independent of Texan action or Houstonian statesmanship. The administration could point to American recognition, which was valuable primarily for the favorable publicity. Men and munitions were flowing freely to Texas anyway. An anxious Congress had above all else demanded a navy, and an agent had been named, but instead of giving bond and going to the United States to buy ships, he had thrown his hat into the presidential election ring.

As election day approached Grayson and one of his most active opponents committed suicide. Whatever their worries were, they probably had nothing to do with the prospective burdens of the office. Vice President Lamar seemed to have the strongest following anyway. Nevertheless this simplified the campaign and the coveted office all but went by default to Mirabeau Buonaparte Lamar, cousin of Gazaway Bugg Lamar and brother of the better known Lucius Quintus Cincinatus Lamar, of the Georgia Lamars.

As if coming from a family characterized by such clusters of flamboyant names were not a sufficient handicap in the rough democracy of the leather laced Republic, Mirabeau B. Lamar added the questionable activity of writing poetry in the Byronic style. In view of these handicaps, it is a monument to his ability that he retained the leadership of his people and gave them as good an administration as he did. That he was "an idealist" is the most damning accusation his critics have ever been able to make.

The fact remains, however, that his background was one of practical politics and frontier leadership. He got his start as secretary to Governor G. M. Troup of Georgia. Weary of editing the Columbus, Georgia, *Enquirer*, he rushed to Texas, literally with sword in hand, to join Houston's retreating and rabble-like army at Groce's Ferry. As a private in a cavalry skirmish on the eve of San Jacinto he saved, with conspicuous bravery, the lives of two comrades. That night he was being addressed as "major" and was at the elbow of the Secretary-of-War as a personal aid. The next day, the sixty Texan cavalrymen deposed their leader and demanded Lamar as their "colonel." He assumed command just in time to make a speech before the battle. To offset the unpopularity of his administration because of his refusal to hang Santa Anna, President *ad interim* Burnet drew the new idol of the army into his cabinet as Secretary-of-War. Seven months after his arrival in Texas he and the other hero of San Jacinto, Sam Houston, were inaugurated as Vice President and President, respectively, of the Republic. Political and personal differences kept their association in these high offices from being pleasant.

Like many Texan leaders of the day, President Lamar (inaugurated December, 1838) felt keenly Van Buren's rejection of the Texan annexation overtures. He and his followers saw but one solution—a permanently independent Texas that was to be expanded at the expense of unoccupied Mexican domains in what is today New Mexico and Colorado. On a second thought Lamar was of the opinion that Van Buren's refusal was fortunate for the future of Texas.

The outlook called for ambitious plans. There should be a national bank and a state maintained system of education. Recognition by France, England and the rest of Europe must be acquired. A centrally located capital should be established.

An army of sufficient size to maintain claims to the wide boundaries should be raised. And last but not least, a navy that could protect Texas after the withdrawal of the French squadron must be procured. "Should the blockade of the Mexican ports," he admonished congress, shortly after his inauguration, December 10, 1838, "by the Navy of France, be raised (and there is no assurance that it will not shortly be) the ships of war of our enemy would again appear on our coast and annoy commerce. The protection of our maritime frontier . . . is a public duty. . . . This duty may effectively be accomplished by a naval force of small magnitude though under the present conditions of our credit and finances not at a moderate expense."[1]

President Lamar's fondness for his navy is often pointed out as being as idealistic and impractical as his love of poetry. If we accept it as evidence we must admit there were many other impractical idealists in the Texas of 1838–39. Proof is found in the attitude of the Senate toward his policy. One third of the Texan Senate and all of the Lower House were elected annually for three- and one-year terms respectively. Thus Texan legislative bodies, until Houston injected a strong personality factor into the Fourth Congress, directly reflected the spontaneous will of the people.

Certainly the Third Congress, elected with Lamar, heartily endorsed and readily passed the essential features of his program. In truth, Congressional enthusiasm for a large Navy exceeded that of the President. Though the Texan Senate knew that on November 13, 1838, Naval Agent Williams, appointed by Houston to succeed Grayson, had signed a formal contract calling for a fleet even larger than that which had been authorized, it *unanimously* passed a secret resolution January 16, 1839, urging that Texas also purchase the recently captured Mexican fleet from France.[2]

The big navy spirit was rampant in Texas during 1838 and most of 1839. There were some who, with exceptionally sound reasoning, thought that a proper coördination of a naval offensive and diplomacy would end the Texan-Mexican war without the use of a single soldier. Texan diplomatic agent Henderson proposed from distant Paris, April 28, 1839, "the necessity of blockading Vera Cruz and such other of the Mexican ports as may be within the province of our Navy as soon as it is afloat and manned. I feel well assured that that course would do more to settle the war with Mexico than any other which Texas could adopt. England would feel herself bound to interfere immediately and bring about a compromise between Texas and Mexico which of course would be upon the basis of the absolute recognition of Texas by Mexico and England too."[3] England's "mediation" that had forced Mexico to accept the French terms so that Admiral Baudin would raise his blockade made Henderson's logic quite acceptable.

If it be conceded that Texas had any prospective need for a fleet it was truly time that she bestir herself. W. M. Shepherd, who had accepted the Navy portfolio after Secretary Fisher's "resignation," had breathed a sigh of relief after the arrival of the French fleet off Vera Cruz, and, in accordance with Houston's pressure for rigid economy, had disbanded the naval personnel down to the skeletonized crew that manned the unseaworthy "receiving ship" *Potomac*. At its lowest ebb this organization consisted of two lieutenants, two midshipmen, a doctor, two pursers, and two seamen. Both seamen were deserters from the United States Navy.[4] Just before the naval expansion under Lamar was started, the ranking lieutenant was cashiered "in consequence of a repeated inebriety."[5] This left Lieutenant Wright the senior line officer.

But such a low ranking officer could not hope to hold seniority long in the large fleet being acquired by Naval Agent Williams. For five-year, ten per cent Texan bonds totaling a face value of £40,350 a Mr. Holford, of England, signed a contract with Williams agreeing to convert into a man-of-war and deliver at Galveston the ocean going, steam side-wheeler *Charleston*.[6] For $560,000 in similar bonds (which could be redeemed by Texas within twelve months for $280,000 in cash) a Mr. Dawson of Baltimore agreed, November 13, 1838, to build a

600-ton full rigged ship, equipped and fitted out as a 22-gun corvette; two 400-ton brigs mounting 16 guns each and three 170 ton schooners mounting 8 or 9 guns each.[7] Such a fleet should rate a post captain with the title of Commodore, several commanders, thirty or thirty-five lieutenants, forty or fifty midshipmen, and a long retinue of surgeons, pursers, gunners, boatswains, masters, master's mates and marine corps lieutenants. Thus President Lamar, between the adjournment of the Third Congress and the arrival of the fleet, found himself with some juicy morsels of naval patronage to hand out.

John G. Tod was a Kentuckian who had climaxed a juvenile runaway episode with a midshipman's commission in the Mexican Navy. Stimulated no doubt by alarmed and influential relatives, Henry Clay procured for him an appointment to the corresponding grade in the American Navy. After a number of years he resigned and in time began pestering the Texan Navy Department for a commission. Lamar seized upon him to supervise the conversion and arming of the S. S. *Charleston*. When he steamed her into Galveston harbor in March, 1839, she was promptly rechristened *Zavala*, in honor of the Yucatecan author and political liberal who had died as the first Texan Vice President.

With equal promptness Tod was sent to Baltimore to supervise the execution of the Williams-Dawson contract.[8] The ships were already being built in the Schott and Whitney yards, Baltimore, on scale drawings provided, in all probability, by American Commodores Barron and Warrington, and Naval Constructor Francis Grice, of the Norfolk Navy Yard. Because of the late delivery of one of the brigs, Tod did not return to Texas until after the fleet was in full operation. He eventually received a commission and commanded the Galveston Navy Yard.

With a pressing matter of a naval constructor out of the way, President Lamar consulted with careful deliberation a 3500-word memorandum, which some naval officer had written for him, on the personnel needs of just such a squadron as was being acquired.[9] Though there were then many good sailors and influential ship operators along the comparatively populous Texan coast, Lamar did not propose to use a single line commission in the new fleet to acquire or keep a political friend.

Barring those of a few young men, who had good records, he even ignored the names on the old list of the first fleet, i.e. those who had been discharged by Houston. Indeed, Commodores Thompson and Hawkins were dead. A like fate had befallen Captain Hurd and one of the Browns. Captain Wheelwright was still in disrepute for having lost the *Independence*. Even so there was an appreciable list of available veterans from the first fleet. There were also many applicants for commissions from elsewhere.

This was particularly true of the coveted post captaincy which carried not only command of the 22-gun corvette but also ex-officio command of the fleet with the resounding courtesy title of commodore. A. C. Allen, an influential man of affairs at Brazoria and a leader in the *San Felipe-Correo* affair back in 1835, considered himself fit timber for that position. Similarly J. D. Boylan, last captain of the old *Brutus*, experienced a desire for further service. More hopeful but less easily satisfied was A. C. Howard of Brunswick, Georgia, "late of the navy & Cap. U.S.R.[evenue] Service,"[10] who thought the Texan Navy could use him as commander-in-chief. Lieutenant G. H. Rankin of Her Britannic Majesty's Navy, then on furlough in New Orleans, seems to have been in a very receptive state of mind for the same position. An even more pretentious application came in the person of Admiral Ribaud, sometime of the French Navy, who brought a letter from Willis Roberts recommending him to Lamar's "hospitality and high consideration."[11]

But all of these were passed over in favor of twenty-nine years old lieutenant Edwin Ward Moore U.S.N. who was then serving aboard the U.S.S. *Boston*, of Commodore Dallas' Gulf squadron. At the age of fifteen he had entered the American Navy as a midshipman. He had waited ten years for the glory that came with the gold stripes of a lieutenant. He did not propose to wait another twenty-five for a captaincy U.S.N. when a post captaincy T.N. could be had immediately.

If a portrait of him exists today, I failed to find it. A half century after serving under him, one of his midshipmen described him as being sturdily built and about five feet and eight inches in height. He had blue eyes, a fair complexion and brown hair. He was genial, liked by his subordinates and was considered an excellent seaman. He was progressive and must have had an inclination for science, for in his declining years, if not sooner, he worked long and hard on an invention that he hoped would revolutionize marine steam engines.

Notwithstanding the aggressive restlessness that motivated his severance from the stagnant United States service, he had been schooled too long in the exactness and forms of the old Navy to adapt himself readily to the makeshift necessities of a navy being built from the water line up. In short, it took him the first year or two of his service in the Texan fleet to learn that under his new flag he could not fully man and fit out ships in crêpe de chine style upon the calico resources of the new Republic. After that he proved to be an officer of unquestionable gallantry and with ability to appreciate readily such naval and diplomatic opportunities as presented themselves. Certainly no one could accuse him of being weak on initiative. On the whole it was a good appointment.[12]

The United States Naval List was also Lamar's favorite recruiting ground for his new roster of commanders and lieutenants. Nearly all of them, like Moore, had served, or were serving as midshipmen, or in higher grades, when they received Lamar's recess appointments. Moore's appointment as post captain, for example, antedated by several months his formal resignation from the United States Navy. At least two of the active naval officers who were recipients of lieutenancies from Lamar apparently refused them when time came for them to vacate their American berths. For both it proved to be a good decision. One of them, Fabius Stanly, eventually became a post Civil War rear admiral, U.S.N. Only eight or nine of the officers on the new list had seen service under Hawkins or Thompson in the old fleet.

Thus an analysis of Lamar's dispensing of naval patronage seems to have been on a non-political basis. He honestly thought the best naval officers available were from the nearby American fleet, and that is where he went to find his line officer personnel. Surgeons and pursers were largely drawn from civil life, but there is every reason to believe that in their selection favoritism played no part. Of course the new midshipmen came from influential families, the recruiting ground for middies the world over.

Before the meeting of the Fourth Congress, November, 1839, Lamar had given recess appointments to forty-four midshipmen, twenty-five lieutenants, four commanders, one post captain and about twenty officers not of the line.[13] This was far under the number called for in his memorandum. Furthermore, the new officers did not draw pay until they were ordered to duty by Lamar's Secretary of Navy, L. P. Cooke. As each new vessel of the fleet arrived at Galveston, a proportional number of officers of proper grade was ordered to duty aboard her.

Lamar began making his naval appointments in March, 1839, as soon as naval constructor Tod delivered the steamer *Zavala*. She and the receiving ship *Potomac* were all that were present in May, 1839, when Baudin's retiring French fleet, with Mexico's squadron still securely under its wing, made a courtesy call at Galveston.

While the dapper, pleasant, one armed Admiral Baudin was assuring the rugged populace that he "would vastly prefer being the humblest member of a well regulated and thriving community like yours than . . . in the sphere of wealth and power in a corrupt and decaying society,"[14] one of his staff officers was looking over the Texan naval establishment. He met a commander, three lieutenants, and eight midshipmen aboard the recently delivered *Zavala*, and noted that a pretentious flotilla was soon expected from the Schott and Whitney yards in Baltimore. France with her unsurpassed instinct for an *entente* or an alliance was deeply interested in the potential military and naval strength of the prospective friend. The Texan coast would be particularly convenient as a base for possible future operations against Mexico. Baudin's favorable reports to his King were largely responsible for formal French recognition of the Republic of Texas, September 25, 1839—the first extended by a European power.

Commander A. C. Hinton's *Zavala* with nine thousand dollars in the purser's safe was next reported in New Orleans trying to enlist sailors not only for herself but also for the prospective Schott and Whitney fleet. The funds in her strong box were insufficient for effective recruiting not to mention a number of changes and repairs Commodore Moore insisted she needed and ordered Hinton to have done. The New Orleans ship chandlers recalled their previous experiences with Texan warships and demanded cash for all work and supplies. Every sailor along the levee knew that paydays in the first Texan fleet had been few and far apart. Thus Hinton's cruise was largely a failure and was followed by abuse and recriminations. Commodore Moore finally had to make a recruiting cruise with one of the larger ships to New York in the winter of 1839–40 before a sufficient number of seamen were enlisted.

In June, 1839, the schooner *San Jacinto*, 170 tons, "four medium twelves and a long 9-pounder, (brass) on a pivot" arrived as the harbinger of the fleet. Her sister schooner, the *San Antonio*, with "6 medium twelves and a single fortified long twelve, a pivot," arrived in August. The third sister, *San Bernard*, identical even in armament with the *San Antonio*, reached Galveston in September.

The 400-ton gun brig *Colorado* (soon rechristened *Wharton*) sixteen medium 18-pounders, was not delivered until October. Two months later, December, 1839, the pride and flagship of the fleet, the *Austin* sailed into Galveston Bay. She was a full rigged ship, 600 tons, and mounted, when delivered, eighteen medium 24-pounders, and two medium 18-pounders.[15] Later her battery was supplemented by the transfer of a few guns from the brig *Archer*. This vessel, for the first few months known as the *Galveston* was the last of the Schott-Whitney contract. A sister of the *Wharton*, she was not delivered until April, 1840, and even then was not sent to sea on a major cruise.

Notwithstanding the late arrival of the *Archer*, the close of 1839 found President Lamar with a fleet, the flagship of which was as large as Commander Mervine's sloop-of-war *Natchez* with which that testy old seadog had browbeaten half the Mexican squadron off Matamoras. With it he could seize supremacy on the Gulf for the Mexicans had not yet taken effective measures to replace the excellent squadron France had captured. True, Lamar's ships were not fully officered, manned and trained for battle by the close of 1839. But as for that matter Mexico's domestic affairs, though improving, were still so badly disorganized that the Mexican army could not have advanced granted that there had been a Mexican squadron to dispute the Gulf with Lamar's still non-functional but potentially strong squadron.

To say that Mexico, immediately after the withdrawal of the French, was still badly disorganized is stating the case mildly. It will be recalled that Baudin had aided and abetted such Federalists as Urrea, Mexía, and Canales in a revolt against Bustamante and his Centralists by raising the blockade on Tampico as soon as the customs house at that point was in the hands of Bustamante's enemies. Thus when Baudin withdrew in the spring of 1839 he left behind a well subsidized revolt throughout the region north and northwest of Tampico.

Political considerations in Mexico City prevented Bustamante from launching a vigorous campaign against the northern Federalists. Should he order the strong Vera Cruz army, now relieved of the French threat, into the troubled area, political pressure would force him to give the coveted command thereof to Mexico's new idol, the one legged Santa Anna. With such an army at his back and new military laurels that would come with a successful northern campaign, Santa Anna would prove more dangerous to the career of Bustamante than were

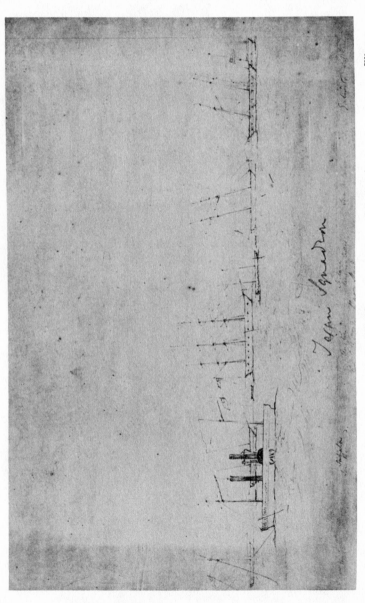

San Bernard   *Austin*, Flagship   *San Antonio*   *Wharton*

Zavala, Steamer   *Santana*, Revenue Cutter   *Archer* (*Galveston*)

COMMODORE MOORE'S SQUADRON, *SAN JACINTO* ABSENT, AT ANCHOR, GALVESTON

From a contemporary sketch by William Bollaert. (Courtesy of Newberry Library, Chicago)

all the Federalists north of Tampico and San Luis Potosí. Should Bustamante place himself at the head of the army in an effort to garner the laurels for himself, he would, under the Constitution, have to vacate temporarily the Presidential Chair. This would leave in his rear the self-same Santa Anna who was an even more accomplished master of palace intrigue than he was a military tactician.

Bustamante chose what appeared to be the lesser of the two evils. He assumed command of the army himself and marched northward, but not until he was sure that Nicolas Bravo would be named to keep the Chair warm for him until his return at the close of what he hoped would be a short and glorious campaign. Admittedly Bravo was not without political ambitions himself, but all the *politicos* in Mexico City knew that Bravo lacked the steel nerve that was required of a Mexican President during the turbulent 'Thirties. Indeed, it quickly developed that Bravo did not have the nerve for even *ad interim* presidential service. Bustamante was hardly out of the city before Bravo refused to function, and the Mexican Supreme Council elevated Santa Anna to the office.

In the field Bustamante was out-maneuvered. The Federalists under Mexía slipped past him and took the open road to Mexico City. Acting President Santa Anna met the situation with one of his rare flashes of dynamic energy. Within a few days a second army was mobilized under his own command. He met Mexía at Acajete, May 3, 1839, and annihilated the Federalist forces. Mexía was shot, and Bustamante's cup of bitterness was filled to the over-flowing. Bustamante remained in the north, however, until a general under his immediate command captured Tampico, June 4, and other subordinates added a few minor gains. His return to the presidency July 19 was not one of triumph. More than ever Santa Anna was the idol of the people.[16]

In the meantime, Canales and Zapata were left to carry on the revolt in the north. Earnestly these Federalists now made overtures to the Texan Government. More than the defeat of

Mexía, the fall of the Tampico embarrassed their cause. The procuring of arms would soon be a serious problem. But President Lamar, now busy watching his new ships arrive at Galveston, gave the Mexican Federalists only a few serious thoughts. He certainly took no steps to aid them openly. Too recently, prominent Federalists had berated the Centralists as grossly incompetent for not having reconquered Texas, and had pledged themselves to Texan subjugation as soon as they were in power. Nevertheless, Lamar did meet Federalist messengers in secret conferences, and he elected to wink at the organizing of a filibustering Texan Legion that was being recruited in Texas to fight under the flag of Canales's recently organized Republic of the Rio Grande. At the same time he sought to take advantage of the situation by sending B. E. Bee to Mexico City to write a treaty with the embarrassed Centralists that would recognize Texan independence.

Within a short time he received word that Bee was not permitted to land on Mexican soil.[17] But Lamar was determined to get a Texan diplomatic agent into Mexico City whether the Centralists wanted to meet one or not. He resorted to the strange subterfuge of handing negotiation instructions to James Treat, whose principal diplomatic qualification seems to have been an abiding patience and a set of United States passports that could be counted upon to get him as far as Mexico City. He arrived at the Mexican capital, November 28, 1839.[18]

About the time that dual citizen Treat arrived in Mexico City, President Lamar was looking a new congress in the face— a congress that had in the membership of the turbulent annually elected lower house none other than Ex-President Sam Houston. "The Great Ex" had made a sort of triumphant tour through the old South and returned to Texas just in time to decide that certain northern Indians, whom Lamar had seen fit to chastise, were better men than Lamar. Besides, how could an ex-president better succeed his own successor than by maintaining a running fire of criticism from one of the congressional floors? Houston's personal following was strong enough to reach political party proportions. Augmented by the inevitable forces of reaction, the opposition was strong enough to have brought political grief to statesmen whom history has credited with being far abler men than Lamar.

Under the leadership of Sam Houston and his henchmen, the reactionary Fourth Congress severely criticized Lamar's inflation of the currency, his visionary educational plans, and his measures to build a capital city on the site of the struggling settlement called Waterloo. Modern Austin now stands as a monument to Lamar's vision, but Waterloo was then being periodically raided by Indians.

Houston's opposition brought quick results. The standing army that had chastised old Indian friends of "The Great Ex" was blotted out by the defeat of the military appropriation bill. This was in spite of the fact that everyone realized the war with Mexico was not over, and that the western frontier had to be protected.

Of course Lamar's ambitious navy program, started though it was in Houston's administration, was vociferously weighed in the balance of parliamentary debate. One of the first congressional resolutions demanded that the President should "inform the Senate by what authority he appointed ninety naval officers during the recess of Congress this present year."[19]

Lamar sought to still the issue by withdrawing the names of his recess appointees for senatorial confirmation. When this failed he tactfully pointed to numerous precedents that had guided him, and submitted a letter from the Secretary of Navy showing that the number he had appointed was still insufficient to officer the squadron. He then ably reminded the senators that Texas was in a state of war and fittingly asked what sort of a resolution the Senate would have passed had he left the ships unofficered and unmanned—but little more than helpless hulks—while such a state of war existed.

His answer was referred to the Committee on Naval Affairs, the chairman of which, Oliver Jones, was one of Houston's loudest voices in the Senate. Nevertheless the other two committeemen, Francis Moore and Harvey Kendrick brought in a majority report which sustained the President. "It will be recalled that at the time these appointments were made the French Fleet was about to be withdrawn from the Mexican Coast, and it was believed the enemy would endeavor to refit their naval forces and attack us again at the most vulnerable point. . . ."[20] The majority report ended, however, by recommending that heavier ships of the fleet be "laid up in ordinary."

Not to be cheated out of this opportunity to attack the administration, Chairman Jones, brought in a one-man, minority report. Precedents he largely ignored. He charged that the President's appointments had gotten so far ahead of the arrival of the ships that ninety-six officers and petty officers of all grades were designated with only ninety-nine sailors and boys for them to command. His point, of course, was economy. Hence he ignored the fact that many of the officers had not been ordered to duty and that their pay did not begin until receipt of such orders. The unsatisfactory relations with Mexico he recognized. But with peace rumors in the air (he had probably heard of Treat's arrival in Mexico City) he felt that the fleet was an unnecessary burden upon the Republic.

For a time it seemed as though the navy would suffer the same fate that had befallen Lamar's standing army. That the Fourth Congress, in the face of Sam Houston's bitterest opposition, finally passed a naval bill which continued that branch of the service is evidence sufficient that the Texans rightfully considered the Navy their first line of defense against Mexico.

But the Navy bill, passed February, 1840, did not provide for keeping the entire squadron in commission. It stipulated that the schooners should remain fully manned to police the coast and to break up smuggling. The heavier men-of-war and the steamer should be left in Galveston with skeletonized crews. But the first hostile Mexican move should automatically authorize the President to man fully a part, or all, of the fleet and send it to sea.[21]

As a result of the attack upon his Naval program, Lamar

never resubmitted his list of officers. Instead he let such officers as he had already appointed and ordered to duty, continue to function in their respective capacities. Thus the Texan Sea Dogs sailed the Gulf for three years without a scrap of paper among them that could be called a commission. If Thomas M. Thompson, sometime *2° Teniete de Marina*, Mexican Navy and late commander of the *Correo de Mejico* (but by this time a beach comber in Tobasco) ever learned this, he must have prayed that one of the ships would be wrecked upon the Mexican Coast so that some Latin prosecutor might revive the maritime legal lore that Messrs. Carlton and Felix Huston had used in the piracy trial he had endured in New Orleans.

CHAPTER NINE

DIPLOMATIC CRUISING • *James Treat Falters* • *Moore Exasperated* • *Off Tampico* • *Yucatan* • *Tobasco Raided*

THE ADJOURNMENT of the turbulent Fourth Congress left President Lamar a rather unhappy statesman. He had seen first one and then the other of his pet policies go down before the onslaught of ex-President Houston and his henchmen. Of his ambitious program and plans, only the navy had survived. And if he followed the spirit of the Naval bill his fleet was to be seriously crippled. In Section 4 of that measure, however, he found a ray of hope. It stipulated that "should Mexico make any hostile demonstration upon the Gulf, the President may order any number of vessels into active service, that he may deem necessary for the public security." Until such a hostile demonstration on the part of Mexico should occur, all of the fleet but the three schooners were to be laid up in ordinary.

The legislative mandate to de-commission the heavy ships of the squadron came at a most embarrassing moment. While the buckskin solons had been tempestuously writing that law into the statutes, various units of the fleet were away on expensive and legally hazardous recruiting cruises to New Orleans and New York. Finally in the latter port Commodore Moore got afoul of United States' neutrality laws and experienced some difficulty extricating himself from the legal meshes. Thus, shortly after the adjournment of Congress, the entire fleet (less the undelivered brig *Archer*) was re-assembled in Galveston, fully officered and manned. Lamar decided that disbanding the crews and laying up the ships so quickly after the strenuous and costly recruiting efforts was out of the question. Most naturally he scanned the horizon for an overt act on the part of Mexico that would justify his invoking the discretionary Section 4 and thereby keep the fleet on a functional basis.

President Lamar was by no means alone in the feeling that it would be folly to disband the fleet. Honorable J. Love was favorably impressed by the ships and crews when he examined the properly manned fleet and advised that it should put to sea at once on a cruise against Mexican commerce as a "demonstration of power and energy on the part of the government, that will give us credit abroad."[1] Senator Francis Moore, of the Naval Affairs Committee, inspected the squadron and was so well satisfied by the potentialities thereof that he advised sending the ships to sea to support the fruitless diplomacy of James Treat in Mexico City. Senator Moore was sure that if the "vessels could be sent on the Coast of Mexico they would do more towards procuring peace than an army of ten thousand men." He also reported that ex-President Houston, then in Galveston, declared himself surprised by the quality of the squadron "and had quite changed his opinion; thinks the vessels ought to be sent to sea immediately, and regrets that he made any opposition to the 'navy bill.' "[2]

Meanwhile President Lamar was still scanning the horizon to the southwest in hopes of discerning enough threats from Mexico to save the fleet. None came until the early summer when Indian forays on the frontier were traced to the activities of General Arista. Now that this very active Centralist General had pretty well destroyed the revolting Republic of the Rio Grande, it was more than natural that he should revert to Filisola's policy of inciting the Indians against the Texans. Furthermore, with the northern revolt in its death throes and many of its leaders refugees from Arista, this commander had become "unremitting in fulminating his threats of invasion for universal extermination"[3] of the Texans.

In addition to Arista's Indian activities and vocal offensive, there were well-grounded reports that Mexican naval agents had bought at least one steamer to be converted into a man-of-war. The same agents were openly in the market for some powerful new steam corvettes, or even frigates, of a type more modern than any previously seen on the Gulf. In the face of these developments, Lamar felt that he would be perfectly justified in keeping the fleet intact. Moreover, Treat's negotiations in Mexico City were proceeding so unsatisfactorily that Lamar felt they should be supported by a naval demonstration.

An examination of Treat's original orders readily indicates why he was getting nowhere with the proud Centralists in Mexico City. According to Lamar's instructions, he was to accept nothing short of "A full, unequivocal, unconditional acknowledgment of the independence of Texas . . . beyond and exclusive of which you will not discuss a single proposition." Furthermore, the recognized boundary of Texas should be "mid-way of the channel" of the Rio Grande from its mouth to the "fountain head of its principle western branch," thence a line due north to the forty-second parallel. But before Treat showed his hand on these absolutely essential limits, he was to feel the Mexicans out with a proposition that the line be run up the channel of the Rio Grande to El Paso, thence due west to the "Gulf of California and along the southern shore of that Gulf to the Pacific Ocean. This boundary will not be strenuously insisted upon but may be intimated as a counterpoise to any extravagant expectations"[4] on the part of Mexico. Since Mexico did not concede the line of the Rio Grande to the United States in 1846 and did not lose as much territory at the end of the Mexican War as Treat proposed with his line running west from El Paso, one does not wonder that his unsupported, ambitious proposals were not being favorably received in the summer of 1840.

In truth, all that kept the Mexicans from summarily dismissing him was the fear that the moment he received his passports, Lamar would immediately ally himself with Canales and his Republic of the Rio Grande. Now that General Arista was getting the situation well in hand in that area, the Centralists could well afford to become even more arrogant with the patient Texan envoy.

Treat should have broken off his negotiations months before and returned to Texas. But there seems to be a sort of tradition among American diplomats that they must bring home some kind of document at all costs. Treat was not inclined to depart from this tradition. He continued his fruitless negotiations right up to the summer of 1840, and even though the position of the Centralists was improving, he showed no disposition to withdraw. Instead he made reports to his State Department and to Lamar that were more re-assuring and optimistic than the situation warranted. Otherwise he might have been re-called.

In the meantime, a new revolt against the régime of the Centralists was breaking out in Yucatan. Throughout its colonial history and during the early days of the Mexican Republic, this interesting peninsula had far less in common with the remainder of Mexico than it does today. And today even the most casual traveller is impressed by differences between it and Mexico as a whole. Where it is not separated from the remainder of Mexico by the Gulf, it is isolated by the jungles of Tobasco. Its warm dry climate and its shrubbery clad, low rugged hills naturally gave its people economic interests distinctly different from those on the mile-high plateau that constitutes most of Mexico.

The proximity of the sea in three directions early gave its people a maritime interest. The British colony of Honduras at its back door had been for over a century a breach in Spain's barrier to direct foreign trade with her colonies. Because of this breach, millions of dollars worth of British goods had flowed into the old Captaincy General of Guatemala and into the Viceroyalty of New Spain. The merchants and mariners of Yucatan were the middle men, and often the smugglers, between the British factors and the remainder of New Spain.

Though Mexican independence had opened Vera Cruz, Tampico, and Matamoras to direct foreign trade, Yucatan in 1840 was still a land of merchants and mariners, though their erstwhile prosperity had steadily declined under the new régime.[5]

The Centralists in Mexico City looked upon the peninsula as a fruitful field for exorbitant taxes and a place whence ships and sailors could be drafted for maritime operations, first against Spain and later against Texas.[6] At the same time the Centralists' government had proved itself, in the eyes of the Yucatecans, incompetent to protect them not only from the forays of the small Texan fleet but even from the insulting audacity of the tiny privateer *Thomas Toby*. Of course the mad, Centralist policy that had caused the French to descend upon the Gulf, brought ruin to the commerce-supported Yucatecans.

Like all citizens of an outlying province that are adversely affected by the policies of a distant government, they saw a remedy in regional autonomy, or states rights. The old decentralizing Constitution of 1824, for which the Texans had at first nominally fought, was rapidly becoming a sacred document in the opinion of the Yucatecans. Unsubsidized by the retiring French and less impulsive than the northern Federalists, they bore their burdens longer. Hence, as the northern revolt was petering out in 1840, the Yucatecans were just getting organized for an even more determined revolt than that which had been subsidized by Baudin and staged by Mexía, Urrea, Zapata and Canales north of Tampico and San Luis Potosi.

By the spring of 1840 the Yucatecan revolt was in full swing. The grip of the Centralist government on the peninsula was quickly reduced to the garrisoned city of Campeche. The jungle lowlands and an improvised Yucatecan navy, such as Texas had in 1835–36, defeated all efforts to reinforce the garrison, and the city fell.

With the Centralist capitulation, June 6, 1840, the entire peninsula fell into the hands of the Federalists, who quickly set up a sovereign government, but continued a lip service to the

Mexican Constitution of 1824.[7] Thus had Yucatan duplicated the actions of Texas in 1835. Whether or not she continued the formula to complete independence might well depend on aid from Texas, for there were many absolute secessionists among the Yucatecan leaders. At the same time Mexico's loss of her one maritime province would be a great factor in protecting Texas from a future invasion.

Needless to say, President Lamar and Mr. Lipscombe, his Secretary of State, were closely watching these trends. They finally came to the justified conclusion that Mr. Treat was being toyed with by the Mexican Centralists. The fleet should be sent to strengthen Treat's diplomacy.

Certainly since Lamar had passed up one good alliance that would have greatly embarrassed the Centralists, he could not afford to pass up the opportunity for an alliance with Yucatan in case Mexico City continued to be obdurate. Furthermore, an alliance with Yucatan, well separated as she was from Texas by several hundred miles of salt water, would not be so likely to lead to subsequent clashes of territorial interests, as a successful Republic of the Rio Grande certainly would have done. Ambitious Canales had included in his transitory republic all of northern Mexico including the Californias, modern Arizona and New Mexico, regions which equally ambitious Texans expected to bring under the Lone Star flag.

"It would perhaps be well," wrote Mr. Lipscombe to Treat, June 13, 1840, just one week after the Centralists lost Campeche, "for you to urge upon Mexico the moderation of this government in not coöperating (thus far) with the Federalists on the Rio Grande as she has been strongly urged to do and might have done with great benefit to herself and detriment to Mexico, that it is a forebearance we cannot practice much longer. . . ."[8] Treat was to pronounce a ten-day ultimatum. If Mexico failed to recognize Texan independence, he was to break off negotiations and withdraw to Point Maria Andrea where a Texan warship would be waiting for him.

This letter was not routed through the usual postal channels by way of New Orleans, but was handed to Commodore Moore for delivery. Nor was the bearer of the dispatch to sail alone. The strong tone of the new instructions was to be backed by a naval demonstration that called for the sailing of the entire fleet. In addition to instructions concerning the delivery of the note, Commodore Moore's orders were to remain on the Mexican coast as a potential threat to Mexican commerce.

As soon as Treat broke off negotiations and sought passage back to Texas, Moore was to begin seizing Mexican ships and close the important ports. Furthermore, if Mexico should break the *de facto* truce then existing between Texas and Mexico by firing upon a Texan ship, Moore was to consider himself at liberty to take aggressive action. In the meantime, the Commodore might well be negotiating with the Yucatecan Federalists preparatory to an alliance against Mexico in case Treat was unsuccessful.[9]

Though Treat's new instructions and Moore's orders were dated June 13 and June 20, respectively, it was July 22 before the advance detachments of Moore's squadron stood to sea. The steamer *Zavala* sailed on that date for Sisal with a letter of introduction, as it were, from Federalist General Canales, just below the Rio Grande, to General Anaya, a leading Federalist in Yucatan. On July 26, Lieutenant Postell's war-schooner *San Jacinto* cleared for Point Maria Andrea, thirty-five miles north of Vera Cruz, with Treat's instructions. Moore, with the *Austin* and *San Bernard* sailed the same day for Sisal.

The *San Jacinto* was off Point Maria Andrea by August 1. The dispatches for Treat were at once sent ashore and posted to the British Legation. When Pakenham received them is not known, but it was August 13 before Treat saw them. That was certainly time enough for everyone in the British Legation and the Mexican Foreign office to provide himself with copies. But perhaps Lamar intended that all of them should have copies.

Moore's orders indicate conclusively that Treat was to get favorable action from Mexico or close his ultimatum within ten days. It was not expected that the *San Jacinto*, after landing the dispatches, would have to remain off Point Maria Andrea more than thirteen days before receiving Treat himself aboard or favorable reports from him. Hence that was the number of days Moore was to keep a ship on that station before he molested Mexican shipping. It is significant that Treat did not get the instructions until the thirteenth day after the *San Jacinto* took station off Point Maria Andrea. When nothing was heard from the Texan diplomat, Lieutenant Postell continued to linger in uncertainty at his assigned post until he had further orders from Moore.

The soundness of Lamar's new diplomacy is pretty well indicated by the commotion this new Texan attitude caused in the Mexican Foreign office and at the British Legation. That it did not bring more immediate and satisfying results may be charged to the unmitigated patience, or gullibility, of James Treat. To beguile him into inactivity, the Centralist Government had to do little more than to make him the beneficiary of its smiles.

British Minister Pakenham, greatly perturbed by the appearance of another hostile squadron in the Gulf, coöperated with the Centralists by soothingly taking Treat under his wing. Clever Pakenham initiated much talk of a formal truce between Texas and Mexico. Instead of calling attention to the *de facto* truce already in existence, Treat became enthusiastic about even such a tame document as this would represent. He seems to have been obsessed with the feeling that he had to get a document. The Mexicans toyed with him further by raising the question as to whether or not he was authorized to negotiate a truce. They probably knew full well that he was not so instructed.[10]

Meanwhile the Commodore was not idle. With the corvette *Austin* and the war-schooner *San Bernard* he had followed the steamer *Zavala*, Commander J. T. K. Lothrop, from Galveston to Sisal. They reached this Yucatecan port July 31. The *Zavala* was gone, as she was supposed to be. She was then establishing a base for the fleet at the Arcas Islands, about a hundred miles

west of the port of Campeche. The letter she had borne from
Canales to Anaya had apparently achieved satisfactory results,
for the Sisal port authorities reported that they had just received orders from their revolutionary headquarters in Merida
to offer "every facility" to Texan men-of-war.

By August 2, the *Austin* and *San Bernard* were off Campeche.
Remembering the Sisal hospitality, Moore hoisted his own
colors instead of the Stars and Stripes—a most unusual procedure for him.

The response was immediate. General Anaya came out to
meet Moore aboard one of the three revolutionist men-of-war.
Anaya surprised Moore by saying that he had not received
the Canales letter. Other communications from friendly Federalists along the Rio Grande were responsible for the hospitality. Moore at once anchored and sent the *San Bernard*, with
Anaya's secretary aboard, back to Sisal to get the letter which
Moore felt was very important, "knowing . . . it had been
written by General Canales after frequent interviews with His
Excellency the President." He and Anaya saw eye to eye on
coöperating against Mexico. The next day, August 3, an equally
satisfactory conference was had with Governor-elect Mendez.

But the Texan Commodore's hands were tied until he was
molested by the Centralists or until he had news from Treat
to the effect that the diplomatic negotiations had failed. While
waiting, he visited the Arcas Islands to see if all was well with
the *Zavala* and her base. Since no news had reached the Arcas
rendezvous, August 18 found the *Austin* and *San Bernard* looking for the *San Jacinto* off Maria Andrea. They found her
August 20. Postell was still without news from, or of, Treat.

Impatiently Moore ran down the coast thirty-five miles to
Vera Cruz. Off that city he hoisted the Stars and Stripes.
Through the night of August 23 and all day of the 24th the
Austin, San Bernard and *San Jacinto* lay within a few miles of
San Juan de Ulúa Castle. Moore hoped he might intercept a
ship from which he could at least learn whether Treat was still
in Mexico. Nothing happened until late in the afternoon of the

second day when Her Britannic Majesty's brig *Penguin* came out. Acting under instructions from Pakenham, her commander gave Moore four letters. They were from Treat. One was for President Lamai, two for Secretary of State Lipscombe and one for Moore.

Of course the Texan Commodore did not know it, but the burden of all four communications was essentially the same. Treat, in his own opinion, was just getting started on the new line of aggressive diplomacy called for in the instructions brought to Mexico by Moore's squadron. He explained that the dispatches had experienced a long delay between Vera Cruz and his hands, hence action on his part had been impossible within the time contemplated in his instructions.

The letter to Moore contained essentially the same information, but also a note of apprehension. He feared rumors of the Texan fleet on the Gulf might impair his negotiations. There were already reports that Mexican ships had been pursued. But Treat explained that because of his confidence in the Commodore he had not "hesitated to assure this government in the most *positive manner* that your instructions were certainly of a pacific character *so long* as my negotiations with the government were *open* and *pending*."[11]

Needless to say the Mexican and the British Legation decided to keep these negotiations *"open* and *pending"* as long as possible. If Moore were greatly apprehensive of Treat's dilatory tactics and disobedience to instructions, he did not say so. On the contrary, by the returning *Penguin*, Moore assured Treat that he had not and would not make a hostile move against a single Mexican ship, though he could have captured "seven or eight" had the situation permitted it.

Before hastening north with Treat's dispatches, however, Moore took advantage of this contact with H.B.M.S. *Penguin* to gather naval information. He was informed by the Englishmen that the Centralists had no armed ships at Vera Cruz, but that the steamer *Argyle*, one of the troop ships that had tried to reinforce the Centralist garrison at Campeche, was in the service of the Mexicans. Furthermore, according to the captain of the *Penguin*, the Centralists were trying to buy a French vessel then in port. They were also expecting the early arrival of their crack corvette, the *Iguala*, which, it was reported, France was returning to them.

Having garnered this intelligence concerning the prospective naval forces of the enemy, Moore left the *San Bernard* off Vera Cruz to maintain contacts with Treat while the *Austin* and *San Jacinto* sailed northward. The latter pressed on to Galveston with the communications for the Texan State Department.

Moore had no intention of returning to Texas with his flagship, however. Instead he lay off the mouth of the Rio Grande for a number of days by way of making a demonstration against Matamoras, the base of the Centralist armies operating against the fast diminishing forces of the Federalist General Canales. And the appearance of Moore off the mouth of the Rio Grande was not without effect. The Centralist general feared that this sudden appearance of the Texan flagship at that point foretold a concerted naval and military offensive in conjunction with Canales. The Matamoras commander was so alarmed that he concentrated an appreciable number of troops at the threatened base, and thus gave a hard-pressed Canales a respite.

Having created this diversion, Moore leisurely cruised southward to contact again his vessels based at the Arcas Islands, which had recently been reinforced by the *San Antonio*, there to await more news from Treat.

Though the *San Bernard*, or one of her sister gun-schooners that occasionally relieved her, lingered off Vera Cruz or Point Maria Andrea for over two full months after the first news from Treat through the British Legation and H.B.M.S. *Penguin*, no news of successful or broken negotiations was forthcoming from the gullible diplomat. All the while Moore's fleet was keeping in pleasant contact with the Yucatecans and making occasional appearances off principal Mexican ports. And to a corresponding degree the fleet was thoroughly alarming Mexican commerce, though no captures were being made.

Impatiently Moore continued to wait for the word from Treat that would permit aggressive action, or for the Mexicans to commit an overt act that would warrant his launching an offensive without further orders from his own government or word from Treat.

Early in October, Moore was off Tampico and disgustedly cursing the devious ways of diplomats in general and Treat in particular, when a terrific storm swept down the coast. By this time he was well acquainted with the geography of the region and met the situation by running under the lee side of Lobos Island. While lying to southward of this tiny protecting island, the foretop lookout sighted, to northward of the island and among the white capped breakers of Banquilla reef, a rather large merchant brig. He had hardly sighted her before distress signals appeared at her yard arm.

Moore at once answered the signals and sent small boats across the tempestuous strip of water to effect a rescue. The seas were running so high that no one could be immediately taken from the stricken brig. All the while, however, Moore kept small boats available for rescue work in case the merchantman should threaten to break up; and a large beacon was kept burning on the north end of Lobos Island.

By the evening of October 6, however, all passengers and sailors, with their baggage, were safely aboard the *Austin*. Then it was learned that the wrecked ship was the Mexican packet *Segunda Fauna* which had sailed from Vera Cruz with mail and passengers September 17 and was standing into Tampico when the storm had caught her and piled her upon Banquilla reef. The twenty-six distressed Mexicans that composed the passengers and crew of the wrecked brig were treated with *"miramiento y humanidad,"* to borrow the language of the Tampico *Disengano*, "even to the degree that the officers gave up their staterooms to some of the passengers."[12]

Moore kept the refugees on board for ten days at the end of which time, October 16, he hoisted the Stars and Stripes, stood close in to Tampico, and landed all the refugees and their personal effects. When they had been ashore long enough to tell the story of the Texan flagship's hospitality, the Lone Star flag was substituted for the American colors.

After this act of mercy Moore apparently felt himself a privileged character off Tampico. But the Mexicans did not like his custom of boarding all inward and outward bound ships. There was extensive newspaper comment when he took from the outbound schooner *Conchita*, General Lemus, a famous Federalist, and his family. The General had recently been captured in the north and was being sent under guard to one of the prisons near Vera Cruz. When the Centralists learned that Lemus, a traitor in their eyes, had been liberated by the still more disliked Texans, their wrath knew no bounds.

Thus when Moore, October 21, sent one of his small boats ashore for water, the Mexicans apparently felt that they owed him no more hospitality for the *Segunda Fauna* rescue, even though the Texan water supply had been diminished by the presence of the distressed Mexicans aboard the flagship. The Mexican garrison waited until the *Austin's* boats were within easy range and gave them an artillery salvo. They got in two more volleys before the panic stricken boat crews could row out of range. No hits were registered, but water was splashed all over the retreating boatmen.

In high dudgeon Moore hastened to Vera Cruz to tell Treat that he had been fired upon and was about to end the *de facto* armistice, diplomatic negotiations or no diplomatic negotiations.

When he arrived off Vera Cruz, he received word that almost simultaneously with being fired upon at Tampico, Treat had at last given up hopes of getting the Mexicans to enter into any sort of agreement whatsoever and was planning to return to Texas as soon as his health would permit. It was near the end of October, however, before he left for the coast to board the waiting war-schooner *San Antonio* for passage to Galveston. He suffered a relapse and died before the ship reached Texas.

Thus doubly free to open hostilities, Moore hastened to the

base at the Arcas Islands to revictual his ships and assign them to blockade stations. But Mexican shipping had long been so apprehensive because of the presence of the Texan squadron that few potential prizes were on the Gulf. Hence, only one prize of any consequence immediately fell into Moore's hands. She was the *Anne Maria*, captured November 2, 1840, off Point Maria Andrea. She with her cargo of flour, flannel, and coffee eventually sold for seven thousand dollars.

It might be added here that this capture was not enough to compensate for the loss of one of Moore's war-schooners. Just three days before the capture of this prize, the *San Jacinto*, trying to ride out a terrific storm at the Arcas Islands base, began to drag her anchor. It meant little that her commander, Lieutenant O'Shaunessy, added one of his cannon to the weight of the anchor. All through the stormy night the little ship continued to drift toward the rocky shore. She struck at 1:50 A.M. and by dawn she was an irretrievable wreck, though the ship's stores and all hands were saved.

But this misfortune and the scarcity of prizes did not dampen Moore's enthusiasm now that he was free to act. He decided to utilize his Federalist guest, General Lemus, who with his family was still aboard the flagship. He would carry him to Yucatan, and with the grateful Lemus as an advocate for a closer alliance between Mexican Federalism and Texas, there should be no trouble in working out a coöperative plan of aggression.

It was particularly important that Moore's fleet be assured of a source of supplies from Yucatan. New Orleans was too distant; and besides the credit of the Texan navy was decidedly low in that port. Commander Lothrop, of the *Zavala*, had already successfully negotiated for fuel and some supplies from Yucatan. Perhaps the *Peninsulares* might be induced to provide supplies without charge as their share of joint operations.

Back on the Yucatecan coast, Moore learned that the *Peninsulares* had not yet declared their full independence but were still carrying on their revolt in the name of the states' rights Constitution of 1824. The Commodore and General Lemus urged the Yucatecans to declare their complete independence so that Texas might go the full limit of a treaty of alliance. The Yucatecan leaders, nevertheless, were not ready to permit their state to "compromise itself by a thing so delicate."[13]

But delicacy did not preclude a *de facto* naval alliance. Not only did the peninsular Federalists desire protection against a soon to be revived Mexican Navy, but they also saw an immediate field of action for a squadron. By virtue of her severance from Mexico, Yucatan's commerce was suffering. Particularly did she feel the loss of commercial contacts with Tobasco, still in Centralist hands and long a point of entry for smuggled merchandise and legitimate imports that passed through the hands of Yucatecan merchants.[14] The ports of Tobasco should be brought under the Federalist colors.

Accordingly, the middle of November, 1840, found the *San Bernard* and the *Austin* being towed by the steamer *Zavala* up the Tobasco River ninety miles to the provincial capital, San Juan Bautista. In company with them was a Yucatecan armed brig. She carried Colonel Sentmena's command consisting of one hundred and forty troops that were to be pitted against the Centralists' garrison of five hundred men. The guns and man power of the Texan men-of-war must have offset the hostile odds, for the Yucatecans took possession of the city after little more than a minor engagement.

A levy of $25,000 was laid on the citizens of the province. The entire amount went into Moore's strong box, but $8,460 was all that ever reached Texas. The remainder went for the procuring of supplies from New Orleans and Campeche. Without these stores, Moore could not have remained longer at sea.

Thanks to this windfall, he continued to operate the corvette, the two schooners, and the steamer off the Mexican coast and in conjunction with the Yucatecans until the end of February, 1841. All of this was very gratifying to the Texans— particularly the phenomenon of the navy bringing into the bankrupt Republic a little hard cash.[15] The *Telegraph* and *Texas Register* spoke glowingly of the cruise.

In truth the cruise just completed had contributed its part toward gaining for Texas even more than the hard cash that moved the local papers to editorial ecstasy. Strangely enough and notwithstanding Treat's lack of aggressiveness in Mexico City, a substantial portion of the Texan gains from this cruise were of a diplomatic character. While Treat was failing to follow up his opportunities, Mr. Hamilton, diplomatic agent in London, was resorting to a most aggressive form of diplomacy with equally gratifying results. Hamilton used the diplomatic threat, offered by Moore's presence on the lower Gulf, that Treat not only ignored but also restrained from action.

It was Hamilton's job to gain English recognition. Success would no doubt lead to recognition by other leading nations of Europe. The way would be paved to supplementary treaties of amity and commerce, which in turn would bolster up the sagging Texas credit and facilitate bond sales under favorable conditions.

Within a few short weeks after arriving in London, the aggressive but not at all times laudable James Hamilton had fully sensed the situation in England. One appreciable faction of the British electorate opposed English recognition because it would be favoring the expansion of slavery. A not so vociferous but nevertheless more influential English faction were holders of Mexican bonds secured by Mexican land. These bond holders saw in the separation of Texas from Mexico the alienation of a large part of their collateral.

Hamilton quickly prepared a brief intended to satisfy both groups opposing Texan recognition. In five blunt, pithy sentences, he listed as many positive reasons why it would be profitable to England to recognize Texas. His most potent arguments were the advantages England would derive from "a judicious commercial Convention" with Texas by which Great Britain would secure "a great cotton producer and important consumer of her Manufactures as her customer & a friendly neutral in the event of a war with United States. . . ."

He then submitted an equal number of negative reasons that were all but threats to the British Lion. Moore's fleet was presented as Exhibit A in his proof that Texas and not Mexico was the power south of United States that had to be reckoned with in the future. Mr. Hamilton set forth his case as follows:

In case England does not recognize [Texas] the following consequences are likely to follow—

1st. In sixty days from this day Vera Cruz, Tampico & Matamoras will be blockaded by the Texian Squadron, which consists of one Corvette, two Brigs, three Schooners & one naval Steamer, now off the Coast of Mexico, while Mexico is destitute of all naval force whatsoever.

2nd. If Texas is informed that Great Britain will not recognize her Independence & that consequently there is no hope of peace with Mexico, she will forthwith join the Federalists, revolutionize the northern provinces of Mexico & make such additions to her Territory as the laws of war would justify under the usages of civilized nations.

3rd. Great Britain has an obvious interest in now avoiding a discriminating duty which will be levied against the productions of all nations which have not recognized Texas & formed Commercial Treaties with her on or before the 1st of Feby. next.

4th. If her Majesty's Government should decline recognizing I must avail myself of the present situation of public affairs in Europe & make the most beneficial arrangement I can with some continental nation giving it exclusive commercial advantages for a valuable equivalent.

* * * * * * * *

Respectfully submitted
J. Hamilton.[16]

Diplomatic agent Hamilton handed the document above quoted to Mr. Palmerston on October 14, 1840, seven days prior to the firing upon Moore's boats at Tampico. Though Treat had been unable to impress the Mexican diplomats with the potentialities of the Texan fleet in the Gulf, the maritime minded Palmerston and the British bond holders fully understood the situation.

A Texan blockade meant money out of British pockets. The further disintegration of Mexico by Federalist revolutionists along the Rio Grande and in Yucatan would mean the further alienation of Mexican resources that stood back of the British owned Mexican bonds. Furthermore, continued Mexican warfare meant continued Mexican inability to pay. For once the profits of peace far exceeded those of war.

Thus on November 13, 14, and 16 (while Commodore Moore was relieving Tobasco of $25,000) Palmerston signed with Hamilton three treaties subject to ratification in Texas within six months. One was a treaty of amity, commerce and navigation. In the second treaty Texas was to assume £1,000,000 of the Mexican foreign debt contracted by Mexico before the secession of Texas. This treaty was to silence the bond holders who saw in the broad Texan prairies part of their collateral for the old Mexican debt. The third treaty was intended to quiet the British abolitionists. It proposed concerted action between the British and Texan navies for the suppression of the slave trade. Belgium and the Netherlands soon followed England's lead on the question of recognition.

Of course the Texas naval supremacy over Mexico and Moore's presence in the Gulf were not entirely responsible for Great Britain's recognition of Texas. Other factors, such as England's interest in a cotton supply outside of United States, contributed to these diplomatic triumphs of Lamar's administration. It cannot be denied, however, that the Texan fleet greatly stimulated British interest in the situation and certainly served notice on all interested that Texas was preparing for an aggressive war if such were necessary to escape the constant threat of a Mexican invasion.

Of even more interest is the direct result of Moore's cruise upon Mexico and Mexican opinion. Though Bustamante had kept Moore idle by toying with Treat, he had done so at terrific political cost to himself and to his administration. Bitterly did his opponents within the Centralist party denounce him for having so much as negotiated with the ungrateful Texans. These critics unquestionably paved the way for Urrea's palace revolution and the ultimate elimination of Bustamante from Mexican public life in October of 1841. Of course the ubiquitous Santa Anna was President Bustamante's successor.

The Mexican journalistic reactions and the reflected effect upon Mexican commerce are also significant.

The *Jalapa Conciliador* at first greeted news of Moore's presence off Vera Cruz with derision. This editor thought the Texans were having dreams "as it seems that Texas lives only by illusions and the forming of castles in the air."[17] However, four days later, October 18, 1840, the same editor was lamenting that Mexican trade and commerce were being stifled by the mere presence of Texan cruisers offshore. The editor then launched an impassioned plea for an adequate Mexican fleet to protect that commerce. By October 22, the Vera Cruz *Censor* was complaining that Mexican commerce was being tied up by the presence of Texan men-of-war, even though no actual captures had been made. The Vera Cruz editor could only lament that on one side, Yucatan, there was revolution and on the other side, Mexico City, there was only inaction.[18] As days went by, the editor of *El Censor* became genuinely alarmed. Texas was not only ceasing to be a boy, he warned, but was rapidly becoming "more robust each day . . . Supreme Government, awake! . . . a little longer and it will be too late."[19]

Though the official daily in Mexico City reprinted many remarks from the provincial papers, its editors had little or no opinions with reference to Treat and Moore's squadron during the autumn of 1840. Too much officially directed criticism might discourage Treat and send him to the coast to unleash the Texan dogs of war. Accordingly, it was not until October 4, 1840, that the *Diario del Gobierno* came out boldly on the matter.

The *Diario* featured a twenty-five hundred word review of the case. The author of this highly impassioned editorial had to go back to Ancient Rome and *Los Tarquinos* to find another historical crisis acute enough to be compared with that in which Mexico then found herself. With the stage thus set, the reviewer proceeded to outline accurately the problems then confronting the Mexican people: "The squadron of Texas dominates our gulf coast from the boundary of the United States to Cape Catoche in Yucatan." And the "Yucatecans are, by a treason most degrading allied with the Texans. . . . Mexicans, arouse yourselves now from this sleep of death! . . . The conservation of Mexican independence depends upon the integrity of her territory."[20]

After the withdrawal of Treat and the arrival of word at Mexico City that the Texan squadron was actually operating with the Yucatecans, the wrath of the Mexican press rose to a frenzy. It reached a climax with the capture and ransoming of San Juan Bautista.

Nevertheless, as the Yucatecan crisis loomed larger and larger, the conquest of Texas, according to the official *Diario*, became more and more a secondary objective. Yucatan had to be conquered before Texas could be more than occasionally raided. Armies could not be maintained in Texas without the maritime resources of Yucatan. Furthermore, Yucatan could not be reconquered so long as the Texan fleet dominated the lower Gulf.[21] Thus the fast tottering Bustamante administration prepared its public for an effort at naval supremacy and laid the foundation for the creation of a really potent fleet during the succeeding Santa Anna administration.

In truth the Mexican analysis of the situation was correct. Until that fleet was created and the Yucatan revolt was crushed, Texas was truly safe from a serious Mexican invasion, even though Canales and his temporary buffer state, the now defunct Republic of the Rio Grande, no longer offered a barrier to the advance of a Centralist army.

We may therefore summarize the results of Moore's first cruise as follows: 1. To an appreciable degree it expedited British recognition of Texas, which was the greatest achievement of Lamar's administration. 2. Though Treat did not make the most of the diplomatic and naval opportunities offered by Texan naval supremacy, through 1840 and most of the following year, Bustamante was forced to weaken his administration by toying with the representative of the despised Texans. To that degree the Texan squadron contributed its part toward Mexican governmental chaos. 3. Mexican commerce was hampered and even tied up in some ports by the threat of Texan action, though few prizes were actually captured. 4. A determined Yucatecan revolt was aided and abetted to such a degree that the Centralist armies were to be busy elsewhere for many, many months, thereby giving Texas a still longer respite.

Thus did Texan naval supremacy throughout two important years pay large dividends to the infant republic.

CHAPTER TEN

YUCATAN RENTS THE FLEET
*Webb's Mission • Alliance • A Mutiny
Houston Vacillates • "Paper Blockade"*

W HEN COMMODORE Moore returned to Texas in February
1841 he found that his compatriots at home had been making
some history on their own account. Unhappily for the proponents of continued naval aggression, the Fifth Congress,
which had been in session since the latter part of 1840, was
almost as unwilling to coöperate with the administration as
had been the Houston-led, reactionary Fourth Congress of
1838–40.

In fact the Congressmen were lulled into quiescence toward
Mexico by the long *de facto* armistice. They had decided that
peace had come to stay, with or without a treaty. So convinced
were the Congressmen of this that the houses deadlocked on
the army appropriations and once again left the military establishment stranded. Nor can it be said that Congress had a
firm administrative leadership. President Lamar had become
so ill that, December 12, 1840, he had asked Congress for a
leave of absence.[1] Hampered by his temporary status as Chief
Executive of the Republic, Vice-President David G. Burnet
could do little else than sign the bills that were sent up to him.

If, by New Year's Day, 1841, plans for further naval aggression against Mexico had been contemplated by anyone other
than Commodore Moore, President Lamar, and the Yucatecans, these plans were killed on January 26. On that date

Vice-President Burnet transmitted to the Texan Senate Hamilton's first and second treaties with England. For reasons not exactly clear the third treaty, with reference to suppression of the slave trade, did not reach Texas until after Congress had adjourned.

The two treaties that did arrive warmed the cockles of every senatorial heart. It will be recalledthat the first treaty covered recognition of Texas and the usual subjects of amity, commerce, and navigation. The second called for British efforts at mediation between Texas and Mexico, which if successful would mean that the Texans would assume a million pounds of the Mexican bonded debt prior to the Texan revolt. Of course all other business was hastily pushed aside, and both treaties were ratified unanimously on the day that they were transmitted to the Senate.[2]

Hence by the time Moore returned from Yucatan, a month or so later, he found the Texan leaders in a happy frame of mind. The peace doves were cooing from the eaves of every public building. Did not one treaty enlist the British pocketbook, one of the pressing factors that had ended the French Pastry War, on the side of the Texans? Mexico would have to give in or be confronted by the irate British navy, which in those days as well as in more recent years, had a habit of looking out for the British bond holder.

In keeping with this new development the returned and rested Lamar could not do other than to send a third agent to Mexico laden with palm branches and instructions. Meanwhile the heavy ships of the Texan squadron were decommissioned and left with skeletonized crews in Galveston harbor. The two war-schooners *San Antonio* and *San Bernard* were left fully manned to patrol the coast, maintain order, keep down smuggling, and conduct some much needed surveys and map making.

President Lamar's final choice for an agent to Mexico fell upon Judge James Webb. Though his instructions and commission were dated March 22, 1841,[3] it was late in May before Webb sailed for Vera Cruz aboard the *San Bernard*.

But the tottering Bustamante régime had learned that there was more domestic danger in toying with Texan diplomats than there was a foreign menace in ignoring them. When the *San Bernard* appeared off Vera Cruz, May 31, the port commandant courteously but promptly refused to let Webb land. Though the Texan agent did communicate with Pakenham, and he in turn called on the Mexican Foreign Office in behalf of the Texans, all was to no avail.[4] Even so, Webb lingered off Vera Cruz, busily engaged upon a futile correspondence with Mexico City, and a more productive correspondence with Yucatan, until the end of June, 1841.

With all hopes dashed insofar as the Centralists were concerned, Webb had the *San Bernard* steered for Yucatan. This was in full accordance with the contingency paragraphs of his instructions. Having failed with Mexico City, he was to seek another alliance with the peninsular Federalists.

While crossing the Gulf of Campeche, the *San Bernard's* topmast was carried away. Her captain felt compelled to lay a course for Galveston, which was reached June 20. Notwithstanding Webb's failure to reach Yucatan, he returned with definite ideas as to conditions on the peninsula and what Texas should do about them.

I am assured that they [the Yucatecans] are now anxious to form such relations on a permanent basis because they feel convinced, that, with our assistance and support, they can, in a short time, put down the central government and establish the Confederacy [of Mexican states] in its stead. . . . Let Texas enter into arrangements at once, with Yucatan and Tobasco, and each party mutually recognize the Independence of the other, and let them conjointly renew and prosecute the War until the Central Government shall be forced into terms. . . . Texas would only be expected to furnish her navy. . . . The captures made . . . would not only pay the expenses incur'd, . . . but would absolutely produce a revenue to the Country. . . . The Federalists of Yucatan and Tobasco have now everything that is necessary to carry on the War successfully, but a Navy, . . . Without a Navy they can make no effectual impression upon the [Centralist's] seaports, and that is the most essential object to be obtained: because it is through the seaports and the revenue derived from their commerce that the [Centralist] Government is sustained—take that and you cut off all their resources and render them hopelessly imbecile.[5]

Lamar was so well impressed by Webb's recommendations that he hastened to Galveston early in July, 1841, for a conference with him. This conference produced a note to the Governor of Yucatan. He was assured that the ports and commercial facilities of Texas were open to Yucatecan ships. It was also urged that a Yucatecan envoy come to Texas for the negotiation of an agreement "mutually beneficial" and calculated to secure "a full and completed acknowledgment of the respective rights of both countries from those who are now our enemies."[6]

It might be added that Lamar's plan for a renewal of naval action against Mexico was not entirely motivated by Webb's rebuffs at Vera Cruz. Palmerston was no longer in the British Foreign office. His successor, Aberdeen, was rather cool toward the Texan treaties and when he learned that the two most favorable to Texas had been ratified while the third one, designed to silence the troublesome anti-slavery factions in England, had not been acted upon, he had seized this as an excuse to withhold England's final ratification subject to Texan action on the slave trade agreement. Thus cold water was dashed upon the warm hopes for an English enforced mediation between Mexico and Texas. Texas was again on her own.

It is also not amiss to add that Lamar's prospective return to naval operations against Mexico was not all of his ambitious program. On June 20, while Webb had been starting for Yucatan, Lamar was watching his Santa Fe expedition depart from Austin. It was to conquer New Mexico, make good Texas claims westward to the Rio Grande, and divert the wealthy Santa Fe trail traffic through Texas. It was not a nearly so well thought out or so practical a scheme as the proposed naval alliance with Yucatan.

The note to the Yucatecan executive brought a quick response. Early in September, 1841, Colonel Martin Peraza, with plenary powers from Governor Barbachano, of Yucatan, presented his credentials to Lamar. Colonel Peraza frankly stated that his presence in Texas had been greatly stimulated by reliable reports that the Centralists, within a month or so, would be in position to send an 18-gun brig and two strong, war schooners (New York built) against his fellow Federalists in Yucatan. Moreover he had a definite plan which he and the Texan Secretary of State quickly organized into a *quasi*-treaty.

This executive agreement was dated September 17, 1841, and covered the following points: (a) Texas would send to sea three or more men-of-war. Their first mission would be to prevent the invasion of Yucatan; after that the greatest possible injury by land or sea to enemy property. (b) Prizes by Texan ships should be adjudicated in Texan ports; those of Yucatecan vessels in the ports of Yucatan. (c) Prize monies, above the legal claims of officers and men making the captures, that might be derived from seized merchantmen, tolls, customs houses, or other property, should be divided equally between the two governments, irrespective of which fleet or force made the seizure. (d) Last but by no means of least importance to the Texans, Yucatan was to pay eight thousand dollars in advance and a like sum at the "expiration of each and every month" that the three or more Texan men-of-war so operated. The agreement might be terminated by either party on little or no advance notice.[8]

On the very next day, September 18, orders were forwarded to Commodore Moore. At his discretion he was to condition, provision, and man *"not less than three"* of the ships under his command. This was to be done by sending ships to New Orleans; but no sailor was to be actually enlisted except on Texas soil or aboard a Texan ship, three marine leagues off shore. If the commander did not think he could outfit and operate at least three vessels on eight thousand dollars per month he was to remain in port and spend no money whatsoever under these instructions. Otherwise he was to proceed to sea as proposed.

After dropping the pilot, he would open a packet of "sealed orders" governing his future actions.[9] For some reason, Moore did not receive these instructions until October 13.

Perhaps the delay was because the Lamar administration had been somewhat disconcerted by the final returns in the September election. It was a presidential year inasmuch as Lamar's term would expire the second Monday the following December, in that year the 13th. Lamar, under the constitution was not eligible to succeed himself and accordingly his faction had backed Vice-President David G. Burnet who was pledged to carry out Lamar's policies. Houston, again eligible to occupy the "White House," had led his own faction on a platform diametrically opposed to that of the incumbent. He had proposed the kindest of treatment to Indians, strict economy in all branches, no participation in Mexican revolutions, and the attainment of peace and recognition from Mexico by negotiations—as though Lamar had not tried negotiations three times.

Notwithstanding all the blather about platforms, the election ran true to frontier form by being an almost one hundred percent personal affair, with the hero of San Jacinto, as Houston was now considered, getting twice as many votes as did Vice-President Burnet. Thus, as Houston himself soon learned, the vote of the people did not reflect approval or disapproval of Lamar's policies. A frontier hero had been returned to office and that was that.

Perhaps Lamar came to this conclusion by October 13, and decided to have Moore go ahead with his commissioning of the three-vessel fleet for Yucatecan service. It was well that he did not delay longer, for December was well advanced before Moore was ready to sail. Indeed, it was not until inauguration day, December 13, that Moore was able to cross the Galveston bar with his 22-gun *Austin* and the two 7-gun schooners, *San Bernard*, Lieutenant D. H. Crisp, and *San Antonio*, Lieutenant William Seeger. Over the bar Moore opened his mysteriously sealed orders. They were nothing more than instructions to sail

to Sisal and carry out the Texan obligations stipulated in the
quasi-treaty with Yucatan.[10]

Moore anchored the three ships off Sisal January 6, 1842.
He and Lieutenant Seeger at once went ashore. They procured
a carriage and were shortly rattling over the dusty highway
toward the Yucatecan capital, Merida, about twenty-five miles
inland from Sisal. Lieutenant Alfred G. Gray, of the *Austin*,
was left in charge of the ships.

The dust of Moore's carriage had hardly disappeared in the
distance before Gray became apprehensive. Everybody in
Sisal was talking about a peace treaty between the Yucatecans
and the Centralists. Right then the peace commissioners were
boarding the American barque, *Louisa*, to return to Mexico
City. Everyone was sure the war was over. If this were true,
reasoned Lieutenant Gray, the Yucatecans had returned to
Mexican citizenship and were now the enemies of Texas. He
even decided that the lives of Commander Moore and Lieutenant Seeger might be in danger.

Gray was a man of action. A party of Texan sailors and
marines were immediately ordered aboard the *Louisa*, and
notwithstanding the obscenity and profanity of her American
skipper, Señor Quintana Roo, representing the Centralists, and
the two Yucatecan commissioners in company with him, were
removed to the *Austin*. Gray told them that they were hostages
pending the return of Commodore Moore.

In due time the truth as to the Centralist-Yucatecan negotiations was ascertained:

The previous October the Mexican President, Bustamante,
long denounced for his failures with France, criticized for his
exorbitant taxes, high tariffs, inability to pay his army and
excoriated for his negotiations with the Texans, found it impossible to continue his régime. He had capitulated and his
arch-enemy, though fellow Centralist, Santa Anna, had been
elevated to the vacant chair. Once again the bombastic and
chameleon like Santa Anna showed marked ability in the realm
of Mexican leadership. Already he had reorganized the taxes.

His pampered pet, the army, was beginning to get full pay. Proposals were being pressed for the subjugation of Yucatan. At the same time he did not propose to take the offensive until he had sufficient naval supremacy to support his army in the Yucatecan campaign. Accordingly Santa Anna had sent his friend, the great Yucatecan patriot Quintana Roo, back to his native land to play a diplomatic game that would keep the *Peninsulares* quiet until Santa Anna was ready to strike. It is doubtful if Quintana Roo was fully aware of the dubious rôle that he was playing.

Nevertheless he had gone to Yucatan and had finally, on December 28, 1841, entered into a preliminary treaty with the Federalists. Well might the Yucatecans be jubilant over its terms. Only nominally would Yucatan continue as a part of Mexico. She would retain all of her recently adopted laws and have complete autonomy over her customs and finances. Revenues collected should remain in that state and be spent for its welfare. Soldiers and sailors could not be drafted from Yucatan. At the same time the peninsula should have full representation in the Mexican Congress.[11]

Should Quintana Roo succeed in getting this document ratified in Mexico City, it would represent a complete victory for the Yucatecans. Pending ratification there would be an armistice. In their jubilance over such a happy peace, the Yucatecans were overlooking the question of the treaty's future in the hands of the Santa Anna directed, Centralist Senate.

While Lieutenant Gray was forcing the hospitality of his ship upon the Yucatecan hostages, Commodore Moore and Lieutenant Seeger were arriving at Merida. There on January 8, 1842, the Texan naval officers were informed by the Yucatecan government of the recently declared armistice.

The news put the Commodore in a blustery frame of mind. Loudly he protested his disappointment. He had come all the way to Merida to work out the details of a joint campaign only to be told by his allies that they had just buried the hatchet with the common foe. It was a breach of faith with Texas!

The Yucatecan Secretary of Foreign Affairs very fittingly put him in his place with a sharp note properly interpreting the character and terms of the *quasi*-treaty with Texas. He insisted that Yucatan could end the agreement when she saw fit. She had not negotiated away her right to make a peace with Mexico.[12]

But if the Yucatecan officials wrote sharply, that was merely for record. Their oral reception was different. Moore and Lieutenant Seeger were told that the tentative treaty of Quintana Roo would not have been signed had it been known that the Texan ships were then actually en route to Sisal. In the meantime Governor Barbachano and his cabinet were eager to have Moore and his squadron remain on the coast until it was seen what action the Centralists would take on the treaty. Should Moore and his ships remain, the Yucatecan government would gladly pay its pledge of eight thousand dollars per month while the fleet was so strategically stationed. Until the Centralists refused to ratify the treaty, however, the Yucatecan forces could not afford to act with the Texans in marauding enterprises similar to the expedition against Tobasco the previous year. Somewhat mollified Commodore Moore agreed to remain on the coast.

Moore had hardly become reconciled to the new situation before he was pulled out of bed at 1 A.M., January 12, to patch up another incipient breach with the Yucatecans. News had just reached Merida of Lieutenant Gray's seizure of the Quintana Roo's party at Sisal. By donning full uniform and calling at the home of His Excellency, the Governor of Yucatan, at the un-Mexican hour of 2 A.M., Moore had everything satisfactorily explained and a release order en route to Lieutenant Gray even before the Yucatecan Secretary of State had learned of the episode.

Shortly after this incident, which in the end gave all hands in both Texan and Yucatecan circles a good and timely excuse to express again their mutual esteem and confidence, Moore returned to his flagship off Sisal.

Hardly had he dispatched his two schooners to Mujeres Island to replenish the fleet's water supply and to ascertain that island's availability as a base of operation, when Moore received word that the American vessel *Sylph* was in distress among the Alacranes, a cluster of barren keys and reefs about one hundred miles to northward. The *Austin* at once sailed to her rescue. Much of the cargo and the lives of all the crew and passengers were saved. Except for this act of mercy, Moore (always something of a scholar) spent his spare time working up his survey notes into an accurate map of the Texan coast.

By January 28, Moore was again off Sisal in company with the *San Bernard* and the *San Antonio*. Three days later the *San Antonio* was sent back to Texas with all the *Sylph* survivors and the correspondence covering Moore's contacts with the Yucatecans. He of course included a full report of his own movements after leaving Texas. He also urged that until Yucatan saw fit to act, a Texan blockade of the Mexican ports be proclaimed. Furthermore, if the steamer *Zavala* were fitted out and sent to him (for towing his sail ships when operating close in shore) he could enforce such a blockade and support the cost of the operations by ransoms from seized cities. The same day that the *San Antonio* sailed northward, the *Austin* and *San Bernard* shook out their sails and laid a course for Vera Cruz.[12]

The *San Antonio* made a fast passage to Galveston. Lieutenant Seeger soon learned that on December 15, 1841, just two days after Moore had sailed, the newly inaugurated President Houston had instructed Secretary of War and Navy, George W. Hockley, to order Moore and his fleet to "return forthwith to the port of Galveston, and there await further orders."[13]

To expedite the transmission of these orders, the pilot boat *Washington* had been chartered and ordered to find Moore as soon as possible. For some reason the *Washington* had not, and never did get in contact with the Texan fleet. A decade later Sam Houston, then in the U. S. Senate, declared that the failure of the *Washington* to reach Moore was due to "peculiar

THE WAR SCHOONER *SAN ANTONIO*, T.N.

The *San Bernard* and *San Jacinto* were sister ships. Each mounted seven 12-pounders and displaced 170 tons. From a contemporary drawing by Midshipman Edward Johns, T.N. (Courtesy of University of Texas, Austin)

influences at Galveston, or some other circumstances."[14] The inference is that the naval operations were popular among the coastal inhabitants of Texas. Accordingly the pilot boat had been deliberately misdirected. Such was probably the case and was no doubt Secretary Hockley's opinion at the time, for he gave copies of the recall orders to Lieutenant Seeger and ordered him to see that Moore received them. The *San Antonio*, however, was to rejoin the squadron by way of New Orleans, where the *Sylph* survivors would be landed and supplies procured for the *Austin* and *San Bernard*.

It was while the *San Antonio* was anchored in the stream opposite New Orleans, February 11, 1842, that the first and only mutiny occurred in the Texas navy. The high ranking officers were ashore. The crew, however, was kept in quarters, for the very good reason that desertions would have been many had a liberal shore leave policy been adopted. It was natural that there should be the usual grousing in the forecastle. Several bottles of hard liquor, smuggled aboard by friendly boatmen, did not contribute toward either mental or vocal contentment. Instead, it stimulated enough courage among some members of the crew that they decided to do something about the situation.

Thus it was that Sergeant of Marines Seymour Oswald accosted Lieutenant M. H. Dearborn and demanded leave for himself and some companions. It was refused. An argument followed. Lieutenant Charles Fuller, ranking officer aboard, came on deck to investigate the cause of the high language. Fuller's presence merely increased the tension of the situation.

Lieutenant Fuller decided to bring order out of the chaos by turning out the marine guard under arms. To a landsman this would appear to have been a foolish move, and as it turned out, it was. Nevertheless, putting the very man on duty to prohibit a breach of discipline that it is feared he is about to commit is a disciplinary device as old as the psychology of command itself.

In this instance, however, Sergeant Oswald did not respond

to the duty assigned. When he went to the locker to issue small arms to his fellow marines, he took not only enough for the guard, but also enough to arm his cronies among the crew.[15] For himself he kept a colt pistol and a hatchet. Thus equipped he approached Lieutenant Fuller. Under the guise of reporting that the marines were armed, he struck at the officer with the tomahawk. The Lieutenant drew a pistol, and a general fight followed which involved a number of seamen and officers.

The fray did not end until Lieutenant Fuller lay dead, Midshipmen Alden and Odell were seriously wounded and the one remaining officer, Lieutenant Dearborn, was "knocked down the cabin hatch and the companion drawn over him."[16]

Oswald and his party at once lowered two boats and pulled for the shore, one toward New Orleans and the other toward Algiers. They were hardly clear when cries from the wounded and imprisoned officers attracted the attention of the watch aboard the nearby U. S. Revenue Cutter *Jackson*.

The American cutter and the city police acted with promptness. Before Lieutenant Seeger had shipped a new crew and loaded his supplies, ten of the mutineers had been apprehended. Two of them were returned to the *San Antonio*, but because of extradition difficulties the remaining eight of them were left in the New Orleans jail.

From New Orleans Seeger ran down to the Arcas Islands, the rendezvous he and Moore had agreed upon when they parted at Sisal. The *Austin* was not there, but a waiting dispatch informed him that Moore would meet him at Laguna. On March 10 both ships reached that point, and the two mutineers were handed over to the Commodore for a court martial.

During the absence of the *San Antonio*, the *Austin* and *San Bernard* had not been idle. It will be recalled that they had laid a course for Vera Cruz the same day, January 31, 1842, that the *San Antonio* had sailed for Galveston. On February 6 they took their first prize, the *Progreso*, Vera Cruz to Matamoras. She was sent to Galveston for adjudication, and with her went the news that a day or so before Moore had looked into Vera Cruz harbor and had seen a steamer and one of the men-of-war the Centralists had long been expecting from the United States. She had been there for "three or four days" and the other was "hourly expected."

At the end of February, Moore found it convenient for his two ships to be back at Sisal whence the Commodore presented the Yucatan Secretary of War and Marine with a bill for eight thousand dollars. He displayed an adroit touch one would expect to find in a person more experienced at collecting bills.

Moore opened by remarking that Yucatan was a little in arrears already. He then told all the bad news for Yucatan that he picked up when off Vera Cruz. Of course he mentioned the new warship and the recently bought steamer flying Mexican Navy colors that he had seen lying under the guns of Castle San Juan de Ulúa. He also insisted that the Centralists were not going to ratify Quintana Roo's treaty. He let but one bit of good news slip in. One of the two new warships for Mexico had been wrecked on the Florida Keys en route from New York. Moore closed with the statement as to where he could be found in case the Yucatecan Secretary of War and Marine wanted to pay him for the next month of service a little in advance of March 8, the date it was due.

The Yucatecan Secretary of War and Marine was none other than General Pedro Lemus, the Federalist General whom Moore had rescued from his Centralist guards aboard the *Conchita* off Tampico the previous year. Lemus forwarded the money, and no doubt smiled as he wrote that the "Governor . . . is pleased with your punctuality." The Governor had, furthermore, heard "casually" that Moore had taken a prize. His Excellency did not remark that half the net proceeds therefrom was Yucatan's, but he did crave such "information as you may consider convenient."[17]

Even with this delicate monetary matter settled satisfactorily, Moore's relations with the Yucatecans did not enter upon an untroubled sea. Newspapers brought from New York by an American barque told of President Houston's radical reversal of all Lamar policies. The press reports did not say that Moore had actually been recalled. Instead there was a badly garbled story about Texan distrust of their Yucatecan allies. It was firmly believed in Texas, according to the New York press, that since the Yucatecans had made peace with Mexico, Moore had been seized at Merida, and that Houston was sending a small merchantman to the fleet with orders to attack Yucatecan commerce.

Of course Moore, still near Sisal and waiting for the return of the *San Antonio*, at once sent out official reassurances to all prominent Yucatecan officials. Nevertheless, the news from New York continued to upset the equanimity of the officials, including the Governor, for several days.

Two days before the *Austin* joined the returned *San Antonio* at Laguna, additional newspapers from New Orleans told of the mutiny aboard the *San Antonio* at that port. This advance news did not put the Commodore in a judicial frame of mind. He immediately resolved to "mete out to the rascals the *uttermost penalties* of the law."[18]

He kept his word. In a court martial convened shortly after the reunion of the two ships at Laguna, one of the culprits was sentenced to be hanged but the court recommended him to the mercy of the administration. The second captive mutineer was granted a trial postponement in order that he might get evidence from New Orleans. Presumably he needed the testimony of some, or all of his unextradited friends then being held in the New Orleans jail.

A year later when Commodore Moore and President Houston were engaged upon their war of words and recriminations, the Texan President accused Moore of murderous severity in the trial of those two mutineers and in his disposal of those who were later delivered to him by the New Orleans authorities. Even the right of the Texan Commodore to court martial mutineers was challenged by the irate Houston. He chose to forget that immediately after the trial of the first two culprits at Laguna, March 14, 1842, Secretary of War and Marine Hockley wrote "your proceedings personally, and of Courts Martials specially, are approved, and the latter confirmed."[19]

When it came to obeying President Houston's recall order of December 15, 1841, now three months old, Commodore Moore did not act with the same alacrity as he did in the matter of naval justice for mutineers. He chose to ignore the order. In none of his dispatches did he set forth very good reasons. The main consideration, however, seems to have been that the Yucatecans were paying the monthly stipend of eight thousand dollars with a fair degree of regularity. Should he depart this sustaining fund would be terminated.

Having chosen to ignore the recall, he lingered until March 28 near Yucatan. On that day he sailed with his entire command for Vera Cruz, which was reached three days later. The same armed merchant steamer and war schooner were still in port. They showed signs of activity, and Moore cleared for action. He was badly disappointed when they did not come out to offer battle.

The American sloop-of-war *Warren* happened to be in port, and she sent out an officer for a visit. From him Moore learned that Lamar's Santa Fe's expedition had been captured to a man. They had been marched southward with marked brutality and were then divided among the dungeons of Mexico City, Puebla, and Perote. The visitor from the *Warren* also reported that a Mr. Lubbock, one of the expedition's leaders, had escaped to Vera Cruz, whence he had sailed in an English vessel to Yucatan in hopes of joining Moore's fleet. The American also volunteered alarming reports as to the progress of Santa Anna's preparations for the reconquering of Yucatan—and then Texas.

Moore detached the *San Antonio* to go to Laguna for Lubbock. It was hoped the Texan would have vital information as to the conditions in Mexico. Meanwhile the *Austin* and *San Bernard* skirted the coast northward to Tuxpan. The run netted two prizes, the *Dolorita* and the *Dos Amigos*, both from

Matamoras. Off Tampico the *San Bernard* was ordered to Galveston with dispatches and reports. In them Moore said nothing suggestive of his returning to the naval base at Galveston. In fact, he made his need of the steamer *Zavala* the subject of a special letter. While Crisp and his *San Bernard* stood for Galveston, Moore doubled back to Yucatan to join the *San Antonio*.

He had been at his old beat off Sisal but a few days when, April 18, the Texan brig of war *Wharton*, 18 guns, hove in sight. She brought a most surprising document. It was a proclamation signed by President Sam Houston, by which the world was informed that all Mexican Gulf ports except those of Yucatan were under blockade. The *Wharton* was there to help enforce it.

To understand President Houston's sudden reversal of policy requires a short digression. During the regular session of the Sixth Congress (chosen in his own election) Houston quickly learned that his ideas of sacrificing national honor to rigid economy were not held in high esteem. Nor was he able to convince the representatives of the people that Indians deserved good treatment. The buckskin constituents as well as the hard, uncouth Congressmen still thought that all good Indians were dead Indians. While Houston's denunciation of Lamar's "meddling" in Mexican revolutions had sounded well during the election, some congressmen and the people still showed a strong inclination for any program that would increase the death rate below the Rio Grande—no matter by what name it might be called. Then, when news of the maltreatment of the Santa Fe prisoners reached Texas, the ire of Congress knew no bounds, and Houston completely lost control. That is, he lost control of everything but the treasury. No matter what had been appropriated, he controlled that important department of government by the simple process of refusing to release funds. Only $20,000, for example, had been appropriated to the Navy because of its revenues from Yucatan. Small though the allotment was, Houston would not permit his treasury department to release any of it.

Houston had scarcely breathed a sigh of relief after the adjournment of his unruly Sixth Congress when he was further embarrassed by the sudden capture, March 5, 1842, of San Antonio, Refugio, and Goliad by a small Mexican army under General Vasquez. San Antonio was but slightly over eighty miles from Austin, the Texan capital Lamar had chosen. Panic swept Texas. Houston himself left the capital in haste to put his wife aboard a vessel bound for Mobile. Orders literally flowed from his pen with reference to mobilization of troops, fortification of Galveston, and forestalling an attack from the sea.[20]

As the light Mexican column was withdrawing to the Rio Grande, Houston decided to counter attack with a blockade of Mexico instead of a more hazardous (and expensive) military pursuit. President Houston even invited ship owners to apply for privateering commissions. Thus it was that all of Moore's acts were approved, and he was reinforced, April 18, by the heavy gun brig *Wharton*.

The fleet was further augmented, April 24, by the return of the *San Bernard*. The dispatches she brought also reflected the new order of things. The President was eager for a quick and vigorous enforcement of the blockade. To do this the administration felt, in the light of Moore's own reports, that certain units of the fleet, particularly the key vessels *Austin* and *Zavala*, had to be refitted and the heavy gun brig *Archer* put in commission. In the meantime, Houston had important business to talk over with Moore. The ships should be sent to New Orleans at once. "Orders will be given that every exertion will be used to fit out the vessels instantly, and if possible, [they will] be ready by the time you join it at New Orleans"[21] after the all important conference with the President.

It was easy for Moore to decide upon prompt compliance with these orders. In the first place they agreed with the line of action he desired. In the second place the Yucatecans had waxed weary of paying the eight thousand dollars for monthly rental on the fleet.

Crafty Santa Anna had not only thrown Texas into a mental chaos by his lightning-like raid of March 6, but he was also telling the Yucatecans that so long as they harbored the Texan squadron near their shores, he could not have his Congress seriously consider the highly favorable Quintana Roo treaty. This suggestion from the Centralists that the presence of the Texan ships was, after all, a boomerang to Yucatecan interests, combined with the shrinking treasury of the *Peninsulares*, explained not only their willingness but eagerness to see Moore return to Texas.

Before he sailed, however, the Yucatecan obligations were paid up in full except for four thousand dollars, which the treasury shortage required that they pay in Yucatecan notes. Good will was expressed all around, and it was made clear to Moore that should the Centralists fail to ratify the Quintana Roo agreement, he would certainly be welcome again upon the coast. As Moore's squadron departed, April 25, 1842, he exchanged farewell salutes with the Yucatecan fleet of two brigs and two schooners, which happened to be standing to sea at the same time—probably for the patrol cruise to their base on Carmen Island. Thus was temporarily ended the Texan-Yucatecan alliance.

CHAPTER ELEVEN

*MOORE CLASHES WITH HOUS-
TON • No Naval Offensive • Mexico's
New Fleet • Yucatecans in Dire Distress*

WHEN THE young Texan Commodore reached Galveston, May 1, 1842, from his second cruise to Yucatan, it was probably with a heart made light by optimism that he viewed his forthcoming conference with the Chief Executive. His outlook had not been so bright since his entrance into the Lone Star service. Six months before, he had sailed just in time to avoid detention by a hostile incoming administration. He had ignored that administration's recall orders. He had gone through a distasteful court martial. At the end of it all, he was having the satisfaction of seeing his every act fully approved. Moreover, on the entire cruise, the fleet had paid its way (except for very important payrolls) in prizes and "lease money" from Yucatan.

He was now returning to an administration recently made friendly to the navy by a Mexican raid on San Antonio. President Houston had publicly and in many communications pledged himself to a war that would bring absolute freedom from Mexico. The new program called for a vigorous blockade made effective by a completely overhauled fleet. The Gulf ports of the United States, as well as the interior cities, were teeming with sympathetic Americans eager to serve in either the Texan army or navy. Not since the capture of San Antonio by the Texans in 1835 had the Lone Star cause been so popular. The new day was at hand.

Furthermore, the conference with President Houston was in tune with the new trend. Moore met the Chief Executive on May 2 in the newly founded city of Houston, temporarily the seat of government since the alarm in Austin caused by the capture of San Antonio. There is no accurate record left of the conference. It is safe to assume, however, that the Commodore outlined the essential ship and personnel needs if Mexico were to feel the full force of a successful naval blockade.

He no doubt pointed out that the brig *Potomac* was still as worthless as ever and available only as a receiving ship. The *Austin* and the *Wharton* had seen more than two years of service in what were essentially tropical waters and had not been drydocked or completely overhauled. Furthermore, each had been through periods when the crews were skeletonized and the ships completely inactive. During such months, they had naturally deteriorated faster than if they had been constantly in active service as had been the war schooners *San Antonio* and *San Bernard*. The 18-gun brig, *Archer*, had been but recently delivered from the builders. She had nevertheless been out of the dock for many months. Her standing and running rigging were not shipshape. Furthermore, she had been stripped of most of her armament to augment the batteries of the flagship *Austin*, the gun brig *Wharton*, and the schooners. The situation with reference to the fine steamer *Zavala*, Moore unquestionably pointed out, was still more pathetic. Since the first cruise, she had been laid up with but little more than a few caretakers aboard. Her bottom had become so leaky that Lieutenant W. C. Brashear had been forced to run her aground in Galveston Bay to keep her from sinking. It was suggested that the immediate expenditure of even a few hundred dollars would temporarily be sufficient to save the ship but more would be needed to make her ready for service. She would, furthermore, be indispensable to a successful blockade.

Concerning the personnel, both commissioned and enlisted, Moore had an equally unsatisfactory condition to report. As the enlistments of most of the men were to expire in a few months, there was no point in going on an extended cruise with forecastles filled with "short timers." It was also regrettable that the Republic was badly in arrears with pay for the men. The officers had served without pay even longer than had the men. Since the acquisition of the new fleet during Lamar's administration, there had been but three pay days for the commissioned personnel. The first was in November, 1839, the second in May, 1840, and the third in May, 1841. It no doubt seemed to Moore that the patience of his subordinates should no longer be imposed upon. It is also probable that Moore reminded the President that he and his officers were still serving without commissions.[1]

Houston listened to the Commodore's needs with a sympathetic ear. It is possible that he also reiterated his frequently published yearning for punitive measures against Mexico and urged the Commodore to expedite the preparations for a vigorous naval offensive. In any case, the very next day his Secretary of War and Marine issued fresh orders to Moore. They urged haste and added that as soon as Moore had refitted at New Orleans "you will proceed to enforce the blockade ordered by the President, dated the 26th day of March, 1842."[2]

Within a few days, Moore was back with his squadron. He was at once greeted with news that was nothing short of astounding. While he had been conferring with the President at the nearby temporary seat of government, his officers had resigned almost to a man. It is needless to say that the long period between pay days was the cause of the trouble. Moore, however, felt that the situation had been aggravated by some of his enemies. As soon as he had met with the restless officers and had fully explained the situation, they agreed to continue in the service. Their willingness to begin a new year without an immediate pay day speaks eloquently, not only of their loyalty to the service, but also to Moore as a commander.

A few days later Moore reached New Orleans with the *Austin* and began making arrangements for fitting out his fleet and giving his officers some pay. To do all this, he had $3236 in cash and $4000 in Yucatecan paper. Both of these sums made up what was left of the Yucatecan subsidy. There was, also, nearly all of the appropriated twenty thousand dollars in Treasury Exchequers worth about fifty cents on the dollar that had been appropriated in the regular session of the Sixth Congress. The President, however, did not release any of this appropriation to Moore. Instead, he gave Moore a power of attorney to establish immediately, in New Orleans, a line of credit up to ten thousand, to be secured by the above mentioned appropriation. Finally there was Moore's personal credit, which was surprisingly good. He eventually raised on his own signature $34,700 for the fleet. This was not done within the next few weeks, however, but over the entire fitting-out period in New Orleans. Even with these limited funds, by June 1, Moore had provisioned the schooners at Mobile, and had had the *Austin* sufficiently overhauled to stand immediate sea duty.

In the effort to get more money he sent the *San Antonio*, Lieutenant Seeger, to Yucatan to convert the four thousand dollars worth of Yucatecan paper into hard cash. He also empowered the Lieutenant to seek a new alliance and a new subsidy from the *Peninsulares*. There were rumors that *El Presidente* Santa Anna, had repudiated the most liberal Quintana Roo agreement as soon as he learned that the Texan fleet had left the Yucatecan coast.

Moore was confident that he would be ready to put to sea as soon as the *San Antonio* returned. His optimism was somewhat shaken, however, by the arrival of the brig *Wharton*, under Commander J. T. K. Lothrop. She had been left at Galveston to protect the coast until her enlisted personnel had all but vanished by desertion and expiring enlistments. When she reached New Orleans, she was not seaworthy and had but nine men before the mast.

She brought fresh orders from Secretary of War and Marine Hockley. The administration was still eager for the fleet to get to sea and enforce the blockade. The *Wharton* was to be among those to sail with the first contingent and had to be fitted out and manned accordingly. The orders brought by Lothrop insisted that Moore should get the *Austin*, *Wharton*, *San Antonio* and *San Bernard* to sea with the "utmost possible dispatch."[3]

Ordinarily such reinforcements should have been welcome, but to the impatient Moore and his depleted resources, the arrival of the *Wharton* was like that of a white elephant. In desperation, the Commodore sent his brother to Houston for at least ten thousand dollars in Exchequer notes, in fulfillment of the promise of which had been made by the administration earlier. The younger Moore was absent at least two weeks of June and finally returned empty handed.

He reported that President Houston had announced a special session of the Sixth Congress. Because he had pledged himself in the press that he would issue no more of the sagging Exchequer notes until this special session had endorsed his policies, the President had expressed an unwillingness to make any such release to the fleet. The President did send, however, a to-whom-it-may-concern document telling the world, in essence, that some of these days Commodore Moore would have ten thousand dollars worth of nice new Exchequer bills with which to pay off naval obligations of the State.[4]

This document was but little more than a repetition of the power of attorney that Moore had already found useless in New Orleans. The Texan Exchequer bills were, at best, no more than promises to pay, and the document furnished Moore was nothing more than a promise of a promise and was therefore hardly acceptable to the close-fisted ship chandlers along the levee. Nor would banks advance against such a document funds with which Moore could recruit personnel. Moore's purchsing power continued in abeyance, and discontent again became rife in the squadron.

It was hoped that the return of the *San Antonio* from Yucatan would alleviate the situation. This tone of optimism had hardly been sounded through the fleet when, July 1, the little warship dropped anchor in the stream. Unfortunately Lieutenant Seeger brought only the cash for the four thousand dollars worth of drafts. Again Moore's heart sank within him.

Lieutenant Seeger did report, however, that the Centralists had really repudiated the Quintana Roo agreement with Yucatan exactly two weeks after the departure of the Texan fleet the previous April. Santa Anna had thus far, however, launched no offensive against Yucatan. Thus the *Peninsulares* hoped that a new agreement might be substituted for the unacceptable Quintana Roo document. In the absence of such a mutually acceptable treaty, Seeger was confident that the Yucatecans would ultimately desire a renewal of the naval alliance with Texas.[5] In the meantime these remote possibilities would not recondition, man, and provision the fleet for the execution of the blockade, for which the Houston administration was clamoring but putting up no money.

Moore decided that he had better make a trip to Texas himself. The summer of 1842, special session of the Sixth Congress was then sitting in the temporary capital at Houston. He hoped that he could do some profitable lobbying for the naval establishment.

Moore met with what appeared at first to be phenomenal success. He reminded the administration and the Senate that he and his officers were still without commissions, but were operating under Lamar's recess appointments of 1839. The Senate confirmed, and the navy department issued, the desired commissions. The Congressmen were, furthermore, liberal with appropriations. They were in a fine frame of mind to appropriate anything that would further a campaign against Mexico. For reconditioning the *Zavala*, still leaky and aground in Galveston Bay, $15,000 was voted; $25,000 for provisioning all ships; $28,231 for the back pay of officers and men; and $29,428.50 for future payrolls—a total of $97,659.50.[6]

This legislation appears a little extravagant compared to the meager twenty thousand dollars that had been voted by the regular session of the same Congress a few months before. In reality, it was downright parsimonious compared to the orgy of appropriating that the same Special Session made for the army. In fact, the military appropriations were so extravagant that Houston brought down upon his head the wrath of the Republic by vetoing it. The populace was still getting disconcerting rumors about mobilized Mexican troops on the Rio Grande, and occasional forays were being felt. Thus the constituents and their representatives felt that Houston should launch a military as well as a naval offensive.

Houston's veto of the army bill withdrew prospective employment from the thousands of adventurers who had rushed to Texas after the capture of San Antonio by Santa Anna's Vasquez the previous March. This vociferous flotsam of the frontier now began flowing back through New Orleans, where Texas and Texan policies were denounced. Naval recruiting fell to nothing, and desertions increased.

By this time Moore had been away from his ships for nearly a month, had seen Congress appropriate the funds that he advocated, and he was now eager to return to New Orleans with the money for the execution of his orders. Thus, on the afternoon that the special session adjourned, he paid the President a visit. Houston told him that he had just signed the appropriation bill "and expressed his gratification in consequence thereof."[7] He then wanted to know when Moore would return to New Orleans and put to sea. Moore explained that it would be useless for him to return to the fleet without a part of the funds recently appropriated. Houston, in harmony with his continued program of keeping the Texan Exchequer bills out of circulation at all costs, said that he would give Moore another to-whom-it-may-concern power of attorney signed by himself. It was the same sort of worthless document that Moore had carried to New Orleans with the fleet, and with which his brother had returned a month before.

This action convinced Moore, whose suspicions had been aroused during the Special Session, that Houston did not intend to execute the naval appropriation act of Congress. Though Houston had signed it, the Commodore reasoned, it was because the President had not the courage to face the public odium that would follow his veto and the resulting disbanding of the fleet in a foreign port. It thus appeared to the sailor as if Houston were trying to manipulate affairs so that abandonment of the squadron would apparently be a result of his own inability to carry out the President's program.

In fairness to Moore's reasoning, during this period President Houston was becoming widely known as the "Tallyrand of the Brazos."[8] Nor can it be said, in the light of Houston's political and diplomatic vagaries throughout his second administration, that the term was a misnomer.

On the other hand perhaps Houston can be excused for dealing with Moore in what was certainly a circuitous if not underhanded manner. Had not Houston's first administration been embarrassed by the insubordination of the Navy Department? Commodore Moore was no doubt viewed as the official child of the President's greatest political enemy, Mirabeau B. Lamar. Furthermore, the Commodore's indifference to the recall orders earlier in the current administration could not have inspired the President with much confidence in Moore's willingness to coöperate with him. Thus the stage was set for the clash of two rugged frontier personalities.

When Moore decided that the President had no intention whatsoever of releasing any funds, he saw red. He turned on his Tallyrandian Chief and told him that "He need not try to humbug me . . . for I would not be humbugged by him." Unless he was given enough money at once to get to sea or maintain the fleet, Moore declared he would return to New Orleans, "disband the navy and leave the vessels to rot in a foreign port, as officers and men could not be kept aboard without rations."[9]

Moore had the President in an embarrassing position. Already the victim of public abuse for having denied the public its demand for a big army, the added odium for an abandoned navy might be more than the administration could stand.[10] At the same time Houston was not in the habit of being told by subordinates that they could not be humbugged by him.

If President Houston violently resented this implied slur upon his ability in the arts of humbuggery, he did not reveal it to Moore. Instead, he kept his poise, and from the events that followed, evidently accepted Moore's refusal to be humbugged as a challenge rather than an insult. He calmed the turbulent Commodore by assuring him that funds would be given him immediately.

The next day, July 30, the naval officer received $18,812 of Exchequer bills. They represented the unexpended portion of the twenty-thousand-dollar appropriation by the regular session of the Sixth Congress. The inference was that the administration would permit him to exhaust the regular appropriation before starting in with the additional funds voted by the recently adjourned Special Session of the same Congress. Houston felt that this was enough money to get the troublesome Moore quietly on his way.

At the same time the "Tallyrand of the Brazos" did not intend that even these limited funds should be put into circulation. Thus when the Exchequer bills were handed to Moore, he was also handed a packet of "sealed orders" to be opened as soon as he had reached New Orleans, but before he had spent any of the money.

"Sealed orders" to be opened by a fleet commander on the high seas is no novelty in naval history, but similarly sealed documents to be opened by a commander at a none too distant drydock is rather unusual. But there was method in Houston's unconventional use of sealing wax. Had Moore known the contents of the sealed orders, he probably would have stayed in Texas and renewed his threat to demobilize the fleet.

The sealed instructions had nothing to do with putting to sea. They merely told the Commodore that he could not spend the Exchequer bills that had been handed to him. He was to permit them to get into the hands only of such merchants, ship chandlers, and such other individuals as were willing to extend credit for an indefinite length of time and who were willing to *hold* a corresponding value of the Exchequer bills as collateral.

Such instructions naturally would limit the use of such bills to larger dealers who could afford to extend indefinite credit to an unstable republic.

Even these dealers would naturally discount such bills to at least one half of their purchase value. To be specific, the Exchequer bills were then worth only fifty cents on the dollar at best. If the merchant received them and agreed to hold them as collateral until the dim distant future when the republic might retire them, he would naturally further discount them to about twenty-five cents on the dollar. At least that was Moore's eventual experience with the Exchequer bills in question. When the Commodore opened and read these instructions in New Orleans, early in August, he probably suspected that he had been at least partially humbugged. Nevertheless, his enthusiasm for getting to sea to press the blockade as he had been ordered combined with the teasing amount of the limited purchasing power were sufficient to keep him in New Orleans with the fleet. At the same time his new purchasing power was not enough to get the fleet to sea.

Houston's motive in publicly joining in the clamor for decisive action against Mexico and at the same time ham-stringing the most effective and economical way of striking Mexico is hard to explain. In fact, most of the conflicting vagaries of his second administration are so many enigmas. The best explanation, however, seems to be Houston's inability, or refusal, to realize that a war costs money. His theory on how wars should be financed is reflected by a letter, during the same period, that he wrote to Mr. M. E. Holliday who wanted to recruit a company of men in the United States and bring them to Texas to help in the chastising of Mexico for her recent reinvasion of Texas. "If you raise your company," Houston wrote, "it must consist of at least fifty-six men, rank and file, completely armed, clothed, and provisioned for six months . . . the *remuneration* for your *expenses* and *services must come from the enemy*.[11]

Houston had lived with the Indians too long. All such people needed for warfare were the simple weapons of the chase, and let the warriors look to the plunder of their enemies for their remuneration. Very likely Houston thought that if he were close fisted long enough with Moore, the Commodore would figure out a way of applying those simple principles to the execution of a naval blockade.

Through the next several months the Commodore was in comparatively close contact with his Department. His reports carried little of his erstwhile optimism. He complained that the recent repairs to the *Austin* had been so scanty that she was beginning to take water at the rate of seventy-three inches a day. The money market was bad, particularly under the hampering restrictions of the sealed orders. In accordance with instructions, he had succeeded in buying the passenger steamer *Merchant* to take the place of the *Zavala*, which a recent examination showed had been neglected until she was now beyond repair. The *Merchant*, however, had been bought on Moore's and another Texan's personal credit and not with the Exchequer bills. From that day, to all practical purposes, the *Zavala* ceased to be on the Texan naval list.

When the Governor of Louisiana would not surrender the *San Antonio* mutineers without a specific letter from and bearing the signature of President Houston, Moore wrote for the request and, of course, for more money. Houston sent the extradition note for the mutineers, dated September 26, 1842, but not any money.

The accompanying dispatches instructed Moore to create a court martial when he saw fit. The blockade had been temporarily suspended, nominally because of Texan inability to get a fleet to sea, but "His Excellency desires that you should spare no exertions to prepare the squadron . . . as it is desirable that it should sail before the gales set in . . . when you will proceed to sea without further orders; and on discharging the pilot . . . you will open your sealed orders, which are herewith transmitted."[12]

About the same time Moore was further depressed by news

from the *San Bernard* at Galveston. Early in September, Lieutenant Crisp had reported her badly worm eaten. Moore had ordered the schooner to New Orleans but the administration would not give Crisp money enough to lay in the essential supplies to make even so short a run as that. Two or three weeks later the *San Bernard* was driven ashore by a gale. Five hundred dollars would have gotten her off and to New Orleans for a drydocking. The administration continued the non-release of funds, and to all practical purposes she, like the *Zavala,* became a deserted, rotting hulk in the Galveston Harbor.[13]

By October 1, 1842, Moore had become greatly concerned about the fate of the other war schooner, the *San Antonio.* Shortly after Moore had discovered the restrictions Houston had placed upon the Exchequer bills given him July 30, and perhaps had fully sensed Houston's Indian theories on war finance, he had sent Lieutenant Seeger and the *San Antonio* on another voyage to Yucatan, by way of Galveston and Matagorda, to communicate with the Yucatecan Federalists who were recently reported to be hard pressed by the Santa Anna's army and navy. The Lieutenant was to see whether the Federalists would not advance him sufficient funds to get the Texas fleet to sea against the common foe.

Two months had now passed and no news had come from the little cruiser. In spite of the series of heavy gales that had swept the Gulf during September and October, Moore continued to wish for the best. Finally in November, word reached Moore that the *San Antonio* had never reached Campeche. Not until then did he give up hope.

The loss of the *San Antonio* was serious in more ways than one. Moore's principal witnesses against the mutineers in the *Austin's* brig went down with the schooner. Worse yet, her failure to reach the Yucatecans had long delayed certain financial assistance. The hard pressed *Peninsulares* were then so eager for Texan aid that they would have paid well for the fleet's services.

Although the Yucatecans had felt quite confident as to their future in the preceding June when Lieutenant Seeger had called on them, the fortunes of politics and war had turned distinctly against them. Not only had Santa Anna refused to reconsider a substitute for the Quintana Roo treaty but he also assumed the offensive much more quickly than the Yucatecans had anticipated. Within six weeks after Moore withdrew from Yucatan the previous April 15, the armed steamer Moore had repeatedly seen at Vera Cruz, reinforced with two other naval acquisitions took the offensive. In an engagement on July 5, the *Peninsulares* lost their best brig, the *Yucateco*, to the Centralist squadron.[14]

This engagement paved the way for Centralist naval supremacy so that a joint military and naval force under General Morales was soon attacking the Yucatecan naval base on the Island of Carmen, near Laguna. The naval base and the three remaining Yucatecan ships fell into the hands of Santa Anna's fleet in August.[15]

Thus far the Centralists' naval supremacy in their operations against the Yucatecans was not so powerful but that it could have been readily brushed aside by Moore's squadron had Houston executed the will of his Congress by releasing the funds necessary for sending it to sea. Such was not to be the case for long.

Only a few months after the ransoming of Tobasco by Moore's fleet on his first cruise, the keels of two powerful Mexican warships had been laid down in two of England's most famous and successful shipyards. Thus while Houston's policies were leaving some of the best Texan ships, such as the *Zavala*, *Archer*, and *San Bernard* rotting on the mud flats of Galveston Harbor, the Mexican navy was being augmented by two of the latest products known to the art of naval architecture.

The *Guadaloupe* was being built in the yards of John Laird. Twenty years later these same shipyards became famous as the producers of cruisers and ironclads for the Southern Confederacy. It is thus interesting to know that the *Guadaloupe* was of iron and therefore was probably the first man-of-war of that material to see service in the western hemisphere. She displaced 775 tons. Designed to operate in shoal waters, she drew but ten feet. She was dependent entirely upon steam. Her battery was as modern as her construction and means of locomotion. It consisted of two long 68-pounders and four 12's.

The other steamer, the *Moctezuma*, was being built in the yards of the Greens and Wigrams. She was a heavy timbered wooden vessel constructed along what were then ultra-modern lines. She displaced 1111 tons and mounted one 68-pounder, two long 32's, four 32-pounder cannonades and a small 9-pounder.[16]

With such heavy guns, and under able management, these two steamers alone were (on paper) far more than a match for the Texan fleet which did not mount a gun heavier than several long 24's.

By April, 1842, the construction of these ships was well advanced. Then it was that their character and ownership became known to Texan Minister Ashbel Smith, in London. They were to sail with guns mounted, and manned by exceptionally large English crews. The *Moctezuma* was to be captained by Commander Cleaveland, R.N., and the *Guadaloupe* by Commander Charlewood, R.N. Confirmed rumors had it that these officers had been granted long leaves of absence to enable them to enter, temporarily, the Mexican service.

In trying to keep the ships from sailing, Minister Smith anticipated every step in logic and every principle of international law that was later invoked by American Minister Charles Francis Adams in trying to keep English built and manned Confederate cruisers from putting to sea. It might also be added that the Mexican briefs to the English Foreign Office supporting the release of the ships anticipated every phase of the subsequent Confederate interpretations of international law and England's own neutrality act.

Ashbel Smith essentially achieved no more and no less than did Charles Francis Adams in his similar rôle twenty years later. The Mexicans were occasioned some delay. The two Royal Navy commanders and their subordinates were ostentatiously and officiously warned that if they entered the Mexican service they would have to terminate their relations with the British Navy. Whether or not they resigned from Her Majesty's service is not revealed in the diplomatic records, but the essential fact remains that they entered the Mexican service. The size of the English crews was supposedly cut down to merchant ship equivalents, and the ships were not permitted to mount their guns in a British port.

Because of this last point a daring Englishman, sympathetic to the Texan cause, sought a privateer's commission from Texan Minister Ashbel Smith. He hoped to capture, by boarding, one or both of the unarmed Mexican ships before they were hardly clear of the Channel. The prizes would then be carried to Texas and adjudicated in Texan courts to be later added to the Texan fleet.[17]

In the interest of a good sea tale, one almost wishes that Ashbel Smith had felt himself authorized to issue the adventurers a letter of marque. On the other hand, had the Texan squadron been off Vera Cruz in October and November, 1842 (in accordance with Houston's alleged desires for an effective blockade) the unarmed *Moctezuma* and *Guadaloupe* could have been intercepted, or cut out, almost as easily as any unarmed craft. As it was, the ships were duly armed and before Christmas, 1842, had joined the Centralists' fleet operating from the captured Yucatecan base on Carmen Island.

Thus augmented, the Centralists' squadron consisted of the steam men-of-war *Guadaloupe*, and *Moctezuma*, the gun brigs *Yucateco* and *Iman*, the war schooners *Aguila* and *Campechano*, and a well armed merchant steamer, the *Regenerador*. With the fleet were a number of supply and troop ships.

Two Centralist armies were being supported in the peninsula by this squadron. One army under General Barragan had been landed at Telchac and was making a drive on nearby Merida. A still larger force under Ampudia was besieging Campeche.

Notwithstanding the draining of this Yucatecan offensive upon his military and naval resources, Santa Anna was able to launch another raid under General Woll against San Antonio. Thus, in September that city again fell into the hands of the Mexicans. The Texan district court was then in session and Judge James W. Robinson, the lawyers, and the court attachés were carried back to Mexico by the retiring army. This raid, the recent successes off Yucatan by the Centralists' fleet, and the alleged successes of Barragan and Ampudia in Yucatan kept the Texan coastal towns in a state of constant alarm.

And well they might be. Had not Santa Anna definitely announced that his first policy was to crush Yucatan and use its maritime resources to maintain the same victorious army on a campaign of conquest in Texas? Thus in Galveston all through the winter of 1842–43, an English visitor reported that the militia was constantly being drilled, and the artillery in the protecting fort kept burnished.[18]

As a result of the second capture of San Antonio within the same year, the populace throughout the state again clamored for a military offensive. Again invoking his Indian ideas of military economy, Houston quieted their clamor by permitting an unpaid, unequipped, abortive expedition of twelve hundred men to march to the Rio Grande. They quarreled. Nine hundred marched home, and three hundred crossed the Rio Grande only to be captured by overwhelming Mexican forces.

While all these stirring events were taking place, Commodore Moore was still experiencing frustrations in New Orleans. As often as he wrote for money, he got an answer urging that he get to sea immediately, but enclosing no money. As the season wore on, letters from the administration did suggest that if he could not get to sea for a cruise against Mexico on the resources furnished, it might be a good idea for him to return to Galveston. Such suggestions were discretionary, however, and at no time, as Houston later claimed, was the squadron ordered back to Galveston.

Had one of his original three war schooners still been afloat, the Commodore would have no doubt made another effort to contact the hard pressed Yucatecans. Instead he continued to do what he could on his own credit and that of friendly Texans.

Longingly he looked forward to December, 1842, at which time the Seventh Congress would be in session. He had hopes that this Congress would force the economizing President to release some of the funds appropriated by the Special Session of the Sixth Congress. Nevertheless January, 1843, was now at hand, and there was no evidence of an administrative response to any such pressure.

Indeed, there was no such pressure. The abortive expedition to the Rio Grande had silenced the Texan jingoists and enabled Houston to capture the leadership of the Seventh Congress in military and naval affairs. His ostentatious dabbling in diplomacy inspired confidence. The warm public friendship that had sprung up between him and the British *Chargé d'Affaires*, Captain Charles Elliot, R.N., was enabling Houston to say, with convincing emphasis, that he was making excellent progress in diplomacy and that a naval blockade would cool the valuable British friendship.

In short, Houston had convinced the Seventh Congress that if he were fully supported in his policies he could, without expeditions into Mexico or without ships on the seas, see Texas through to a satisfactory destiny by means of inexpensive diplomacy. Thus, Moore in New Orleans, notwithstanding continued reports of Centralists' success in Yucatan and apprehensive alarms on the Texan coast, was to wait in vain for the funds that he had hoped congressional pressure would force Houston to release. At the same time, the Commodore knew nothing of Houston's shift to naval pacifism under the benign influence of Captain Elliot, R.N. His orders to blockade Mexico had never been rescinded.

When a month's session of the Seventh Congress revealed no change in the close-fistedness of the Texan treasury, Moore, with the financial aid of a friend, chartered the tiny, fast

schooner *Two Sons* and sent her January 17, 1843, with offers
to the Yucatecans. Moore asked for an immediate grant of
twenty thousand dollars and eight thousand dollars a month.
In return he offered to force the withdrawal of the two Centralist armies by driving off the fleet that supported them.

The voyage of the *Two Sons* got a quick response. Colonel
Martin Peraza, who had closed the previous alliance with
Lamar, quickly arrived in New Orleans with $7213.00 in hard
money. Under date of February 11, 1843, he and Moore closed
a treaty-like contract very similar to the document Peraza had
previously signed with Lamar.[19] The Commodore was elated.
Provisioning and recruiting went forward rapidly under the
stimulus of even this small amount of *hard* cash. On February
24, 1843, Commodore Moore was writing Governor Barbachano
of Yucatan that he would be at sea within a week.

But the day after he wrote that optimistic note, there arrived
in New Orleans Colonel James Morgan and Mr. William Bryan.
They introduced themselves as being two of three naval commissioners who had been voted plenary power in a secret act
of the Seventh Congress to do with the navy whatsoever they
saw fit. A two-to-one decision was to settle every question of
policy they might consider. In the absence of a member, one
of the remaining two might act alone, provided he were unop-
posed by his colleague.[20] As it actually happened, the third commissioner, S. M. Williams, who as naval agent had drawn the
contract under which the fleet had been built, refused to serve.
Thus, Morgan and Bryan were left to act in harmony, with the
former playing the more aggressive rôle.

Moore was not aware of the fact nor did either commissioner
take him immediately into his confidence in the matter, but the
same Houston sponsored congressional act that had created
the commission had also secretly provided for the sale of the
squadron at whatever figure it would bring. Moore was told
that there was a secret act, but that was all. When he later
learned the truth, he charged that Houston had procured its
passage only by telling Congress that both the previous regular

appropriation of twenty thousand dollars and that of the regular session of $97,659.00 had been expended and that the fleet still was not seaworthy.

Irrespective of this charge, it is true that the two commissioners lost a great deal of their enthusiasm for selling the navy after they came in contact with Moore. Instead of summarily relieving him of his command, as the administration had anticipated they would, Morgan and Bryan left Moore in charge. They furthermore temporized with him when he showed a strong inclination to put to sea in accordance with his agreement with the hard pressed Yucatecans.

In view of this turn of affairs the commissioners wrote a full report to Secretary of War and Navy G. W. Hill and awaited developments. The desired additional instructions dated April 4, 1843, came in the form of orders to be transmitted to Moore at once. The Commodore was to be informed that he was suspended from all command and ordered, in arrest, to report to the Department in person. Moreover all outstanding orders sealed and otherwise were revoked, with italics. In case Moore continued to be cantankerous and sailed anyway, or had already sailed, the commissioners were armed with the discretionary use of a proclamation dated March 23, 1843.

This was probably the strangest document ever dictated or penned by an American executive. It declared that Moore and all his men were pirates, and invited the nations of the world to seize "the said Post Captain E. W. Moore, the ship *Austin* and the brig *Wharton* with their crews and bring them, or any of them, into the port of Galveston, that the vessels may be secured to the Republic and the culprit or culprits arraigned and punished by sentence of a legal tribunal. The Naval Powers of Christendom will not permit such a flagrant and unexampled outrage. . . . "[21] Of course the commissioners were not to publish this document unless it were necessary to bring Moore to heel.

When Colonel Morgan gave Moore his orders to report back to Texas, "in arrest," the Commodore suspected that the plenary power of the commissioners enabled them to leave him in command should they see fit. Moreover the Commodore had a trump card no one had suspected. "If I obey this order," he told Colonel Morgan, "and leave the vessels in the port of New Orleans; every officer under me will resign; the vessels will be left at the mercy of the sailors, who will be sure to mutiny and destroy them; which they threatened to do once before when I could not pay them off."[22]

Morgan was impressed. Well he might have been, for Moore was speaking in all sincerity and for the good of the service. At last he abandoned once and for all his hopes of sailing to Yucatan. He promised that if left in command, he would sail the ships to Galveston where their chances at being saved, upon demobilization of the personnel, would be greater than in New Orleans. Colonel Morgan, the more dominant of the two commissioners, accepted this promise and expressed the opinion that the sooner they started for Galveston the better. Furthermore, he would (to save the government the expense) go along as a passenger. The Colonel wanted to keep the Commodore under his eye. After getting Bryan's approval and agreeing that all these arrangements should be put in writing to make everything regular and shipshape, Moore went about getting his ships under way.

Behind a steam tug they stood for the mouth of the river, April 15, 1843, so that they were off Balize before dawn of the 17th. Fog delayed them through the 18th. On the evening of that day, the schooner *Rosario* three and one half days from Campeche, anchored nearby to await the lifting of the fog.

She brought dire tidings. The Yucatecans and Santa Anna were about to settle their difficulties. Centralist General Ampudia had stopped bombarding Campeche and was in daily conference with the Federalists. General Barragan's army was again on the coast at Telchac. His troops were being withdrawn under the protection of the new steam-frigate *Moctezuma* which was to escort them to Campeche. Of course Barragan's army was not needed at Campeche for peace negotiations were already under way at that point. The concentration was prepara-tory to an invasion of Texas by way of Galveston, just as soon as the peace pipe had been smoked by the *Peninsulares*.

Already Ampudia was urging the Yucatecans to join him against the traitorous Texans. Had not Commodore Moore falsely taken money from and signed the treaty with Colonel Martin Peraza the preceding February and failed to put in his appearance? Even worse, the *Rosario* reported that high Yuca-tecan officials attributed Moore's long absence to a Centralist bribe. Colonel Morgan, as well as Moore, considered the situa-tion really alarming.

Furthermore the reports were correct. With peace in Yuca-tan, naval supremacy in the hands of Santa Anna and six thou-sand Centralist troops about to be launched against Galveston there was something to worry about. Such a movement, made jointly with another offensive against San Antonio would put the Lone Star Republic in a more critical position than it was in when San Jacinto was fought.

If anything, Colonel Morgan was even more alarmed than was the Commodore Moore. He decided that the situation was sufficiently grave to warrant his assuming to the fullest the wide discretionary powers given to the naval commissioners in the secret act of the Seventh Congress. He resolved "to save the Republic, if I could."[23]

His formula—no doubt worked out by Moore—was Nelsonic in concept if not in scope. A quick run to Telchac would enable the *Austin* and *Wharton* to engage and vanquish the powerful *Moctezuma* and smaller craft that were to convey Barragan's army to Campeche. The Texan ships would then hasten to Campeche and in conjunction with a small improvised Yucate-can fleet blockaded in that port, attack and vanquish the main Centralist squadron off Campeche. With Santa Anna's war fleet thus whipped in detail, no reinforcements or supplies could be sent to Barragan or Ampudia. Their armies could not even be united. Hence they in turn could be defeated in detail by the reorganized Yucatecan land forces.

Any modern naval or war college faculty would have declared the plan perfect, subject to the conventional provisos that the enemy be encountered at the anticipated points—Telchac and Campeche—and in conveniently weakened detachments.

CHAPTER TWELVE

NAVAL BATTLES OFF CAM-
PECHE • On to Yucatan • Mutineers
Punished • Combat • Last Anchorage

WHEN MOORE cleared the mouth of the Mississippi, April 19, 1843, and steered for Yucatan, he had an inkling as to what card Houston would play when he heard the news. Colonel Morgan had showed him the unpublished proclamation declaring him a pirate. Now that the most aggressive commissioner, Morgan, had been converted to his views and confidences, Moore naturally assumed that Houston would publish the proclamation himself. To prepare the Texan public for such probable action by Houston, Moore sent, by a passing ship, an open letter to the editor of the Texas *Times:*

In the event of my being declared by proclamation by the President as a pirate, or outlaw; you will please state over my signature that I go down to attack the Mexican squadron, with the *consent* and full *concurrence* of Col. James Morgan . . . who is going with me, believing as he does that it is the best thing that can be done for the country.

This ship and brig have excellent men on board and the officers and men . . . are all eager for the contest. We go to make *one desperate struggle* to turn the tide of ill luck.[1]

But while en route to make the desperate effort, Moore chose to dispose of the *San Antonio* mutineers, who had been in confinement aboard the *Austin* since their delivery to Moore by the Lousiana authorities some weeks before. Of course he had had ample time to try them before his departure, but mutineers

181

dangling from the yardarms of his flagship while in the stream at New Orleans would have completely killed his painfully difficult recruiting program. No, it would be better to do it at sea, where there were no territorial complications and where a commodore was master of his domain.

The sinking of the *San Antonio* the preceding fall with all on board had weakened the case against the accused to a great degree. The prosecution's key witnesses, Lieutenants Seeger and Dearborn with Midshipmen Odell and Alden, were no longer available. The officer detailed as judge advocate for the court, which really began its deliberations before the ships were clear of the river mouth, managed to break down the resistance of one Frederick Shepherd who agreed to turn "state's evidence."

This made the trail short and gruesome. From Shepherd it was learned that the mutiny had almost broken out while the *San Antonio* was cruising with the *San Bernard* off Yucatan during January, 1842; that mutineers from the two craft were to have seized the *San Antonio* and sold her to the Mexicans, and that the actual outbreak in New Orleans was but the sudden fruition of a half planned conspiracy.[2]

The confession of Shepherd saved his life, but it brought to F. Williams fifty lashes with cat-o'-nine-tails and one hundred each for W. Barrington and E. Kenan. But they were lucky. Private Antonio Landois and Corporal Simpson, of the marine guard, along with seamen J. Hudgins and I. Allen were given death penalties.

April 26 the flagship hove to for the brief ceremony of hanging the culprits from the yardarms until dead. As fate would have it, Seymour Oswald, the marine sergeant who had precipitated the mutiny by his unexpected attack upon Lieutenant Fuller, had escaped from the New Orleans jail just before the delivery of the prisoners to Moore, and thereby evaded justice altogether. Shepherd, who had bought immunity with a confession, was killed three weeks later by a shell from the *Guadaloupe* or *Moctezuma*.

With this object lesson as to the strength and majesty of

Texan martial law in the memories of the *Austin's* 146 men and the *Wharton's* 86, Moore pressed on to Telchac to intercept the *Moctezuma*. But the light and variable airs that delayed the Texan fleet's arrival off that little port until April 27, had given the *Moctezuma* time to rejoin the remainder of the squadron off Campeche.

The next day Moore was off to Sisal where he communicated with his Yucatecan friends. He learned, to his chagrin, that he had missed the detached Mexican ships, including the *Moctezuma*, only twenty-four hours. But the warmth with which Governor Barbachano received him and the rapidity with which he broke off armistice negotiations with Santa Anna's Ampudia, who was closely besieging Campeche, was gratifying.

Down the coast Moore sailed at once to the vicinity of Campeche. Dawn of April 30 revealed the powerful steam frigates *Moctezuma* and *Guadeloupe* in company with the brigs *Yucateco* and *Iman*, and the schooners *Aguila* and *Campechano*—the entire Centralist fleet, less the armed steamer *Regenerador*.

Though the Texan Commodore as a naval officer is open to criticism, in the light of his own correspondence, for playing the orders from one date or source against orders of another date or source and ending by obeying, with frequent indifference to consistency, those that pleased him most, it cannot be said that he faltered in the presence of the enemy. Some officers would have hesitated. The *Austin's* two 18's, sixteen medium 24's, and two medium 18's supplemented by the *Wharton's* one long 9 and fifteen medium 18's were opposed by three long Paixhan 68's, two long Paixhan 32's, four long 12's and one long 9, all mounted on the most modern of steam frigates designed for operating among the shoals and lagoons of the Mexican coast. The batteries of these steamers were supplemented by one long 32 and six 18's aboard the heavy war schooner *Aguila*; one long 18 and sixteen short 18's aboard the brig *Yucateca*; a 12 and eight 6's aboard the brigs *Iman* and *Campechano*.

Making some allowance for the fact that Texan figures have

been followed as to the armament of the sail ships in the Centralist fleet, Moore, with his ships manned by almost exactly half their full war strength, would have been justified in approaching the blockaders with extreme caution and trepidation, if not waiting for another night when a union with the Yucatecan schooners at Campeche might have been made under cover of darkness.

But not Moore. Too long had he already waited for a sight of the enemy. By 6:30 A.M., he had maneuvered sufficiently to pick up the sea breeze that was setting in. By seven he was almost within gunshot and at once converted the impending battle into a joust of Nordic versus Latin by hoisting, in addition to the Texan ensign at the mizzen, the United States and English ensigns on the foremast. The main truck was reserved for his own broad pennant. With this effusion of color, the crews broke into three cheers.[3] Apparently the Englishmen serving under Commanders Charlewood and Cleaveland, respectively of the *Guadaloupe* and *Moctezuma*, soon decided that it was a game two could play. They added Spanish and English colors to the already displayed Mexican ensigns.[4]

The affair soon degenerated, however, into a running brush, for the Mexican fleet stood southward, with the steam frigates covering the retreat of the sail squadron. Thus frequent broadsides were exchanged with the steamers from 7:50 to 8:20 when they steamed southward in the wake of the Centralist sail contingent. Firing ceased at 8:26 A.M., shortly after which the Texans were joined by the Yucatecan schooners *Sisaleno* and *Independencia* which, with five other tiny craft in company, mounted two long 12's, five long 9's, and one long 6. This little Yucatecan flotilla, which had been seen approaching since 7:10, may have stimulated the Mexican withdrawal. It was commanded by none other than Commodore J. D. Boylan, who had sought a commission from Lamar when the new fleet had been bought and who had commanded the Texan War schooner *Brutus* during Commodore Thompson's cruise of 1837.

When the combined flotillas had come to anchor seven miles

THE TEXAN FLAGSHIP *AUSTIN*

Built 1839; crew, 300; armament, 18 medium 24-pounders, 2 medium 18's; displacement, 600 tons.
From a contemporary incomplete drawing by Midshipman Edward Johns, T.N. (Courtesy of University of Texas, Austin)

northwest of Campeche, because of the dying breeze, and Commodore Moore had piped all hands to grog, the enemy steam frigates were seen bearing down. The Texans again beat to quarters. With the larboard springs on the anchor chains, Moore was able to present his starboard batteries in spite of the flat calm.

At the same moment a northwest breeze sprang up, the anchors were slipped and all moved off on the starboard tack toward Campeche. The steamers drew in closer and several broadsides were again exchanged. One 68-pound shot took effect upon the after shroud of the mizzen rigging about eight feet above the dead eye, narrowly missing Commodore Moore and Lieutenant Gray. It was the only projectile to strike the *Austin*. The *Wharton* received a shot abaft the fore chains, starboard side, which caused the only Texan casualties—two killed, four wounded.[5]

By 11:45 A.M. the squadrons had separated to a distance at which the firing was ineffective, and the Yucatecan-Texan fleet continued to Campeche. The *Guadeloupe* and *Moctezuma* threw a parting shot or two and again retired to the southwestward. Colonel Morgan reported a few days after the battle that the Mexican loss had been some twenty killed, including Commander Cleaveland, of the *Moctezuma*. Furthermore "we have driven their fleet from Lerma, raised the blockade of Campeche, placed General Ampudia and his besieging army in a very perilous situation inasmuch as he cannot now communicate with his fleet."[6]

At Campeche, Colonel Morgan went ashore to assume a diplomatic rôle while Boylan and Moore perfected signals and made plans for a decisive naval victory.

The effects of this initial brush upon the attitude of Yucatan were instantaneous. Señor Mendez, who had been negotiating the proposed armistice with Ampudia, was given ground on which to reopen hostilities. It seems that Ampudia had agreed to let the temporary cessation of hostilities for negotiations extend to the Texans also when it was learned from overland that Moore was on the coast. The firing of the first shot by the Mexican squadron in an effort to prevent a juncture of the Texans and Yucatecans was a breach of faith, hence Mendez declared the negotiations at an end, and the land fighting was resumed. That Moore had added materially to the troubles of Santa Anna and the corresponding safety of Texas there can be no doubt. This alone was enough to justify the cruise.

Meanwhile Commodores Moore and Boylan took steps to engage the Mexican fleet in a decisive action. For several days after the initial brush, the two commodores sallied forth and showed their teeth, but the Mexicans on each occasion declined an action. Within a few days the Mexicans were reinforced by the armed merchant steamer *Regenerador*, one long 32 and two long 9's, after which it was Moore who seemed to have been inactive. But shortly the *Regenerador*, with all the sail contingent, except the *Aguila*, stood for Telchac to finish the troop movement that the *Moctezuma* had left uncompleted. This division of the enemy and a favorable wind gave Moore his chance to fall upon the two steam frigates and heavily armed *Aguila*.[7]

At 5:20 A.M., May 16, the *Austin* and *Wharton*, followed by the Yucatecan flotilla, stood to sea to engage the enemy. By 6:20 the enemy were about five miles away and bearing West Southwest, but upon the approach of Texans they headed off shore. But Moore's ships must have been faster than the *Aguila* in the prevailing airs of that day, and the steam frigates were naturally reluctant to leave her, for by 10:40 A.M. Moore was close enough that an action was obviously at hand.

He hoisted the same ensigns that he flew in the previous engagement. The *Moctezuma* then broke out a Mexican ensign and trumped Moore's display of the English and American flags at his fore with English and Spanish flags at his main and fore masts respectively. The *Guadaloupe* considered her color scheme complete without the Spanish ensign, but a vacant halyard was found for the crosses of merry England.

By 11:30 A.M. the Yucatecan contingent was well out of the incipient action in that they were two and a half miles astern, but already the long guns of both Texans and Mexicans were beginning to speak. The projectiles from the medium 24's and 18's of the Texans continued to fall short until 11:40. However, the *Austin* was beginning to take punishment from the enemy long guns.

First and last in the fourteen-mile running fight to South-westward with the Texans pursuing, the *Austin* felt the effects of seventeen hits on hull and rigging. Most of them were 68-pound projectiles from the *Guadaloupe*, though the *Aguila* and *Moctezuma* each registered two or three hits. Thus by 3:00 P.M., the *Austin's* rigging had suffered so badly that when the wind freshened at that hour, Moore had to wear the ship and present his larboard batteries to relieve the strain on his rigging. On this course he was unable to close for a continued action.

Naturally Moore did not permit Commander Lothrop's un-injured *Wharton* to pursue the three hostile ships alone, hence both vessels withdrew to Campeche. At no time had the Yuca-tecans participated in the action and but seldom were any Texan weapons other than the long guns effective, though once, early in the action, Moore managed to lay the *Austin* between the two steam frigates for a few seconds of effective, simultane-ous firing from both the larboard (port) and starboard batteries. Through most of the action the ranges were so far that only the fire of one long 12 on the *Wharton* could be contributed to the *Austin's* aid.[8]

In spite of the *Austin's* being so badly cut up by the *Guada-loupe's* long 68's that she was practically forced to give up the pursuit, the Texans claimed a signal victory. Moore claimed that he chased the enemy for fourteen miles during the course of the action. Colonel Morgan, who witnessed the battle from the water front of Campeche enjoyed the spectacle until Moore had chased the enemy out of sight.[9]

One is not surprised, however, to find that the Mexican com-manders were equally enthusiastic about their victory over the Texans. Eight days before the battle, in spite of the fact that the Texans had joined the Yucatecans after the short engagement April 30 and had continued to come and go at will, not to mention having cut Ampudia off from his fleet, official dispatches in the Mexico City press declared that the Texan fleet was blockaded in Campeche and was therefore harmless.[10] Nevertheless, Commodore Tomas Marin's official report of the main action of May 16, 1843, does not disagree materially with that of Moore, which has been followed above. About the only differences are in the parts emphasized. Where Moore made references to sundry direct hits, Marin reported but four damaging balls that reached the *Moctezuma* and six that affected the *Guadaloupe*. The effects of all could be "remedied immediately as all were of little consideration."[11] Marin was as sure that Moore's ships were sorely wounded as the Texan was sure that the *Guadaloupe* had felt the evil effects of the "shell shot abaft her wheel house."

Commodore Marin made no references to casualties, hence the Mexican fisherman who visited the *Guadaloupe* and then reported to Moore that she alone suffered about seventy killed and wounded may have been correct, particularly since the Mexican ships were fully manned and therefore more crowded than the Texan men-of-war. Moore's casualties were three killed and twenty-one wounded for the *Austin*, and two deaths from a bursting gun on the *Wharton*.

But the biggest difference in emphasis was Moore's italicized assertion that he chased the Mexicans for fourteen miles before 3:00 P.M., whereas Commodore Marin dwelt with satisfaction upon the Texan retirement after that hour—"with precipitation to their refuge which is the shallow water where they remain under the guns of the plaza."[12]

Though the claims of each on this last point are essentially true, the fact remains that each still had a formidable foe to deal with when the day was done. The battle showed beyond controversy, however, that so long as the Marin feared to lay his ships within range of the comparatively short ranged medium length guns that constituted the major portion of the Texan broadsides, Moore could come and go when he saw fit and could dominate any position he chose to defend. Certainly the Mexicans had shown no stomach for even long range fighting, at which they had an obvious advantage, in that they had permitted Moore to retrace his steps for fourteen miles without molesting him at a distance.

But the question of complete naval supremacy was never to be settled. The approaching Yucatecan summer with its ills for the unacclimatized Centralists, Barragan's failure against Merida and the renewed vigor of the rebels with the arrival of the Texans, and the semi-nullification of such naval advantages as the Mexicans had enjoyed before Moore appeared on the scene, were all leading toward another Centralist-Yucatecan truce with terms very advantageous to the latter.[13]

Meanwhile back in Texas there had appeared at Galveston, about two weeks before Moore's departure, the San Antonio judge who had been captured and carried back to Mexico by General Woll in the raid on San Antonio, September, 1842. As a ruse to get back to Texas, Judge Robinson had proposed to Santa Anna that he be released to negotiate a truce with Texas for the Centralists on the incongruent terms of Mexican sovereignty but absolute autonomy for Texas. It was a chance for Santa Anna to save his face, play for time, or both; hence Robinson was released. Houston pretended to be contemptuous of the plan, but with powerful English aid to Texas and additional worries for Santa Anna in Yucatan, thanks to Moore's cruise, Robinson's negotiations grew into a genuine truce the following summer.

The Robinson negotiations, with England and the United States participating, were in full swing when Houston heard that Moore and Morgan were at large with the *Austin* and *Wharton*. Apparently in mortal fear that this was a menace to English and American commerce and amity, Houston at once released his copy of the Piracy Proclamation that he had given to Commissioners Bryan and Morgan. It was published May 6, in the press of Texas, so that it eventually appeared in the leading news sheets of the day.

The contents of this interesting manifesto have been characterized in the preceding chapter. It is enough to include here a reminder that in it Moore and his men were, to all practical purposes, outlawed as pirates; and the neutral powers were, with sycophantic terms unbecoming to the Houston of mythology, invited to apprehend the ships and bring Moore and his men before the Texan bar of justice. And to make sure that England and the United States knew exactly how the Administration viewed Moore (as if the Piracy Proclamation were not enough), almost duplicate communications were dispatched to Washington and London, in which Moore and any acts he might do were vigorously repudiated.

The first inkling Moore had of the publication of the Proclamation came to him about May 28. Lieutenant Gray, of the *Austin*, had been detached a week or ten days before to command the borrowed Yucatecan gun boat *Independencia*. His mission was to harass the Mexican forces off Telchac to keep the Mexican forces divided. May 28 he was back with a prize laden with supplies for the Centralist and with the rumor that insofar as Sam Houston was concerned, they were all pirates. Moore decided to fight on until the rumor was confirmed or denied. In the meantime relations with Yucatan had begun to forecast a termination of the monthly financial support that had been promised. On June 1, Moore asked Governor Barbachano to cover accounts for supplies he had contracted. It was twenty-four days before His Excellency saw fit to reply.

On the same day that Moore sought to draw his fleet's emoluments for the month of May, Colonel Morgan stepped aboard the *Austin* with an official copy of Houston's Proclamation. He and the Commodore decided to remain on the coast until they had heard from their most recent reports to the Department in hopes that perhaps their actions might be approved as had been those of Moore earlier in Houston's administration. At the same time they did not deem it proper to attack the enemy until their actions had been sustained. Moore later considered this very unfortunate indeed, for on June 14, the enlistments of the

Englishmen on Mexico's new steam frigates expired and they left the Centralist service to a man. This made the ships easy prey, Moore thought, for a night attack, but he and Morgan kept the peace.

No dispatches of confirmation had come by June 24, but on that date Barbachano wrote to inform Moore that the full amount of $8000 for the month of May would not be paid. Moore's work had been appreciated and had been of the utmost importance, but he had failed to arrive as early as his and Colonel Peraza's contract had stipulated. The State would pay the recent accounts totaling $29,000, and assume the carpentry bills Moore had contracted locally for repairing the *Austin*. An additional $2000 would be paid, and Yucatan would consider the slate cleaned and the contract ended.

And well the Yucatecans could afford to end the agreement. The Centralists were admitting the futility of their entire campaign, which had started eight months before with such brilliant successes, by withdrawing fleet and soldiers from Campeche as well as from Telchac. Now that they had withdrawn, Moore did not have to wait longer for powder with which "to fight our way back,"[14] but since the rigging of the *Austin* had been sadly damaged by a bolt of lightning June 25, he lingered a few days longer. But by June 29 all accounts were practically settled, the residue of the $2000 was in sight and a new fore topmast had been shipped. Accordingly the *Austin* and *Wharton* sailed for Galveston.

With the splash of the anchors and the clatter of the chains as they raced out the hawse pipes when the *Austin* and *Wharton* found their berths off the Navy Yard at Galveston, July 14, 1843, the history of the Texas Navy as an operative organization ends.

There is no temptation to repeat further the oft told tale of how the Lone Star Republic stumbled on to the Robinson truce with Mexico that very summer and to annexation early in 1845. But old friends such as Moore, his officers, and the ships that remained of the once pretentious fleet Lamar had assembled cannot be summarily dismissed. At the same time a minute, detailed account of Moore's controversies with his enemies and the tortuous path each of the four remaining ships took to Davy Jones's Locker would be anticipating the work of the biographer and the antiquarian. Thus, in spite of wealth of material that is available on the subject, the destinies of the ships and personnel will be disposed of rather briefly.

Moore immediately began seeking a trial before a court of any character, naval, military or civil; but so popular was the returned Commodore with the coastal constituents that Houston dared not try the alleged pirates. Instead the President chose to inform Post Captain Moore, Commander Lothrop and Lieutenant Snow that they were dishonorably discharged from the Navy. The action against Lothrop was because he had not succeeded Moore at New Orleans in accordance with a letter Morgan's secretary had given him and which Morgan had retrieved before Lothrop had read it. Snow had irritated the President by his having joined Moore at New Orleans from the grounded *San Bernard* with some equipment from that craft. By these dismissals without judicial procedure to support him, Houston was unquestionably overstepping even his status as commander-in-chief of the Army and Navy.[15]

Not until the latter half of 1844, however, did Moore, by a special resolution of Congress, get a court.[16] Though Houston had declared him dishonorably discharged, Congress considered him still in the Navy for it was a court martial that tried him. It was composed of high ranking military officers because of the absence of naval officers that ranked above Moore. The charges were: neglect of duty; misapplication of money; disobedience of orders; contempt and defiance of the laws; treason; and murder. The prosecution offered twenty-two specifications. Moore was acquitted on all but four and they were a part of those supporting the charge of disobedience to orders.[17] No penalty was handed down. Houston's answer to this practical vindication was: "The President disapproves the proceedings of the Court in toto."[18] Lothrop and Snow were never tried.

Since the ships were laid up in ordinary to be cared for by a contractor, Moore, like the other naval officers, except for one or two who were assigned the duty of checking the work of the caretakers, was without active duty until the end of the Republic.

Annexation was hardly achieved before he began an agitation to the effect that since United States had annexed Texas and her navy, he and his fellow officers were *ipso facto* officers in the American Navy of date and grade as stipulated in their Texan commissions. It was the signal for a bitter pamphlet and epistolic war that dragged on into the 'fifties and suffered a revival every time a friend of Moore's mentioned the subject on the floor of Congress. Commanders Buchanan, du Pont and Magruder, U.S.N., had no intentions of sitting supinely by while an adventurer, whom they long had ranked by many files, slipped into a coveted post-captaincy. To block him they wrote and had printed at their own expense, for distribution among Congressmen, more than one dissertation upon the virtues of seniority versus selection, with special reference to themselves and the bumptious Texan Commodore. The modern student becomes disgusted with the pettiness of all concerned, particularly on the part of the three commanders, but he is grateful for the historical information that was thus preserved as a by-product of their controversy.[19]

With a Supreme Court decision on their side[20] and the bitter opposition to Moore of the strategically situated Houston, then in the American Senate, the United States naval officers had their way. The Federal Government finally, in 1857, sought a compromise by appropriating enough money to pay each of the nine or ten survivors of those who had been officers in the Texan service at the time of annexation a sum equivalent to what an officer of corresponding grade, would have drawn "when waiting orders" during a period of five years in the American navy.

Even before this date, Moore had reached a settlement of his claims against Texas. When, as a state, the erstwhile Republic was making its financial adjustments during the pros-

perous year of 1848, Moore was voted $11,398.36 for his ad-
vances on the fleet and $3,500.00 back pay. This did not satisfy
all his claims for as late as 1856 he was voted an additional
$5,290.00 provided he would sign a release of all claims against
the state.

The fate of the ships was as drab as that of the officers. In
spite of the fact that the Eighth Texan Congress, 1844, repealed
Houston's secret act of 1843 authorizing their sale, they were
not long to continue as men-of-war. The first move made by
the United States toward Texan annexation was an announce-
ment of an Amercian naval concentration in the Gulf to protect Texas. The Texan demand that this be done is further evidence, if more be needed, of the importance the Texans at-
tached to the Gulf in connection with their own military safety.
With this concentration the need for a Texan fleet definitely
vanished. Thus the ships remained out of commission at Galveston until annexation was achieved, at which time they became
the property of the United States.

That was where Commander Randolph, U.S.N., found the
Austin, Wharton, Archer, and the hulk *San Bernard* when he
went to Texas in the summer of 1846 to make a report upon
their deplorable condition.[21] The following August the chief of
the Bureau of Construction advised the sale of all. Only the
Austin could be of any possible service to the American Navy
and that in the unromantic rôle of a receiving ship at Pensacola.[22] But even this proposed status as a pseudo-man-of-war
was soon denied her, for two years later the Commandant at
Pensacola expressed regret that so rapidly was the *Austin* leak-
ing that she was unfit for use even as a receiving ship.[23]

In the meantime the *Archer, Wharton* and the hulk of the
San Bernard had been sold "as unfit for service."[24] What their
future may have been is not recorded, but the epitaph of the
flagship and pride of the Texan fleet was written into the Annual
Report of the Secretary of Navy in 1849: "The sloop *Austin*
has been broken up, being unworthy of repairs."[25]

APPENDIX I

NOTES AND CITATIONS

CHAPTER I

TEXAN MARITIME TROUBLES

1. DAVID CROCKETT, *Life* (1865 edition), 345.
2. H. H. BANCROFT, *History of Mexico*, V, 152.
3. E. C. BARKER, *Texas and Mexico, 1821–1835*, 108.
4. Ministerio de Hacienda, Circular Numero 21, *Austin Papers*, I, 696.
5. Inclosure, Austin to Terán, June 30, 1828, *Ibid.*, II, 66; Austin to Ceballos, Sept. 20, 1828, *Ibid.*, 109–110, and Austin to Terán, Sept. 20, 1828, *Ibid.*, 120.
6. GEO. FISHER to Austin, May 18, 1830, *Ibid.*, II, 391.
7. S. RHOADS FISHER to Austin, Jan. 10, 1831, *Ibid.*, II, 583.
8. V. FILISOLA, *Memorias para la Historia de la Guerra de Tejas*, I, 184–89.
9. COL. FRANCIS W. JOHNSON, *Texas and Texans*, I, 68 ff.
10. *Ibid.*, 77, quoting D. L. Kokernot.
11. V. FILISOLA, *op. cit.*, 209.
12. CAPT. W. J. RUSSELL, in the *Texas Almanac*, 1872, 168 ff.
13. COL. FRANCIS W. JOHNSON, *op. cit.*, 77.
14. E. C. BARKER, *Life of Stephen F. Austin*, 397–403.
15. H. H. BANCROFT, *North Mexican States and Texas*, II, 124–28.

CHAPTER II

THE WAR BEGINS AT SEA

1. E. C. BARKER, *Life of Stephen F. Austin*, 460, quoting printed address of Brazoria Ayuntamiento signed by Edwin Waller, Wm. H. Wharton, *et al.*
2. *Memoria de la Marina*, 1834, p. 8.
3. E. C. BARKER, "Difficulties of a Mexican Revenue Officer in Texas," *Texas State Historical Association Quarterly*, IV, 198 quoting Ugartechea to Tenorio, June 20, 1835. This study is an excellent record of Tenorio and his difficulties.
4. This account of the heretofore overlooked *Moctezuma-Ingham* episode is drawn from the June 15, 1835, dispatches, accompanied by undated clippings from the New Orleans *Bulletin*, of Consul General Martinez in the Mexican Foreign Office Archives, Sección 3, Caja 1, Expediente 3516.
5, Testimony of J. W. Zacharie in John Winthrop's *Report of the Trial of Thomas M. Thompson*, 17.
6. Declaration of Lieut. Ocampo, Sept. 21, 1835, H. R. Docs., 25th Cong., 2nd Sess., No. 351, p. 712.
7. J. H. BROWN, *Life and Times of Henry Smith*, 63.

8. Deposition of A. C. Allen, Mexican Foreign Office Archives, Sección 5, Caja 16, Expediente 8732.
9. Resolutions of Nacogdoches, Aug. 15, 1835, *Austin Papers*, III, 100.
10. AUSTIN to Mary Austin Holley, Aug. 21, 1835, *Ibid.*, 101–03.
11. THOMAS M. THOMPSON to Capitan de Marina Lopez, October, 1835, "Parte Oficial," *Diario del Gobierno*, Nov. 2, 1835.
12. Deposition of W. A. Hurd, Mexican Foreign Office Archives, Sección 5, Caja 16, Expediente 8732.
13. CONSUL GENERAL MARTINEZ to Departamento de Relaciones Exteriores, Sept. 23, 1835, Mexican Foreign Office Archives, Sección 3, Caja 1, Expediente 3516. Also see John Winthrop, *Report of the Trial of Thomas M. Thompson*.
14. ALEX. DIENST, "The Navy of the Republic of Texas," *Texas State Historical Association Quarterly*, XII, 171, quoting New Orleans *Courier*, Jan. 18, 1836.
15. H. R. Docs., 25th Cong., 2nd Sess., No. 351, p. 723.
16. November 2, 1835.
17. Mexican Foreign Office Archives, Sección 3, Caja 1, Expediente 3516.

CHAPTER III

LEGISLATION AND LETTERS OF MARQUE

1. *Memoria de la Marina*, 1834, 7–8.
2. *Memoria de la Guerra y Marina*, 1835, 36–38, and Presupuesto numero 9.
3. E. C. BARKER, "The Work of the Permanent Council," *Texas State Historical Association Quarterly*, VII, 249–71.
4. *Journal of the Consultation*, 11, 26.
5. The most widely available copies of the Texans' constitution-like *Plan of the Provisional Government*, a most interesting document, are in F. W. Johnson's *Texas and Texans*, I, 306–12 and in Ben P. Poore's *Federal and State Constitutions of the United States*, II, 1747–52.
6. *Proceedings of the General Council*, 13.
7. *Ibid.*, 8.
8. *Ibid.*, 27.
9. ALEX. DIENST, "The Navy of the Republic of Texas," *Texas State Historical Association Quarterly*, XII, 179–80.
10. HALL to Austin, Nov. 23, 1835, *Austin Papers*, III, 264–65.
11. *Proceedings of the General Council*, 10.
12. ALEX. DIENST, *op. cit.*, 184–86.

CHAPTER IV

THE NAVY AND SAN JACINTO

1. H. P. N. GAMMEL, *Laws of Texas*, I, 931.
2. AUSTIN and ARCHER to Smith, Jan. 20, 1836, *Texan Diplomatic Correspondence*, I, 59.
3. *Niles Register*, XXXIV, 8–9.

4. *Telegraph and Texas Register*, Sept. 8, 1838.
5. ALEX. DIENST, "The Navy of the Republic of Texas," *Texas State Historical Association Quarterly*, XII, 203.
6. W. M. GOUGE, *The Fiscal History of Texas*, 42.
7. *Proceedings of the General Council*, 291–92.
8. CONSUL MARTINEZ (New Orleans) to Minister of Foreign Affairs, April 2, 1836, Mexican Foreign Office Archives, Sección 5, Caja 16, Expediente 8729.
9. Depositions of C. Antonio Ramirez, Aug. 6, 1837 and of Pablo Martinez, Aug. 6, 1837, Mexican Foreign Office Archives, Sección 6, Caja 1, Expediente 9.
10. COMMODORE H. L. THOMPSON to "The Honorable Naval Department," Aug. 29, 1837, Archives, Texas State Library, Navy MSS.
11. H. H. BANCROFT, *North Mexican States and Texas*, II, 201–59 and G. L. Rives, *The United States and Mexico*, I, 311–61 for good authentic treatments of the Mexican advance. See also V. Filisola, *Memorias para la Historia de la Guerra de Tejas*, II.
12. F. W. JOHNSON, *Texas and Texans*, 386–96.
13. ALEX. DIENST, *op. cit.*, XII, 265.
14. CONSUL MARTINEZ (New Orleans) to Mexican Legation, Washington, D. C., Mar. 14, 1836, Mexican Foreign Office Archives, Sección 5, Caja 16, Expediente 8716; and to Minister of Foreign Relations, *Ibid.*, Expediente 8729. For Texan accounts of the *Liberty's* cruise see Alex. Dienst, *op. cit.*, XII, 249 ff.
15. ALEX. DIENST, *op. cit.*, 250 quoting Houston's Proclamation of March 31, 1836.
16. ESPINO to General Fernandez, April 3, *Diario del Gobierno*, April 30, 1836.
17. C. T. NEU, "The Case of the Brig Pocket," *Texas State Historical Association Quarterly*, XII, 276.
18. U. S. CHARGÉ ALCEE LA BRANCH to R. A. Irion, Nov. 29, 1837, *Texan Diplomatic Correspondence*, I, 271.
19. FRANK C. HANIGHEN, *Santa Anna, Napoleon of the West*, 105–07.
20. HOMER S. THRALL, *Pictorial History of Texas*, 519.
21. V. FILISOLA, *Memorias para la Historia de la Guerra de Tejas*, II, 477.
22. *Ibid.*, 478.
23. *Ibid.*, 482–83.
24. V. FILISOLA to Departamento de Guerra y Marina, May 31, 1836, *Diario del Gobierno*, June 26, 1836.
25. Ex. Docs., 24th U. S. Cong., 2nd Sess., No. 35, p. 29.
26. *Telegraph and Texas Register*, Aug. 2, 1836.
27. ALEX. DIENST, *op. cit.*, XII, 251.
28. *Treaties and Conventions*, 834; C. T. Neu, *op. cit.*, 294.
29. T. J. GREEN, *Journal of the Texan Expedition against Mier*, 485–87.
30. RAMON M. CARO, *Verdadera Idea*, 60–66.
31. ALEX. DIENST, *op. cit.*, 195, 256, 263, citing the New Orleans *Commercial Bulletin*, July 18, 1836.
32. *Diario del Gobierno*, Aug. 5, 1836.

33. *Memoria de la Guerra y Marina*, 1839, 25. There were no annual *Memorias* between 1835 and 1839.
34. *Texas Almanac*, 1861, 45.
35. Mexican Foreign Office Archives, Sección 3, Caja 15, Expediente 5389.
36. *Ibid.*, Sección 3, Caja 13, Expediente 5007.
37. G. L. Rives, *The United States and Mexico, 1821–1848*, I, 372–73.
38. W. M. Gouge, *The Fiscal History of Texas*, 54–55, quoting reports of the Naval Affairs Committee and of the Acting Secretary of Navy.

CHAPTER V

THE MEXICAN BLOCKADE

1. E. C. Barker in F. W. Johnson's *Texas and Texans*, I, 471.
2. José Maria Tornel, *Tejas y las Estados-Unidos en sus Relaciones con la Republica Mejicana*, in Castañeda's *The Mexican Side*, 357.
3. Archives, Texas State Library, Navy, MSS.
4. Francisco de Lopez to District Judge for Nuevo Leon, April, 1837, H. R. Docs., 25th Cong., 2nd Sess., No. 75, p. 24.
5. Gen. Nicolas Bravo to Consul D. W. Smith, April 13, 1837, *Ibid.*, also in Mexican Foreign Office Archives, Sección 6, Caja 1, Expediente 1.
6. Testimony of Lieut. Peck, Court Martial of Commander Mervine, Aug. 1837, H. R. Docs., 25th Cong., 2nd Sess., No. 75, p. 31.
7. Espino to Mervine, April 15, 1837, *Ibid.*, 39.
8. Gen. Nicolas Bravo to Ministerio de Guerra y Marina, April 17, 1837, in *Diario del Gobierno*, May 4, 1837.
9. Mexican Foreign Office Archives, Sección 6, Caja 1, Expediente 1.
10. *Diario del Gobierno*, May 11, 1837.
11. Gen. Vicente Filisola to Ministerio de Guerra y Marina, June 8, 1837, (with copies of his correspondence with Dallas) in *Diario del Gobierno*, June 18, 1837.
12. *Diario del Gobierno*, July 31, 1837.
13. Tornel, *Tejas y los Estados-Unidos en sus Relaciones con la Republica Mejicana*, translated in Castañeda's *The Mexican Side*, 360.
14. Lieut. J. W. Taylor, T. N., to S. Rhoads Fisher, Sec. of Navy, April 21, 1837, in the *Telegraph and Texas Register*, June 8, 1837.
15. Mexican official reports in *Diario del Gobierno*, May 11, June 3, and July 26, 1837.
16. William H. Wharton to Sam Houston, April 22, 1837, Wharton MSS.
17. *Diario del Gobierno*, May 11, 1837.
18. *Memoria de la Guerra y Marina*, 1839, p. 26.

CHAPTER VI

THE TEXAS NAVY COUNTER ATTACKS

1. Houston to the Texan Congress, May 31, 1837, *Secret Journals of the Senate of the Republic of Texas*, 60–63; also *Texas House Journal*, 1st Texan Congress, 2nd Sess., 84–87.

2. *Telegraph and Texas Register*, Sept. 9, 1837.
3. H. L. THOMPSON to "The Honorable Naval Department," Aug. 29, 1837, Archives, Texas State Library, Navy MSS.
4. *Ibid.*
5. J. D. BOYLAN to Navy Department, Sept. 1, 1837, Archives, Texas State Library, Navy MSS.
6. Deposition of Antonio Ramirez, Mexican Foreign Office Archives, Sección 6, Caja 1, Expediente 9.
7. H. L. THOMPSON, "Answer to Questions," Sept. 20, 1837, Archives, Texas State Library, Navy MSS.
8. Deposition of Purser Wells, Sept. 1837, Archives, Texas State Library, Navy MSS. See also deposition of Surgeon Dunn and the charges and specifications of Lieutenants Davis and Simons, *Ibid.*
9. P. W. HUMPHREYS to Thompson, Sept. 24, 1837, Archives, Texas State Library, Navy MSS.
10. Deposition of Pablo Martinez (Master of the *Abispo*), Aug. 11, 1837, Mexican Foreign Office Archives, Sección 6, Caja 1, Expediente 9.
11. J. D. BOYLAN, *op. cit.*
12. Depositions of Pablo Canesa and Antonio Corral, Aug. 18, 1837, Mexican Foreign Office Archives, Sección 6, Caja 1, Expediente 9.
13. COMMODORE JOSÉ DE ALDANA to Commander, Departamento de Vera Cruz, Aug. 19, 1837, *Diario del Gobierno*, Sept. 11, 1837.
14. *Diario del Gobierno*, July 25, 1837.
15. Details of this engagement are from H. L. Thompson, *op. cit.*, J. D. Boylan, *op. cit.*, and José de Aldana to Commander, Departamento de Vera Cruz, Aug. 30, 1837, *Diario del Gobierno*, Sept. 11, 1837. The *Telegraph and Texas Register*, Sept. 2, 1837, gave a very inaccurate account of the battle.
16. *Secret Journals of the Senate of the Republic of Texas*, 90.
17. *Diario del Gobierno*, June 18, 1837.
18. F. B. WRIGHT to the Secretary of Navy, Sept. 20, 1837, Archives, Texas State Library, Navy MSS.
19. *Diario del Gobierno*, June 18, 1837.

CHAPTER VII

THE FRENCH IN THE GULF

1. BARON DEFFAUDIS to Mexican Foreign Office, March 21, 1838, *Contestaciones entre Francia y Mejico*, 3.
2. LUIS G. CUEVAS, *Exposición del Ex-Ministro sobre las Diferencias con Francia*, 29.
3. P. BLANCHARD et A. DAUZATS, *San Juan de Ulúa*, 283.
4. H. H. BANCROFT, *History of Mexico*, V, 191.
5. "Convention Conclue entre le Contre-Amiral C. Baudin et le General Don Manuel Rincon," Nov. 28, 1838, P. Blanchard et A. Dauzats, *San Juan de Ulúa*, 331–32.
6. H. H. BANCROFT, *op. cit.*, V, 197 ff.

7. Notes of Lieutenant de Vaisseau E. Maissin, *San Juan de Ulúa*, 519–20, also 337.
8. R. A. Irion to J. P. Henderson, Aug. 7, 1838, *Texan Diplomatic Correspondence*, III, 1217–18.
9. Manuel Dublan y J. M. Lozano, *Legislación Mejicana*, III, 617–9, 692. See also *San Juan de Ulúa*, 483–89.
10. The outstanding American commentator upon and witness of the French operations was Lieutenant (later Admiral) D. G. Farragut, U. S. N., who commanded the U.S.S. *Erie* at Vera Cruz. See L. Farragut, *David G. Farragut, Life and Letters*, 132 ff. H. H. Bancroft, *History of Mexico*, V, 186 ff. offers the best secondary account in English. M. Rivera, *Historia Antigua y Moderna de Jalapa*, III, 356 ff. is perhaps the best Mexican account.

CHAPTER VIII

A NEW PRESIDENT AND A NEW NAVY

1. M. B. Lamar, "Message to Both Houses," *Lamar Papers*, II, 356.
2. *Secret Journals of the Senate of the Republic of Texas*, 127.
3. J. P. Henderson to Texan Secretary of State James Webb, April 28, 1839, *Texan Diplomatic Correspondence*, III, 1248.
4. Lieut. Taylor to Lamar, Dec. 9, 1838, *Lamar Papers*, II, 315.
5. Sec. of Navy Cooke to Lamar, Dec. 28, 1839, Harriet Smithers MS. for *Journals of the Fourth Texas Congress*.
6. *Memorial of James Holford to the Legislature of Texas*, 2.
7. W. M. Gouge, *The Fiscal History of Texas*, 198. See also copy of contract in *House Journal*, 5th Texan Cong. 1st Sess., 202–04.
8. Alex. Dienst, "The Navy of the Republic of Texas," *Texas State Historical Association Quarterly*, XIII, 9.
9. "Remarks upon the Navy," 1838, *Lamar Papers*, II, 227 ff.
10. A. C. Howard to Lamar, June 17, 1839, *Ibid.*, V, 295.
11. Willis Roberts to Lamar, June 20, 1839, *Ibid.*, 296.
12. W. Callahan, *List of Officers, U. S. Navy and Marine Corps*, 1775–1900, p. 388; Alex. Dienst, *op. cit.*, 14.
13. *Secret Journals of the Senate of the Republic of Texas*, 137.
14. Alex. Dienst, *op. cit.*, 6.
15. E. W. Moore, "Statement of Texas's Naval Force," *Lamar Papers*, IV, 26.
16. H. H. Bancroft, *History of Mexico*, V, 206–19.
17. Lamar to the Senate, Dec. 10, 1839, *Secret Journals of the Senate of the Republic of Texas*, 148.
18. A. K. Christian, *Mirabeau Lamar*, 140.
19. Harriett Smithers MS. for *Journals of the Fourth Congress*, Republic of Texas.
20. Majority Report, Naval Affairs Committee, undated, *Ibid.*
21. H. P. N. Gammel, *Laws of Texas*, II, 364.

CHAPTER IX
DIPLOMATIC CRUISING

1. J. Love to Lamar, Mar. 15, 1840, *Lamar Papers*, III, 353.
2. F. Moore to Lamar, March 9, 1840, *Ibid.*, 349.
3. Lipscombe to Treat, June 13, 1840, *Texan Diplomatic Correspondence*, II, 644.
4. Burnet to Treat, Aug. 9, 1839, *Ibid.*, II, 471.
5. J. Suarez y Navarro, *Informe sobre las Causas y Carácter de los Frecuentes Cambios Políticos Ocurridos en el Estado de Yucatan*, 8–9, 56–62.
6. S. Baqueiro, *Ensayo Historico sobre las Revoluciones de Yucatan*, I, 15, 35–38.
7. *Ibid.*, 29–35.
8. Lipscombe to Treat, June 13, 1840, *Texan Diplomatic Correspondence*, II, 645.
9. Lamar to Moore, June 20, 1840, *Ibid.*, 651–52.
10. Treat's Correspondence with his State Department and with Commodore Moore Aug., 1840 to Nov. 1840 may be examined in *Texan Diplomatic Correspondence*, II, 684–714.
11. Treat to Moore, Aug. 21, 1840, *Ibid.*, 692–93. The italics are Treat's.
12. *Diario del Gobierno*, Oct. 31, 1840, quoting the Tampico *Desengano* of Oct. 17, 1840.
13. S. Baqueiro, *op. cit.*, 44.
14. *Diario del Gobierno*, Sept. 22, 1840.
15. The extant source materials showing the detailed movements of the various units of Commodore E. W. Moore's squadron from the date of its sailing, July 22, 1840, until the return of the last ship in the early spring of 1841 are fragmentary at best. The ships' log books must have been lost in one of the capitol fires. The ship movements described in this chapter are based upon: E. W. Moore, "Statement of Texas's Naval Force," 1843, *Lamar Papers*, IV, 27 ff.; Moore's Report of Dec. 24, 1841, Archives, Texas State Library, Navy MSS.; Reports of Lieut. W. S. Williams (Capt. of the *San Bernard*), Sept. 16, 1840, and Nov. 1840, *Ibid.*; Report of Commander J. T. K. Lothrop (of T.S.S. *Zavala*), Nov. 3, 1840, *Ibid*. The Texas State Library also has a valuable record in Alfred Walke's *Midshipman's Journal, Jan. 22, 1840–Oct. 20, 1840*. It is not a personal diary but is an instructional work book and as such approximates a ship's log. Also valuable are "Diary of Midshipman James L. Mabry," *Galveston News*, Jan. 16 and subsequent issues, 1893; Moore to Cooke, Aug. 28, 1840, *House Journal Appendix*, 5th Texas Cong. 1st Sess., 234 ff.; Prize Returns, Archives, Texas State Library, Navy MSS.; Lieutenant O'Shaunessy (of the *San Jacinto*) to Moore, Nov. 2, 1840 (on the wreck of his command), *Ibid.*; E. W. Moore's pamphlet, *Brief Synopsis of the Doings of the Texas Navy*, 1–4; and Lieutenant Tennison's *Journal*, Dienst Collection, Univ. of Texas.
16. E. D. Adams, *British Interests and Activities in Texas*, 53, quoting Hamilton to Palmerston, Oct. 14, 1840.

17. Published in Jalapa, Aug. 14, 1840 and reprinted in *Diario del Gobierno*, Aug. 20, 1840.
18. *Ibid.*, Aug. 29, 1840.
19. *Ibid.*, Sept. 7, 1840.
20. *Ibid.*, Oct. 4, 1840.
21. *Ibid.*, Oct. 6, 1840 to Feb. 24, 1841.

CHAPTER X

YUCATAN RENTS THE FLEET

1. *Senate Journal*, 5th Texas Cong., 1st Sess. 65–66.
2. *Secret Journals of the Senate of the Republic of Texas*, 195–97.
3. MAYFIELD to Webb, Mar. 22, 1841, *Texan Diplomatic Correspondence*, II, 723–26.
4. COMACHO to Packenham, June 8, 1841, *Ibid.*, 357–58.
5. WEBB to Lamar, June 29, 1841, *Ibid.*, 762–63.
6. LAMAR to the Governor of Yucatan, July 20, 1841, *Ibid.*, 793.
7. PERAZO to Roberts, Sept. 16, 1841, in Moore's *To the People of Texas*, 15.
8. ROBERTS to Perazo and Perazo to Roberts both of Sept. 17, 1841, *Ibid.*, 18–20.
9. Sec. of War and Navy B. T. ARCHER to Moore, Sept. 18, 1841, *Ibid.*, 12–13.
10. Secret Orders and Enclosures, Sept. 18, 1841, *Ibid.*, 13–21.
11. Tratados de 28 de Diciembre de 1841, S. Baqueiro, *Ensayo Historico sobre las Revoluciones de Yucatan*, Sección de Documentos, I, 38–41.
12. MOORE's relations with the Yucatecan officials and the movements of his ships are well covered by his two-hundred page pamphlet, *To the People of Texas*, 20–43. It is a documentary work in that it contains little other than Commodore Moore's official correspondence from 1841 to the last cruise of a Texas warship, July 1843. For these years, it is the most valuable single source concerning the Texas Navy.
13. HOCKLEY to Moore, Dec. 15, 1841, *Ibid.*, 43.
14. HOUSTON in the U. S. Senate, July 15, 1854, *Cong. Globe*, Appendix 33rd Cong., 1st Sess., 1081.
15. New Orleans *Picayune*, Feb. 13, 1842.
16. E. W. MOORE, *Reply to the Pamphlet by Commanders Buchanan, du Pont, and Magruder*, U. S. N., 25–26.
17. LEMUS to Moore, Feb. 25, 1842, Moore, *To the People of Texas*, 38.
18. MOORE to Lemus, March 8, 1842, *Ibid.*, 41.
19. HOCKLEY to Moore, April 14, 1842, *Ibid.*, 51.
20. MARQUIS JAMES, *The Raven*, 321–24.
21. HOCKLEY to Moore, April 14, 1842, Moore, *To the People of Texas*, 50–51.

CHAPTER XI

MOORE CLASHES WITH HOUSTON

1. On condition of fleet and personnel at this time see Moore to Hamilton, Dec. 2, 1842, Moore, *To the People of Texas*, 114; Moore to Hockley,

April 4, 1842, *Ibid.*, 49; Moore, "Statement of Texas's Navy," 1843, *Lamar Papers*, IV, 27; and Moore to Hamilton, Nov. 15, 1844, *Memorial of James Holford to the Legislature of Texas*, 14.

2. HOCKLEY to Moore, May 3, 1842, Moore, *To the People of Texas*, 63.

3. HOCKLEY to Moore, May 29, 1842, *Ibid.*, 71.

4. HOUSTON to All Whom the Present May Come or Concern, June 18, 1842, *Ibid.*, 73.

5. Decreto Formal de General Santa Anna Nulificando los Tratados, May 7, 1842, S. Baqueiro, *Ensayo Historico sobre las Revoluciones de Yucatan*, Sección de Documentos, I, 53–54; and Moore to Hockley, July 2, 1842, Moore, *To the People of Texas*, 75.

6. H. P. N. GAMMEL, *The Laws of Texas*, II, 813.

7. MOORE, *To the People of Texas*, 82.

8. MARQUIS JAMES, *The Raven*, 338, quoting Lamar.

9. MOORE, *To the People of Texas*, 83.

10. H. K. YOAKUM, *History of Texas*, (Wooten Edition), 393.

11. MARQUIS JAMES, *op. cit.*, 323, quoting Houston to M. E. Holliday, May 6, 1842. The italics are mine.

12. ACTING SECRETARY HAMILTON to Moore, Sept. 15, 1842, Moore, *To the People of Texas*, 95.

13. To all practical purposes, the *San Bernard* at this time disappears from the Texan Naval list, though she was not finally dropped until after a survey by an officer of the U. S. Navy at the time of annexation.—See Commander Randolph, U. S. N., to Bureau of Construction, June 5, 1846, Archives, U. S. Navy Dept. Library, Class 3, Area 8.

14. S. BAQUEIRO, *Ensayo Historico sobre las Revoluciones de Yucatan*, I, 70.

15. *Ibid.*, 72–107.

16. *Memoria de la Guerra y Marina*, 1845, Plan Numero 13.

17. See M. P. RUSSELL to Smith, June 2, 1842; Russell to Smith, June 4, 1842; Smith to Russell, June 22, 1842; Pringle to Smith, June 29, 1842; undated memorandum; Smith to Earl of Aberdeen Sept. 14, 1842; Smith to Sec. of State Anson Jones, Sept. 19, 1842; and Aberdeen to Smith, Sept. 27, 1842, all in *Texan Diplomatic Correspondence*, III, 982–1037.

18. MRS. M. C. HOUSTON, *Texas and the Gulf of Mexico*, II, 245.

19. Contract between Moore and Perazo, Feb. 11, 1843, Moore, *To the People of Texas*, 125–26.

20. Appendix, *Secret Journals of the Senate of the Republic of Texas*, 316–17.

21. The most available copy of the Proclamation is in Alex. Dienst's "The Navy of the Republic of Texas," *Quarterly of the Texas State Historical Association*, XIII, 110–11.

22. Extract from testimony of Col. J. Morgan, Moore's court martial, Dec. 1844, *Doings of the Texas Navy*, 10.

23. *Ibid.*, 12.

CHAPTER XII

NAVAL BATTLES OFF CAMPECHE

1. Moore to Pinkard, April 19, 1843, *British Correspondence Concerning Texas*, 193–94.
2. Report of the Court to Moore, April 18, 1843, *Doings of the Texas Navy*, 28–29, and Moore to Sec. of War and Navy Hill, May 10, 1843, Moore, *To the People of Texas*, 149.
3. Minutes of the Action, April 30, 1843, *Ibid.*, 151.
4. Elliot to Aberdeen, May 29, 1843, *British Correspondence Concerning Texas*, 199.
5. Minutes of the Action, *op. cit.*, 153.
6. Morgan to Hill, May 9, 1843, *Doings of the Texas Navy*, 18.
7. Moore to Hill, May 20, 1843, Moore, *To the People of Texas*, 159.
8. Minutes of the Action, May 16, 1843, *Ibid.*, 160–62. See also Walke's *Journal*, Archives, Texas State Library, Navy MSS. and Tennison's *Journal*, Dienst Collection, Univ. of Texas.
9. Extracts from Morgan's testimony, Moore's court martial, *Doings of the Texas Navy*, 16.
10. José Rivera to Departamento de Guerra y Marina, May 8, 1843, *El Siglo Diez y Nueve*, May 28, 1843.
11. Tomas Marin to Commandancia General de la Esquadra del Mar del Norte, May 17, 1843, *Ibid.*
12. *Ibid.*
13. S. Baqueira, *Ensayo Historico sobre las Revoluciones de Yucatan*, Sección de Documentos, 62–64 and E. Ancona, *Historia de Yucatan*, III, 390–410.
14. Moore, *To the People of Texas*, 170.
15. The laws and regulations of the United States for governing the navy had been adopted as those of Texas. Under them no officer could be dismissed without a court martial.
16. H. P. N. Gammel, *The Laws of Texas*, II, 1030.
17. See Judge Advocate T. Johnson to Moore, Dec. 7, 1844, and the latter's remarks thereon.—*Doings of the Texas Navy*, 23–24.
18. *Ibid.*
19. See Buchanan, du Pont and Magruder, *In Relation to the Claims of the Late Texas Navy;* Moore, *Reply to the Pamphlet . . . in Relation to the Officers of the Late Texas Navy;* Buchanan, du Pont and Magruder, *To the House of Representatives in Relation to the Late Texas Navy;* Moore, *Doings of the Texas Navy;* Moore, *Reply to . . . in Relation to the Late Texas Navy;* Moore, *Letter to Senator Pearce of Maryland;* and Houston, *Documents Relative to the Dismissal of Post Captain E. W. Moore from the Texan Navy.*
20. Brashear vs. Mason, 6 Howard 92.
21. Randolph to the Bureau of Construction, June 5, 1846, Archives, Naval Records and Library, U. S. Navy Dept.

22. MORRIS to the Secretary of Navy, Aug. 15, 1846, *Executive Letters*, Naval Records and Library, U. S. Navy Dept.

23. LATIMER to the Navy Dept., May 16, 1848, *Letters of Commandants of Navy Yards*, Naval Records and Library, U. S. Navy Dept.

24. *Report of the Secretary of Navy*, 1848, p. 25.

25. *Ibid.*, 1849, p. 630.

APPENDIX II

BIBLIOGRAPHY OF WORKS AND MATERIALS CONSULTED

BIBLIOGRAPHICAL AIDS

BOLTON, H. E., *Guide to Materials for the History of the United States in the Principal Archives of Mexico*, Washington, 1913.

GRIFFIN, A. P. C., *Bibliography of American Historical Societies* (Vol. II of Annual Report, Amer. Hist. Assn. for 1905), Washington, 1907.

GRIFFIN, G. G., *Writings on American History* (A series of volumes published annually since 1906, for most part by Amer. Hist. Assn. as a part of its annual reports), New Haven and Washington, 1906——.

HAFERKORN, H. E., *The War with Mexico, 1846–1848, A Bibliography*, Washington, 1914.

HARBECK, C. T., *A Contribution to the Bibliography of the History of the United States Navy*, Cambridge, 1906.

KAISER, J. B., *Finding List of Books, Texas State Library*, Austin, 1911.

Naval Historical Society, *Catalogue of the Books, Manuscripts and Prints and Other Memorabilia in the John S. Barnes Memorial Library*, New York, 1915.

RAINES, C. W., *A Bibliography of Texas*, Austin, 1896.

VAN TYNE, C. H. and LELAND, W. G., *Guide to the Archives of the Government of the United States in Washington*, Washington, 1907.

LETTERS, JOURNALS AND MANUSCRIPTS

Account Book of the Austin, 1841–1843, Texas State Library, Austin.

Austin Papers, Austin, Texas. (Most of these, with an excellent calendar of the entire collection have been edited by Dr. E. C. Barker and published by the Amer. Hist. Assn., Reports for 1923.)

Commandants of Navy Yards, Letters, Naval Records and Library, Navy Department, Washington, D. C.

Executive Letters, Naval Records and Library, Navy Department, Washington, D. C.

Lamar Papers, Austin Texas. (Most of these, with calendar, have been published, under the editorship of C. A. Gulick, by the Texas State Library, Austin, 1921–1927.)

Midshipman's Journal of Midshipman Edward Johns, T. N., Texas U. Library, Austin.

Midshipman's Journal of Midshipman Alfred Walke, T. N., Texas State Library, Austin.

Miscellaneous Letters, Naval Records and Library, Navy Department, Washington, D. C.

Navy Papers, Texas State Library, Austin.

Pursers' Accounts, Texas Navy, Texas State Library, Austin.

Tennison's Journal (as a Midshipman and Lieutenant, T.N.), Dienst Collection, Texas U. Library, Austin.

ARCHIVES AND COLLECTIONS

Archivo General de la Secretaria de Relaciones Exteriores, Mexico City.
Archives Section, Naval Records and Library, Navy Department, Washington.
Archives Section, Texas State Library, Austin.
Archives Section, Texas U. Library, Austin.
Biblioteca de Marina y Guerra, Mexico City.
Dienst Collection, Texas U. Library, Austin.
Unpublished MSS. Collection, Rosenberg Library, Galveston, Texas.
Wharton Collection, Houston, Texas. (Clarence R. Wharton's private collection of old newspapers, rare books, transcriptions from original materials elsewhere and unpublished MSS.)

OFFICIAL AND SEMI-OFFICIAL PUBLICATIONS

ADAMS, E. D. (Editor), *British Diplomatic Correspondence Concerning the Republic of Texas, 1838–1846*, Austin, 1918.
American State Papers, Documents, Legislative and Executive, of the United States from the 1st Session of the First Congress, 38 vols., Washington, 1832–1861. (See particularly Exec. Docs., 25th Cong., 2d Sess., No. 12; H. R. Docs., 25th Cong., 2d Sess., No. 75 and No. 351; and the Annual Reports of the Secretaries of the Navy.)
BLANCHARD, P., et DAUZATS, A., *San Juan de Ulúa ou Relation de l'Expédition Française au Mexique sous les Ordres de M. le Contre-Amiral Baudin, Suivi de Notes et Documents, et d'un Aperçu Général sur l'Etat Actuel de Texas*, par M. E. Maissin, Paris, 1839.
Congressional Globe, Washington.
Contestaciones entre Francia y Mexico, un Supplemento al Diario del Gobierno de Mexico, Num. 1066, Mexico City, 1838.
Diario del Gobierno de la Republica Mexicana, Mexico City.
DUBLAN, MANUEL, y LOZANO, JOSÉ MARIA, *Legislacíon Mexicana, o Colección Completa de las Disposiciones Legislativas Expedidas desde la Independencia de la Republica*, Mexico, 1876. (Vols. I to V carry Mexican legislation through the period of this work.)
GARRISON, G. P., *Diplomatic Correspondence of the Republic of Texas* (Amer. Hist. Assn. Reports for 1907–1908), 3 vols., Washington, 1908–1911.
GAMMEL, H. P. N., *The Laws of Texas, 1822–1902*, 10 vols., Austin, 1898–1902.
HOUSTON, SAMUEL, *Rules and Regulations Promulgated by the President for the Direction of the Army and Navy of Texas*, Houston, Texas, 1838.
Journal of the Consultation Held at San Felipe de Austin, Oct. 16, 1835, Houston, Texas, 1838.
Journal of the General Council of the Republic of Texas Held at San Felipe de Austin, Nov. 14, 1835, Houston, Texas, 1838.
Journals of the Senate, Republic of Texas, Printed in various newspaper plants of the Republic, but for the most part in Houston, Washington and Austin, 1837–1845. (See also Winkler, E. W.)
Journals of the House of Representatives, Republic of Texas, Printed as were the Journals of the Senate, 1837–1845.

Journals of the House of Representatives, Appendixes, Washington, Texas, 1843–1845.

Mexican Ministers of War and Navy, *Memorias de la Guerra y Marina, 1822–1845,* Mexico City, 1823–1845.

Mexico, Legation in U. S., *Correspondencia que ha Mediado entre la Legación Extraordinario de Mexico y el Departamento de Estado de los Estados Unidos Sobre el Passo del Sabina por las Tropas que Mandaba el General Gaines,* Mexico, 1837.

Mexico, Ministero de Relaciones Exteriores, *Lord Aberdeen, Texas y California, una Colección de Documentos,* Mexico City, 1925.

Ordinances and Decrees of the Consultation, Provisional Government of Texas and the Convention which Assembled at Washington, March 1, 1836, Houston, Texas, 1838.

Peña y Reyes, Antonio de la, *Don Manuel Eduardo de Gorostiza y la Cuestión de Texas, Una Colección de Documentos,* Mexico City, 1924.

Poore, Ben P. (Editor), *Federal and State Constitutions of the United States,* Washington, 1878.

Suarez y Navarro, Juan, *Informe sobre las Causas y Carácter de las Frecuentes Cambios Políticos Ocurridos en el Estado de Yucatan,* Mexico, 1861.

Winkler, E. W. (Editor), *Secret Journals of the Senate, Republic of Texas,* Austin, 1911.

PERIODICALS

Austin City Gazette, 1837–1839. (File used not complete within these dates.)

Colorado Gazette, 1839–1842.

Congressional Globe, 1835–1850.

Diario del Gobierno de la Republica Mexicana, 1832–1848.

El Siglo Diez y Nueve (Mexico City), 1842–1848.

Matagordo Bulletin, 1837–1839. (File used not complete within these dates.)

Miles Register, 1835–1845.

New Orleans Daily Picayune, 1835–1843.

New Orleans Delta, 1835–1843.

Telegraph and Texas Register (Houston, Texas), 1835–1842. (File used not complete within these dates.)

The Quarterly of the Texas State Historical Association (Austin), 1896–1912. (Continued from 1912 to date as *The Southwestern Historical Quarterly.*)

PAMPHLETS

Action of the Legislature of the State of Texas in Reference to the Charge of Defalcation Against Commodore Moore, and the Construction Put upon the "Annexation Resolution" by the United States, Washington, 1849.

Buchanan, F., du Pont, S. F., and Magruder, G. A. (Commanders U. S. N.), *In Relation to the Claims of the Officers of the Late Texas Navy,* New York, undated.

———, *To the House of Representatives,* New York, undated.

Caro, R. M., *Verdadera Idea de la Primera Campaña de Tejas,* Mexico City, 1837.

CASTAÑEDA, CARLOS E. (Translator), *The Mexican Side of the Texan Revolution*, Dallas, 1928. (An excellent and valuable translation of a collection of rare Mexican pamphlets from the pens of leaders of the disastrous Campaign of 1836. Some of the Mexican pamphlets in this list are included in this work.)

CUEVAS, LUIS G., *Exposición del Ex-Ministro que la Suscribe sobre las Diferencias con Francia*, Mexico City, 1839.

FILISOLA, VICENTE, *Defensa*, Mexico City, 1836.

FISHER, S. RHOADS, *To the People of Texas*, 1836.

HOUSTON, SAMUEL, *The Texan Navy, Speech . . . Delivered in the U. S. Senate July 31, 1846, on the Bill Authorizing the President to Increase the Naval Establishment of the U. S. by Adding thereto the Naval Establishment of the Late Republic of Texas*, Washington, 1846.

HOUSTON, SAMUEL, *Speech . . . on Bill for Relief of Yucatan, Delivered May 8, 1848*, Washington, 1848.

Memorial of the Officers of the Late Texas Navy to the Congress of the United States, Washington, 1850.

MOORE, E. W., *A Brief Synopsis of the Doings of the Texas Navy*, Washington, 1847.

———, *Reply to the Pamphlet by Commanders Buchanan, du Pont and Magruder*, Washington, 1850.

———, *Reply to the Pamphlet by Commanders Buchanan, du Pont and Magruder in Relation to the Late Texas Navy*, Washington, 1850.

———, *To the People of Texas, An Appeal: In Vindication of his Conduct of the Navy*, Galveston, 1843. (Very valuable in that it is essentially a compilation, totaling over 200 pages, of the Commodore's correspondence with the Navy Department and the President during the second administration of Sam Houston.)

Reply to the Objections Urged by Three Commanders of U. S. Navy to the Incorporation of the Officers of the Late Texas Navy in the Navy of the United States, undated.

SANTA ANNA, Antonio Lopez de, *Manifesto que de sus Operaciones en la Campaña de Tejas*, Vera Cruz, 1837.

TORNEL, J. M., *Tejas y los Estados Unidos en sus Relaciones con la Republica Mejicana*, Mexico City, 1837.

URREA, JOSÉ, *Diario de las Operaciones Militares . . . la Campaña de Tejas*, Durango, 1838.

WINTHROP, JOHN, *Report of the Trial of Thomas M. Thompson for a Piratical Attack upon the American Schooner San Felipe*, New Orleans, 1835.

MAGAZINE ARTICLES AND HISTORICAL STUDIES

ALMONTE, JUAN N. (Castañeda, C. E., Translator), "Statistical Report on Texas," *Southwestern Historical Quarterly*, XXVIII, 177–221.

BARKER, E. C., "The Work of the Permanent Council," *The Quarterly, Texas State Historical Association*, VII, 249–71.

———, "The Texan Declaration of Causes for Taking up Arms against Mexico," *The Quarterly, Texas State Historical Association*, XV, 173–85.

———, "Difficulties of a Mexican Revenue Officer in Texas," *The Quarterly, Texas State Historical Association*, IV, 190–202.

CONDRON, S. H., *The First Texas Agency at New Orleans in 1836*, Texas U. Graduate School Thesis, unpublished.

COVINGTON, NINA, *The Presidential Campaigns of the Republic of Texas, 1836 and 1838*, Texas U. Graduate School Thesis, unpublished.

DIENST, ALEXANDER, "The Navy of the Republic of Texas," *The Quarterly, Texas State Historical Association*, XII, 165–203; 247–75 and XIII, 1–43; 85–127.

FULLER, G. F., "A Sketch of the Texas Navy," *The Quarterly, Texas State Historical Association*, VII, 218–230.

HOWREN, ALLEINE, "Causes and Origin of the Decree of April 6, 1830," *Southwestern Historical Quarterly*, XVI, 378–422.

LUKER, J. E., *The Diplomatic Relations Between Texas and Mexico, 1836–1842*, Texas U. Graduate School Thesis, unpublished.

MANNING, W. R., "Poinsett's Mission to Mexico," *American Journal of International Law*, VII, 781–822.

MARSHALL, T. M., "Diplomatic Relations of Texas and United States, 1839–1843," *The Quarterly, Texas Historical Association*, XV, 267–293.

NELSON, L. M., *The Second Texas Agency at New Orleans, 1836–1838*, Texas U. Graduate School Thesis, unpublished.

NEU, C. T., "The Case of the Brig *Pocket*," *The Quarterly, Texas State Historical Association*, XII, 276–295.

SMITHERS, HARRIETT, *The Diplomatic Service of Ashbel Smith to the Republic of Texas, 1842–1845*, Texas U. Graduate School Thesis, unpublished.

BIOGRAPHIES AND MEMOIRS

BARKER, E. C., *The Life of Stephen F. Austin*, Dallas, 1925.

BROWN, John H., *Life and Times of Henry Smith*, Dallas, 1887.

CALLAHAN, W., *List of Officers of the United States Navy and the Marine Corps from 1775 to 1900*, New York, 1901.

CHRISTIAN, A. K., *Mirabeau Buonaparte Lamar*, Austin, 1922.

CROCKETT, David, *Life of David Crockett, the Original Humorist, etc.*, London, 1865.

FARRAGUT, L., *Life of David Glasgow Farragut, Embodying His Journal and Letters*, New York, 1879.

FILISOLA, VICENTE, *Memorias para la Historia de la Guerra de Tejas*, 2 vols., Mexico City, 1848.

GREEN, T. J., *Journal of the Texan Expedition against Mier*, New York, 1845.

HOLLEY, MRS. MARY AUSTIN, *Texas*, Lexington, Ky., 1836.

HOUSTON, Mrs. M. C., *Texas and the Gulf of Mexico, or Yachting in the New World*, 2 vols., London, 1844.

JOHNSON, F. W., *A History of Texas and Texans*, 5 vols., Chicago, 1914.

JONES, ANSON, *The Republic of Texas*, New York, 1859.

KENDALL, G. W., *Narrative of an Expedition . . . from Texas to Santa Fé*, London, 1845.

PORTER, D. D., *Memoir on Commodore Porter*, Albany, 1875.

Robinson, Fayette, *Mexico and her Military Chieftains*, Philadelphia, 1849.
Santa Anna, Antonio Lopez de, *Memoirs of General Antonio Lopez de Santa Anna* (Translated by W. W. Watkins), Texas U. Thesis, unpublished.
Stapp, W. P., *The Prisoners of Perote*, Philadelphia, 1845.
Thompson, Waddy, *Recollections of Mexico*, New York and London, 1846.

HISTORIES

Adams, E. D., *British Interests and Activities in Texas*, Baltimore, 1910.
Ancona, Eligio, *Historia de Yucatan desde la Èpóca Más Remota Hasta Nuestros Dias*, 5 vols., Merida, Yucatan, 1878–1905.
Ballesca, J. (Editor), *Mexico, Su Social Evolución*, 2 vols., Mexico City, 1900.
Bancroft, H. H., *History of Mexico*, 6 vols., San Francisco, 1886–1888.
———, *History of the North Mexican States and Texas*, 2 vols., San Francisco, 1886.
Baqueiro, Serapio, *Ensayo Historico sobre las Revoluciones de Yucatan desde el Año 1840*, 1871.
———, *Rosgo Biografico del General D. Sebastian Lopez de Llergo y Calderon, General en Jefe de las Tropas de la Peninsula de Yucatan en los Años 1840, 1842, 1848*, Merida, 1898.
Barando, Joaquin, *Recordaciones Historicas*, 2 vols., Mexico City, 1907.
Barker, E. C., *Mexico and Texas, 1821–1835*, Dallas, 1928.
Dommartin, Hippolyte du Pasquier de, *Les Etats Unis et le Mexique*, Paris, 1852.
Gambrell, Herbert P., *Mirabeau Buonaparte Lamar, Troubadour and Crusader*, Dallas, 1934.
Gouge, William N., *The Fiscal History of Texas*, Philadelphia, 1852.
Hanighen, Frank C., *Santa Anna, Napoleon of the West*, New York, 1834.
Kennedy, Wm., *Rise, Progress and Prospects of the Republic of Texas*, 2 vols., London, 1841.
Lanz, Manuel A., *Compendio de Historia de Campeche*, Campeche, 1905.
Manning, W. R., *Early Diplomatic Relations between United States and Mexico*, Baltimore, 1916.
Miller, E. T., *A Financial History of Texas*, Austin, 1916.
Morphis, J. W., *History of Texas*, New York, 1874.
Negrete, Emilie del Castillo, *Invasión de los Norte Americanos en Mejico*, 4 vols., Mexico City, 1890.
Newell, Chester, *History of the Revolution in Texas*, New York, 1838.
Niles, J. M., *History of South America and Mexico*, 2 vols., Hartford, 1844.
Rippy, J. F., *The United States and Mexico*, New York, 1926.
Rives, G. L., *The United States and Mexico, 1821–1848*, 2 vols., New York, 1913.
Smith, Justin, *The Annexation of Texas*, New York, 1911.
Stiff, Edward, *A New History of Texas, Being a Narrative of the Adventures of the Author in Texas*, Cincinnati, 1847.
Thrall, Homer S., *A Pictorial History of Texas*, St. Louis, 1879.
Wharton, Clarence R., *El Presidente*, Austin, 1926.

———, *History of Texas*, Dallas, 1935.

———, *San Jacinto, Sixteenth Decisive Battle*, Houston, 1930.

WOOTEN, D. G. (Editor), *A Comprehensive History of Texas*, 2 vols., Dallas, 1898.

YOAKUM, H. K., *History of Texas, 1685–1846*, 2 vols., New York, 1856.

ZAVALA, LORENZO DE, *Ensayo Historico de las Revoluciones de Mejico*, 2 vols., Paris, 1832.

INDEX

Aberdeen, Earl of, (George Hamilton Gordon), cool toward Texan treaty, 144

Abispo, Mexican merchantman, prize, 86

Acajete, battle of, federalists defeated, 115

Adams, Charles Francis, his neutrality arguments anticipated by Texans, 172, 173

Adventure, Mexican merchantman, prize, 85, 86

Aguila, Mexican warship, 173; in battles off Yucatan, 183–187

Ariel, U. S. merchant steamer, 12

Alacranes, islands, visited by Texas fleet, 86, 87; *Sylph* wrecked upon, 150

Alamo, mission, fortress, 34, 35, 46, 52, 53, 57

Alamo, Mexican warship; *see Vencedor del Alamo*

Aldana, Commodore José de, Mexican navy, cruises in search of *Brutus* and *Invincible*, 88; engages Commodore Thompson off Galveston, 89–92, 96

Alden, Midshipman, Texas navy, wounded in San Antonio Mutiny, 152, 182

Allen, A. C., Texan ship owner, 25, 36; desires rank in Texas navy, 110

Allen, I., hanged for mutiny, 182

Almonte, Col. Juan N., Mexican army, 21, 54

Ampudia, Gen. Pedro de, centralist, besieges Campeche, 173, 178, 179, 185

Anáhuac, garrison and customs officers at, 9–12; Texans blockade Bradburn in, 13, 14; vacated by Mexicans, 17; reoccupied; 21, again vacated, 22

Ana Maria, Mexican transport, 24

Anaya, General, federalist leader, Yucatan, 126, 128

Anna Maria, Mexican merchantman, prize, 133

Arcas, islands, rendezvous for Texan fleet, 127, 128; *San Jacinto* wrecked at, 133

Archer, Dr. Branch T., Texan leader, 78

Archer, Texan war brig, arrives at Galveston, 114; Moore's need for, 157; in need of repairs, 160; property of U. S., 194

Argyle, steamer, Mexican troop ship, 129

Arista, General Manuel, Mexican army, captured at Vera Cruz, 100; incites Indians against Texas, 121, 122; gets federalists well in hand, 123

Army, Texan, spontaneously organized October, 1835, 33, 34; provided for in plan of provisional government, 36; defeated by Urrea, 46; "delaying action" at Alamo, 47; new volunteers, 52; retreat before Santa Anna, 53–55; victory, 56; inactivity and quarrelling in, 63; decline of, 105; Lamar favors large army, 107; discontinued by 4th Cong., 117; denied appropriations by 5th Cong., 141; Houston vetoes appropriations for, 165; abortive invasion of Mexico, 174

Atenzingo, rioting in, 97

Austin, armed coasting schooner, 13

Austin, Capt. John, emissary to Brazoria, 14; commands Texans at Velasco, 15; dies, 20

Austin, Stephen F., concerned over closed ports, 7; alarmed over tariff of 1827, 8; to Mexico City, 20, 21; returns from Mexico, 26; present at *San Felipe-Correo Affair*, 27–29; commands before San Antonio, 33, 34; diplomatic mission to U. S., 35

Austin, Texan sloop-of-war and flagship, described, 113, 114; to Sisal, 126, 127, 128, 130; off Tampico, 131, 132; on Tobasco raid, 134; second cruise to Yucatan, 146, 147, 150, 152, 154, 155; need for refitting, 157; in need of repairs, 160; to New Orleans for fitting, 161, 163, 169, 177; begins last cruise, 179, 181, 183; in naval battles off Campeche, 184–188; returns to Galveston, 190, 191; becomes part of U. S. navy, 194

Ayuntamientos, Texan, 18–20

Baltimore, new Texan fleet built at, 108, 109

Banquilla reef, *Segunda Fauna* wrecked upon, 131

213

Privateering, failure of to aid Texans, 40; *see* Letters of Marque, *William Robbins*, *Terrible*, *Thomas Toby*

Progreso, Mexican schooner, prize, 152

Provisional Government, Texan, 36, 37, 40, 41

Pulaski, steamer, Texan efforts to purchase, 93, 94

Quintana Roo, Yucatecan statesman, centralist, negotiates with federalists, 147–149, 158

Rafaelita, prize of the *Brutus*, 88; *see Correo de Mejico*

Rambler, Amer. schooner, 49; *see Liberty* and *William Robbins*

Ramirez, ye Sesma, Gen., Mexican army, 45

Randolph, Com. V. M., U. S. N., reports on condition of Texan fleet, 194

Rangers, Texas, 58, 59, 63

Rankin, Lieut. G. H., British navy, seeks post-captaincy Texas navy, 110

Ransom, Commodore H. L. Thompson demands of Campeche, 85, 86; levied on San Juan Bautista, 134

Red Rover, armed coasting schooner, 13

Reform Laws of 1833, 20

Regenerador, Mexican war steamer, 173; in battles off Yucatan, 183, 186

Republic of the Rio Grande, 116, 121, 123

Ribaud, Admiral, French navy, seeks commission Texas navy, 110

Richmond, 54

Rincón, General Manuel, Mexican army, 100

Roberts, Willis, recommends Admiral Ribaud to Lamar, 110

Robbins, William, Texas privateer, 38–40; *see Liberty*

Robinson, Judge J. W., captured by Woll, 174; negotiates with Santa Anna, 189

Rodgers, Commodore John, U. S. navy, 81, 82

Roo, Quintana, negotiates with Yucatan federalists, 147–149, 158

Rosario, schooner, brings news from Yucatan, 178–179

"Runaway Scrape," 53

Russell, Capt. William J., emissary to Brazoria, 14; commands *Brazoria*, 15, 16

Sabine, Texan merchant schooner, 12

Saltillo, 45

Sam Houston, Texan merchantman, 88, 89

San Antonio, provincial capital of Texas, 4; garrisoned by Ugartechea, 21, 22; Cos commands at, 33; surrenders, 35; captured by Santa Anna, 45, 46; evacuated by Filisola, 59; captured by Vasquez, 157; captured by Woll, 174; mentioned, 24, 31, 38, 49, 53, 60

San Antonio, Texan war ship, arrives at Galveston, 113, 130; on cruise, 132; kept in commission, 142; second cruise to Yucatan, 146, 150; to New Orleans via Galveston, 150; mutiny aboard, 151, 152; rejoins *Austin*, 154–156; in need of repairs, 160; to Yucatan for cash, 162, 163; returns from Yucatan, 163; lost, 170; mentioned, 181, 182

San Antonio Trail, 3, 6

San Bernard, Texan war schooner, arrives at Galveston, 113; sails for Sisal, 126–128; off Vera Cruz, 130; on Tobasco raid, 134; to Mexico with Webb mission, 142–144; second cruise to Yucatan, 146, 150, 152, 155; to Galveston, 156; rejoins fleet off Yucatan, 157; in need of repairs, 160, 163; worm eaten and unseaworthy, 170

Sanderson, H., ship chandler and creditor to Texas Navy, 94

San Felipe, capital, Austin's colony, 25, 35, 52, 54, 55

San Felipe, Texan gun runner, 26; captures *Correo de Mejico*, 27–30, 32, 38, 41

San Jacinto, battle of, 55, 56; effects of Mexican defeat, 57–59; Col. Lamar at, 106

San Jacinto, Texan war schooner, arrives at Galveston, 113; Galveston to Point Maria Andrea, 126–128, 130; wrecked on Arcas Island, 133

San Juan Bautista, on Rio Grande, 46

San Juan Bautista, Tobasco, pays $25,000 ransom, 134, 139

San Juan de Ulúa, castle, Vera Cruz harbor, 98, 99

San Luis Potosí, 45, 115

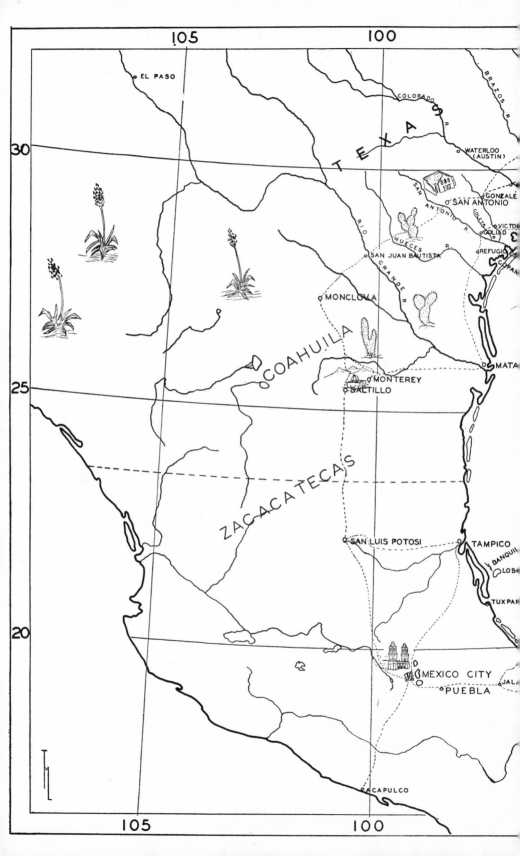